The Economics of Russia's War in Ukraine

The Economics of Russia's War in Ukraine provides a thorough analysis of the Russo-Ukrainian war, tracing its historical roots and exploring its multifaceted dimensions. This book emphasizes economic, geopolitical, and humanitarian impacts, highlighting Ukraine's resilience amid challenges. At the same time, this study examines the EU's dynamic responses to economic crises and energy transition, the consequences of the war on global trade dynamics, and the significant influence of geopolitical events on financial markets. It underscores the EU's commitment to aiding Ukraine, enhancing its security, and increasing defence spending in response to evolving geopolitical complexities. The impact of the invasion on financial markets and the vulnerabilities of the banking sector are closely examined, highlighting the complex relationship between geopolitics and the global economy. Findings suggest that the priorities for the post-war reconstruction of Ukraine include addressing human capital and demographics, employment opportunities, environmental protection, infrastructure and housing reconstruction, security and mine clearance, waste recycling, agriculture and food security, digital transformation, social protection and healthcare, and education and research. This book therefore argues that a comprehensive, integrated approach with international support is crucial for Ukraine's recovery and sustainable economic growth.

The Economics of Russia's War in Ukraine will be useful for scholars, students, professionals, policy makers, all interested in economics, international relations, security, and global studies, as well as all those wishing to have a thorough and clear understanding of the backdrop of Russia's invasion of Ukraine in February 2022 and its influence on Europe.

Nataliya Struk is a Doctor of Economic Sciences, Professor of Accounting and Auditing Department in the Faculty of Economics, Ivan Franko National University of Lviv, Ukraine.

Maryana Prokop is an Assistant Professor at the Institute of International Relations and Public Policies, Jan Kochanowski University of Kielce, Poland.

Oleksandra Struk is an Assistant Professor at the Institute of Political Science, Faculty of Social Sciences, University of Warmia and Mazury in Olsztyn, Poland.

Routledge Studies in the Modern World Economy

Economic Development Parables
From Siam to Thailand
Winai Wongsurawat

The ASEAN Digital Economy
Towards an Integrated Regional Framework
Edited by Paul Cheung and Xie Taojun

The Future of Multilateralism and Globalization in the Age of the U.S.–China Rivalry
Edited by Norbert Gaillard, Fumihito Gotoh, and Rick Michalek

Nuclear Power Safety and Governance in East Asia
Edited by Soocheol Lee, Weisheng Zhou and Kiyoshi Fujikawa

Inequality and Public Policy
Towards Visible Equality and Equal Opportunity
Bhanoji Rao, Suresh K.G. and Pundarik Mukhopadhaya

The Governance of Economic Development
Investment, Innovation, and Competition in China
Anson Au

The Economics of Russia's War in Ukraine
Impact Analysis of Economic Policy and Finance
Nataliya Struk, Maryana Prokop and Oleksandra Struk

For more information about this series, please visit: www.routledge.com/Routledge-Studies-in-the-Modern-World-Economy/book-series/SE0432

The Economics of Russia's War in Ukraine

Impact Analysis of Economic Policy and Finance

Nataliya Struk, Maryana Prokop and Oleksandra Struk

Routledge
Taylor & Francis Group
LONDON AND NEW YORK

First published 2025
by Routledge
4 Park Square, Milton Park, Abingdon, Oxon OX14 4RN

and by Routledge
605 Third Avenue, New York, NY 10158

Routledge is an imprint of the Taylor & Francis Group, an informa business

British Library Cataloguing-in-Publication Data
A catalogue record for this book is available from the British Library

ISBN: 9781032564173 (hbk)
ISBN: 9781032564197 (pbk)
ISBN: 9781003435433 (ebk)

DOI: 10.4324/9781003435433

Typeset in Times New Roman
by codeMantra

Contents

Preface ix

1 **The Effect of the War on the Ukrainian Economy** 1
NATALIYA STRUK

Introduction 1
1.1 Prerequisites for Russia's Full-Scale Invasion of Ukraine 3
1.2 Historical Background: Main Reasons for Russian Aggression against Ukraine 6
1.3 Economic Reasons for Russia's War with Ukraine and Their Impact on Geopolitics 10
1.4 Economic Consequences of Russia's Full-Scale Invasion of Ukraine 14
1.5 Assessment of the State of Ukraine's Economy during the War 16
Conclusion 28

2 **The Effect of the War on European Economy** 35
OLEKSANDRA STRUK

Introduction 35
2.1 EU Response to Russia's Invasion of Ukraine 36
2.2 Effects of War in Academic Discourse: Lessons from the History 42
2.3 European Economies within War in Ukraine: General Overview, Data Analysis, and Some Forecasts 45
2.4 EU Energy Dependency 52
2.5 Ukrainians on the EU Labour Market 60
Key Takeaways 67

3 **Ukraine's Relevance to European and Global Trade from 2013 to 2022: The Evolution of Ukraine's Trade Policy in the Context of the Annexation of Crimea and Russian Military Aggression in 2022** 75

MARYANA PROKOP

Introduction 75
3.1 Methodological Assumptions 76
3.2 Events Impinging on the Dimensions of Ukraine's Trade Policy from 2013 to 2022 (Selected Aspects) 78
3.3 Ukrainian Trade from 2013 to 2022 (General Aspect) 82
3.4 Commodity Structure of Ukrainian Exports to the EU and Russia 88
3.5 Ukraine's Trade Exchange with Countries of the World 96
3.6 Importance of Ukraine for the EU Market 105
Conclusion 108

4 **The War in Ukraine Impacting European Financial Market and Banking Sector** 115

OLEKSANDRA STRUK

Introduction 115
4.1 A Brief Overview of the European Financial Market 116
4.2 World Uncertainty and Economic Policy Uncertainty versus Financial Stability in Recent Studies 117
4.3 Investors' Market Expectations versus War in Ukraine 122
4.4 European Stock Market versus War in Ukraine 123
4.5 Banking Sector versus War in Ukraine 130
Final Considerations and Conclusions 135

5 **Non-Military Involvement of the EU and the US in the Russian–Ukrainian War and Re-Definition of UE, UK, US Countries' Security Policy** 142

MARYANA PROKOP

Introduction 142
5.1 EU, UK, and US Aid Policy towards Ukraine 143
5.2 EU, US, and UK Security Policy after the Russian Aggression against Ukraine 149
Conclusion 158

6 Ukraine's Economic Recovery: Key Priorities for the Future 162
NATALIYA STRUK

Introduction 162
6.1 Analysis of the State of Economic Recovery in Ukraine during the War 165
6.2 Priority Areas for the Reconstruction and Development of Ukraine's Economy after the War 175
Conclusion 180

Postface 184

Index *195*

Preface

Russia's invasion of Ukraine has led to an increase in economic uncertainty and puts the global economy at risk. Commodity and energy prices have increased sharply as uncertainty about supply disruptions has grown. In addition, sanctions and trade restrictions have been imposed on Russian banks, businesses, and individuals. According to the IMF, more than 7 million Ukrainians – about one-fifth of the population – have left the country or been displaced, thereby putting pressure on the social protection system. All of this is likely to contribute towards greater uncertainty in the economy, among businesses, households, and financial markets, particularly in EU states. Therefore, the main purpose of the study is to assess the economics of Russia's war in Ukraine in terms of impact analysis of economic policy and finance.

Obtained results of the study will enable us to answer the following questions: How does the war affect the Ukrainian economy? How does the war affect the economy of European states? What is the impact of the war on the global trade, financial, and banking sector in the EU? Will the war in Ukraine mark a new era for European defence policy? And finally, how much would it cost to rebuild Ukraine?

Our main objectives include:

- to define preconditions and analyse consequences of the war for the Ukrainian economy,
- to study the impact of war on the economy of European states,
- to examine consequences of the war for global trade,
- to examine how European financial markets deal with the current situation,
- to study the non-military involvement of the EU and US in the Russian-Ukrainian war and re-definition of the EU security policy,
- to outline the strategic directions of economic development for Ukraine's recovery.

The case study of the Ukrainian economy during the war will enable us to present what solutions were introduced in Ukraine in order to ensure economic efficiency in the given conditions, as well as to identify the most relevant measures, which can be used by other countries, under the conditions of the real threat of war, in the form of comprehensive guidelines. The authors use a multidimensional approach to the study of consequences of hostilities in Ukraine for the economies of the EU states. For this purpose, the research will cover an analysis of trade between Ukraine and European countries, as well as the influence of the situation in Ukraine on the European financial and energy sectors. The given approach will enable us to determine to what extent Ukrainian resources covered the demand of European markets and to what extent the war reduced the given flow of goods and services. Noteworthy, we would like to show how Russian aggression in Ukraine has changed the approach of the European countries to security policy and the degree to which they are committed to supporting Ukraine in its struggle for independence. The most significant merit of the publication is its comprehensive approach covering the entire functioning of the state's economy under conditions of military threat, as well as their implication nature, which means usefulness in practical terms for other states in similar conditions.

The proposed investigation is innovative in its nature, because it contains a scientific study on the impact of war in modern times on the economy of European states. The study is relevant and valuable, because there is no other scientific work presenting these issues. Moreover, it is a good case representing the dependence and interconnection of states nowadays. We would like to show how bad an idea is to start war today, how much costs it generates and is ineffective from the perspective of the economy. Future wars could be prevented only through a change of paradigm, where the primary goal is not a net profit, but the sustainable development of countries' economies, based on fair distribution of public goods, limited consumption of resources, respect for the environment and environmental protection.

Chapter 1 presents the intricate dimensions of the Russo-Ukrainian conflict, delving into its historical context and global repercussions. Unravelling the roots of the conflict from the mediaeval state of Rus, the study highlights the unique identities shaped by linguistic, cultural, and political differences over centuries. The collapse of the Soviet Union in 1991 marked Ukraine's independence, but historical interference by Moscow has contributed to a complex relationship, leading to a detailed examination of military engagements from 1991 to the full-scale attack in 2022.

The study characterises the war as a clash between two civilisations, emphasising the contrast between Ukrainian values of freedom, democracy, and respect for human rights and the authoritarianism evident in Russian actions. Vladimir Putin's efforts to control Ukraine underscore Moscow's strategic importance, with the study revealing the substantial risks posed by Russia's aggressive military strategy globally. The research emphasises the war's threats to democratic systems, increased global military expenses, reduced social expenditures, exacerbated food supply issues, and contributed to mass migration.

Furthermore, the study presents diverse economic motives for Russia's invasion, focusing on Ukraine's natural resources and its global economic role. Key economic points, including Russia's control over eastern Ukrainian deposits and the strategic importance of lithium, are explored. Authors highlight the potential triggers for Russia's invasion, driven by global attention and competition for access to Ukraine's resources. The economic consequences, spanning various sectors such as agriculture, energy, and metallurgy, are meticulously analysed. The first chapter thus contributes vital insights into the multifaceted nature of the conflict, urging a nuanced understanding for effective strategies on the global stage.

Chapter 2 is dedicated to a thorough examination of the repercussions of the war in Ukraine on the European economy. Addressing key research inquiries, the study delves into various aspects, including the EU's response to Russia's invasion, the evolution of the EU's strategic approach, and the role of international cooperation. Drawing lessons from historical perspectives on economic outcomes of wars, the research scrutinises the specific impacts on EU Member States and the intricate dynamics of the energy crisis triggered by the conflict.

Thus, the results of the study provide responses to the following research questions: What was the EU response to Russia's invasion of Ukraine? How has the EU's strategy evolved in response to Russia's invasion, and what role did international cooperation play? What are the economic outcomes of wars in light of lessons from history and how do they relate to the situation in Ukraine? How did the war in Ukraine impact the economies of EU Member States? How did the energy crisis triggered by the war affect the EU economy, and what emergency measures and strategies were implemented in response? How successful was the temporary protection programme for Ukrainian refugees, especially in terms of integration, employment, and skills recognition? What is the economic impact of Ukrainian refugees on the labour force and GDP growth in host countries? Through a combination of quantitative and qualitative research methods, encompassing data analysis, synthesis, interpretation, as well as a structural-functional approach and comparative analysis, the chapter offers a comprehensive analysis. Leveraging scientific studies, statistical data, international reports, and web sources, the study contributes to a nuanced understanding of the complex economic landscape shaped by the war in Ukraine.

Chapter 3 covers an analysis of the trade with Ukraine as well as its importance for the global and European markets. The Russian military invasion of Ukraine in February 2022 had a profound impact on global trade dynamics, particularly within Europe, due to the significant roles both Ukraine and Russia played in the global market for goods and services. The outbreak of the conflict presented notable challenges for Ukrainian trade with European nations and the rest of the world, exacerbated by Russian missile attacks causing destruction to critical infrastructure, industrial facilities, and raw material stocks. Moreover, a considerable population migration, including emigration, further disrupted Ukraine's trade relations with Europe and beyond. In response to Russian aggression, various sanctions and restrictions were imposed against Russia as a means of economic pressure and condemnation of its hostile actions. European countries and the US deliberately shifted away from economic cooperation with Russia, including trade partnerships. Ukraine's gradual departure from the Russian market for goods sales since 2013 was driven by economic instability, Russian activities in eastern Ukraine, the annexation of Crimea, and the 2022 military aggression. The aim of this study was to analyse trade between Ukraine and EU countries and selected countries of the world, in order to establish the importance of Ukrainian trade for European and world markets.

Therefore, efforts are made to address the following research questions: what is the importance of Ukraine in trade with the EU and selected world countries between 2013 and 2022 and to what extent Russian military aggression implied on the dimension of Ukraine's trade with Europe and the world? What place does the EU hold in Ukrainian trade between 2013 and 2022? What is the place of Ukraine's trade with the EU between 2013 and 2022? What place does Russia hold in Ukraine's trade between 2013 and 2022? What is the importance of Ukraine in the trade of the world (excluding the EU and Russia) between 2013 and 2022? Whether and to what extent is there a change in the scope of trade between Ukraine and the EU after the Russian military aggression against Ukraine? Whether and to what extent is there a change in the scope of trade between Ukraine and countries of the world after the Russian military aggression against Ukraine? Whether and to what extent is the structure of exports/imports between Ukraine and the EU changing after the Russian-Ukrainian war? Whether and to what extent is the structure of exports between Ukraine and the countries of the world changing after the outbreak of the Russian-Ukrainian war? Whether and to what extent do the EU countries with the highest share of Ukrainian exports determine the overall share of Ukrainian exports in the EU economy?

The combination of geopolitical uncertainty, higher commodity prices, sanctions imposed on Russia and regional business disruptions has contributed to increased volatility and risk aversion. Volatility on the financial market has been caused by higher global commodity prices, oil and gold prices. The rotation to value stocks and the declining performance of crypto-assets also indicate growing investor appetite for lower-risk assets. The chapter will contain an analysis of how the Ukraine-Russia war rattled EU financial markets.

Chapter 4 undertakes a thorough analysis of the effects of the Ukraine conflict on Europe's financial market and banking sector, with a specific emphasis on the EU. The research questions guiding this exploration encompass the nature of the European financial market, the impact of war-related uncertainties on stock market performance, and the role of economic policy measures in shaping investor expectations. Employing a mix of quantitative and qualitative research techniques, including data analysis, synthesis, interpretation, and comparative analysis, the chapter scrutinises the European stock market's response to the war's initiation and observes trends in performance and volatility. Additionally, it investigates the multifaceted impact of the military conflict on different sectors within the European stock market, exploring both immediate and long-term consequences for various industries. Furthermore, the chapter examines how the ongoing conflict influences different channels of the banking sector in Europe. Drawing on a comprehensive array of scientific studies, statistical data, and international reports, this chapter provides a nuanced and insightful exploration of the intricate interplay between the conflict in Ukraine and the financial landscape of Europe. Thus, the main research questions are as follows: What is the nature of the European financial market? What is the impact of WUI and EPU on stock market performance, particularly in the context of war-related uncertainties? How do investors' expectations and market sentiments change in response to geopolitical events, and what role do economic policy measures play in shaping these expectations? How did the European stock market respond to the initiation of the war, and what trends were observed in their performance and volatility? In what ways did the military conflict in Ukraine affect various sectors in the European stock market, and what were the immediate and long-term consequences for different industries? How does the ongoing conflict in Ukraine impact different channels of the banking sector in Europe?

In Chapter 5, the authors focus on non-military means used by the EU and the US in the context of the threat posed by Russian aggression against Ukraine, as well as an analysis of the extent to which the security policy of European countries has changed. The conflict in Ukraine has fundamentally reshaped perceptions of state security, presenting the global community with the challenge of ensuring stable and effective security policies and aid for Ukraine. Russian activities within Ukrainian borders, notably missile strikes, have caused widespread destruction of cities and critical infrastructure, posing significant threats to civilian life and prompting large-scale migration of Ukrainians seeking safety abroad.

The international community has vehemently condemned Russian military actions and advocated for their cessation, sparking national-level discussions in many countries about enhancing their own security measures. European leaders and the US, siding with the invaded state, have pledged comprehensive humanitarian, financial, and military support for Ukraine. These Russian actions not only undermine the security environment in Europe but also constitute a direct assault on established international norms, order, and adherence to international law. EU Member States, concerned for their security, have implemented measures to bolster their defence capabilities and have actively engaged in aiding Ukraine. The author undertook the task of answering two research questions: To what extent have the EU countries, UK and US been involved in assisting Ukraine? Have European countries taken steps to strengthen their own security, and to what extent?

Chapter 6 is devoted to the main priorities for restoring Ukraine's economy after the horrific damage caused during the war. Restoring the economy under martial law is an extremely challenging task for professionals of various levels of responsibility. Large-scale post-war economic recovery can only begin after victory. The main prerequisite for economic recovery is that Ukraine receives reliable security guarantees that will make it impossible to resume hostilities in the future. Obviously, sustainable economic growth and development can only take place on a solid security foundation. Security is by nature a public good that must be provided by the state and the international community. Once this basic condition is met, the key objectives of post-war economic recovery should be to rebuild property and infrastructure destroyed or damaged by the war; restore economic activity of business entities as soon as possible; return refugees and internally displaced persons to their previous places of residence (if possible); and create the basis for sustainable economic growth.

Reparations from Russia and assistance from the international community should be the most important sources of funding for Ukraine's post-war reconstruction. Ukraine's diplomatic efforts should be focused on obtaining EU candidate status, and subsequently full membership. In other words, Ukraine's post-war reconstruction programme should be aligned with the goals of EU membership.

Without waiting for the end of the war, it is important to identify the main priorities for Ukraine's economic recovery and development. In the area of humanitarian aid, it is necessary to ensure access to basic needs (food, clean water, healthcare) for the affected population, provide temporary housing and support for internally displaced persons. A separate priority is the restoration and rebuilding of critical infrastructure (roads, bridges, energy facilities, communication networks), repair, and modernisation of utilities. In the area of employment, it is advisable to create employment opportunities for people and implement short-term employment programmes for the affected people. Stabilising the country's financial sector and ensuring access to banking services, managing inflation and stabilising the local currency are absolute priorities. In the social services segment, it is appropriate to focus on restoring and improving educational services and strengthening social protection programmes to support vulnerable groups. In the area of security and the rule of law, it is advisable to restore the proper legal basis for a favourable environment for economic activity. Another priority is environmental restoration, in particular, the implementation of measures aimed at eliminating environmental damage, as well as successful practices of long-term environmental restoration. In the area of international cooperation, it is necessary to seek and coordinate international assistance for economic recovery, and to interact with international organisations, donor countries, and non-governmental institutions to mobilise resources and expertise. The identified priority areas are interconnected and often require a comprehensive approach to implement. That is why the purpose of Chapter 6 is to highlight various aspects of Ukraine's economic recovery and development in the wartime and post-war periods. Specific strategies and measures in each situation should be adapted to the unique context of the war in Ukraine and the changing needs of the population.

The primary audience for this work encompasses scholars, academic staff, and students, particularly those immersed in the disciplines of economics, international relations, security studies, and global affairs. Additionally, individuals seeking an in-depth comprehension of the contextual foundations underlying Russia's invasion of Ukraine in February 2022 and its repercussions on Europe will find this study valuable. Moreover, the academic discourse extends its relevance to policymakers within European states. Given its intricate analysis of the prevailing circumstances, including their implications on the European Union's economy, the work provides pertinent recommendations and outlines potential strategies for navigating the crisis amid the ongoing conflict.

In contrast to existing publications addressing economic crises or the challenges posed by the COVID-19 pandemic in contemporary Europe, the circumstances confronting Ukraine present a distinctive scenario. The strategies devised by Ukraine, alongside those implemented by European nations, offer novel insights. The efficacy of these approaches stands as a valuable repository of knowledge for other economies grappling with crisis situations. The unique nature of Ukraine's experience contributes a nuanced perspective, providing potential lessons and applicable strategies that extend beyond the conventional frameworks established by earlier crisis scenarios in Europe.

1 The Effect of the War on the Ukrainian Economy

Nataliya Struk

Introduction

Russia's large-scale war against Ukraine, which began in 2022, has become the subject of intense scholarly attention and is expected to be the focus of numerous academic studies. The war has elicited mixed reactions, with some perceiving it as inevitable, while others were caught off guard. The roots of this war can be traced back to the aggressive invasion of the eastern regions of Ukraine by Russian armed forces in 2014, followed by the subsequent occupation of the territory of Crimea. This historical context created the preconditions for the unfolding of a situation that has caused concern among world leaders and representatives of international organisations. The collapse of the Soviet Union in 1991 marked the emergence of 15 sovereign states and the fall of the multinational communist empire that had existed for seven decades. This event also accelerated the fragmentation of the multi-ethnic Russian Empire, a geopolitical entity with a history spanning more than four centuries.

In the post-Soviet space, some former republics maintain close cooperation with Russia through various organisations. The Baltic states, on the other hand, have sought European integration by becoming members of the European Union and NATO, while Georgia, Moldova, and Ukraine have consistently pursued similar goals.

Although Russia claims to be a passionate defender of the defenceless, the reality reflects a pattern of not only supporting one side in armed conflicts but also helping others to create an image of peacemaker. Such actions often lead to increased confrontation. To substantiate this claim, the chapter outlines a series of military clashes involving Russia from 1991 until the full-scale attack on Ukraine in 2022, documented by the Disinformation Action Centre on August 6, 2022.

The narrative culminates in a contemporary context that highlights the expansion of Russian mercenaries in Africa and other regions. The hybrid war from 2014 to 2021 and the full-scale war in 2022 caused significant losses in Ukraine, affecting cities, villages, infrastructure, industrial facilities, agriculture, and the environment.

The author emphasises the urgent need for a thorough study of global risks at the international level and prompt action to eliminate the potential for geopolitical

DOI: 10.4324/9781003435433-1

conflicts. It is pointed out that armed conflicts between states are significantly underestimated, as evidenced by Russia's unexpected full-scale war against Ukraine in 2022. The consequences of this war went beyond national borders, affecting not only Ukraine but also countries around the world. The mention of weapons of mass destruction further emphasises the seriousness and global implications of such conflicts. This research aims to provide a comprehensive understanding of the multifaceted dimensions of the Russo-Ukrainian conflict, extending beyond the immediate geopolitical landscape. The chapter seeks to shed light on the historical, political, and cultural intricacies shaping the dynamics between Russia and Ukraine, with a focus on the conflict's origins and its implications for global stability. The overarching goal is to contribute to effective strategies in addressing the immediate crisis and preventing similar occurrences on the global stage.

Research Questions:

1. What are the historical, political, and cultural intricacies that have shaped the dynamics between Russia and Ukraine, leading to the Russo-Ukrainian conflict?
2. How have divergent paths over centuries resulted in unique identities for Ukrainian, Russian, Belarusian, and Lithuanian peoples, influencing the geopolitical landscape of the region?
3. What role did the collapse of the Soviet Union in 1991 play in Ukraine's independence, and how has historical interference by Moscow contributed to the complex relationship between Russia and Ukraine?
4. How can the military engagements involving Russia from 1991 to the full-scale attack on Ukraine in 2022 be characterised, and what are the global implications of the Russo-Ukrainian war?
5. In what ways does Vladimir Putin's persistent effort to control Ukraine underscore Moscow's strategic importance, and what risks does Russia's aggressive military strategy pose globally?
6. How does the war impact democratic systems, increase global military expenses, reduce social expenditures, exacerbate food supply issues, and contribute to mass migration?
7. What are the economic reasons for Russia's invasion of Ukraine, with a focus on the strategic importance of Ukraine's natural resources and its role in the global economy?
8. How have various economic sectors, including agriculture, energy, and metallurgy, been affected by Russia's invasion, and what are the overall economic consequences during and after the war?
9. What measures has Ukraine implemented to ensure financial stability during the conflict, and how have economic indicators, such as GDP growth, inflation, and foreign exchange reserves been affected?
10. Despite the challenges, in which economic sectors did Ukraine exhibit resilience, and how crucial was international financial assistance in stabilising the economy during and after the conflict?

The theoretical and methodological basis of the study is formed by general scientific and philosophical methods of scientific knowledge, dialectical, systematic, and empirical approaches to the study of the impact of war on the economy of Ukraine. Statistical methods were used for an analytical assessment of the state of Ukraine's economy during the war. The bibliographic method of research allowed us to systematise and summarise the achievements of scientists and experts to identify unresolved scientific and applied problems.

The information base of the study includes legislative and regulatory documents of the Ukrainian government and international institutions, materials of the State Statistics Service, the NBU, Eurostat, the World Bank, the EU, the UN, etc., scientific works (monographs, articles, reports of scientists on the topic of the study), and Internet resources.

1.1 Prerequisites for Russia's Full-Scale Invasion of Ukraine

The extensive military campaign launched by Russia against Ukraine in the year 2022 stands as a subject of considerable scholarly scrutiny and is expected to be the focus of numerous academic investigations. There are those who considered the conflict inevitable, while others were taken aback by it. The aggressive invasion of Russian military forces in 2014 into the eastern regions of Ukraine, coupled with the subsequent occupation of the Crimean territory, has laid the ground for this protracted state of war. World leaders and representatives of international organisations have articulated expressions of apprehension in response to this unfolding situation. Notably, the perception that Russia's use of force in neighbouring countries (following the dissolution of the Soviet Union on December 25, 1991) has, arguably, served to embolden the state towards future aggressive endeavours.

It is essential to highlight that the collapse of the Soviet Union gave rise to 15 sovereign nations. This resulted in downfall of the multinational communist empire, which spanned seven decades, as well as precipitated the fragmentation of the polyethnic Russian Empire, a geopolitical entity with a history extending over four centuries. Likewise, the European theatre saw similar occurrences of imperial disintegration in the 19th and 20th centuries, specifically with the Ottoman and Habsburg Empires. The October Revolution and subsequent Soviet governance merely deferred the inevitable disintegration of the Russian Empire for several decades (Kappeler, 1993).

Some former republics of the Soviet Union continued close cooperation with Russia, forming various organisations. However, the Baltic countries became members of the European Union and joined NATO. Georgia, Moldova, and Ukraine consistently aspired to the same objectives.

Russia claims to be a staunch defender of the defenceless. In reality, it frequently not only supports one side in armed conflicts but also aids others (to cultivate a peacekeeper image). Frequently, such actions lead to heightened confrontations. In order to prove this assertion, we will outline a series of military clashes involving Russia, starting from 1991 and extending to the full-scale attack on Ukraine in 2022 (Center for Countering Disinformation, 2022, August 6).

The Yugoslav Wars (1991–2001): Approximately 1,600 Russian military personnel were part of the UN forces in Yugoslavia. In 1999, around 4,000 were deployed to Kosovo.

The War in Georgia (South Ossetia) (December 1991–January 1993): Russian military forces engaged in combat and supplied weapons to Abkhazia and Georgia before the conflict began. Prior to the war, Russia armed all parties involved (i.e. Abkhaz, Georgian, Ossetian), escalating the conflict. Despite the loss of over 2,000 Caucasian volunteers, the Georgian side suffered around 169 military casualties. Russia lost 46 out of 500 soldiers. Among the civilian population of Georgia, 224 peaceful residents were killed. Over the next decade, the country faced ongoing political turmoil and recurring economic, financial, and social crises.

Armed Conflict in Moldova (Transnistria) (November 1990–July 1992): Moldova suffered 286 casualties, while Transnistria lost 826 individuals, including 310 civilians. From a total of six Russian battalions comprising over 3,000 combatants, 24 casualties were recorded. Despite international recognition of Transnistria as part of Moldova, it does not control the territory.

War in Abkhazia (August 1992–September 1993): Russia deployed 1,800 military personnel to Abkhazia, with 73 casualties. Overall, approximately 16,000 people, out of a pre-war population of 537,000 in Abkhazia, lost their lives, and around 250,000 became refugees.

Civil War in Tajikistan (May 1992–June 1997): 33,600 Russian military personnel participated, resulting in 302 casualties. Tajikistan and the United Tajik Opposition suffered over 60,000 casualties. After the war, Tajikistan experienced complete devastation, and its economy and society regressed by ten years. Nearly 1.2 million people became refugees within and outside the country.

First Chechen War (December 1994–August 1996): According to official data, Russian army losses were reported as 4,379 killed, 1,906 missing in action, and 19,794 wounded. However, according to the Soldiers' Mothers Committee of Russia, the actual casualties were over 14,000 (a common practice, as the Russian government tends to downplay real losses). Regarding Chechen losses, Russia acknowledges the deaths of 17,391 Chechen military personnel and 40,000 civilians.

Second Chechen War (August 1999–April 2009): During this war, approximately 7,400 Russian military personnel and 600 Russian civilians lost their lives. Among the Chechen casualties were 14,113 military personnel and over 50,000 civilians.

South Ossetia Armed Conflict and Russia's War in Georgia (August 2008): A total of 19,000 Russian military personnel were deployed, resulting in 67 fatalities and 283 injuries. Simultaneously, the losses of the Georgian army included 410 servicemembers, 14 policemen, and around 2,000 civilians injured. The number of refugees reached over 118,000.

Annexation of Crimea (Ukraine) (since February 2014): Approximately 25,000 Russian military personnel were introduced with no reported losses. More than 100,000 individuals were displaced. Despite the military, geopolitical, internal political, and economic adverse consequences, Ukraine lost two-thirds of its naval fleet.

War in Donbas (Ukraine) (since April 2014): From 2014 to 2021, Ukraine suffered over 13,000 deaths and more than 30,000 injuries. Russia's losses included 5,650 deaths and approximately 13,500 injuries. A significant number of refugees emerged from the eastern part of Ukraine.

Russian Military Operation in Syria (since September 2015): Over 68,500 Russian military personnel participated, resulting in 283 fatalities, the loss of 19 aircraft, and helicopters. The conflict led to the death of nearly half a million civilians, with over half of the population (12 million people) becoming refugees. Today, 90% of Syria's citizens live below the poverty line.

Second Nagorno-Karabakh War (since November 2020): The Azerbaijan army, in a 44-day conflict, seized control of a part of the territory that had been under Armenian control since 1994. Approximately 7,000 military personnel, over 160 civilians, and hundreds of others were killed during the hostilities. Following Russia's intervention, the leaders of Azerbaijan and Armenia signed a ceasefire agreement. Pursuant to this agreement, Russia deployed around 2,000 military personnel, 90 armoured vehicles, and 370 units of military equipment to the Nagorno-Karabakh region. Despite the specified number of soldiers and military equipment in the agreement, the region witnessed the presence of Russian tanks, combat helicopters, and Grad rocket launchers. It is worth noting that during a military operation in September 2023, Azerbaijan armed forces fully regained control over Nagorno-Karabakh. In December, Armenia and Azerbaijan exchanged prisoners of war and agreed to move towards a peaceful settlement. However, there are still barriers that need to be overcome to ensure lasting peace.

Intervention in the protests in Kazakhstan (January 2022): At the request of the president of Kazakhstan, Russia deployed 1,480 military personnel to suppress the protests. This demonstrated to the world the readiness of Russian forces for potential intervention in Ukraine.

Currently, Russian mercenaries are expanding their military presence in Africa, Libya, Sudan, the Central African Republic, Madagascar, and Mozambique.

The hybrid warfare from 2014 to 2021 and the full-scale war in 2022 inflicted significant losses on Ukraine. Cities, villages, infrastructure, industrial facilities, agriculture, and the environment are being destroyed. What is even worse, lives of people are being devastated.

The statement by S. Korsunsky, the Extraordinary and Plenipotentiary Ambassador of Ukraine to Japan, is relevant nowadays. He suggests that the Chechen Wars should have served as the 'first warning' to the world about how political issues are resolved in a country where a 'KGB maniac' is in power. In Europe, there are still numerous separatist movements, but no one has thought of resolving such issues through carpet bombings as in Grozny. The world should have drawn conclusions then, but it did not (Korsunsky, 2022).

A thorough examination of global risks at the international level is essential, and swift action must be taken to address the potential for geopolitical conflicts. Current realities demonstrate that the likelihood of armed conflicts between states is significantly underestimated. The use of weapons of mass destruction confirms this. Hence, the full-scale war of Russia against Ukraine in 2022 has been surprising for many. The burden of war lies not only on Ukraine but also on most countries worldwide. The consequences of the war have transcended national borders and become global.

1.2 Historical Background: Main Reasons for Russian Aggression against Ukraine

Concerning the identification of the reasons for the war between Russia and Ukraine, there are many, and they are profound. Historically, the neighbourly relations between Russia and Ukraine have always been complex.

> History should be remembered, but not rewritten… It is not by chance that Putin, explaining the aggression, used the narrative about the supposed creation of Ukraine by Lenin. Unable to see and approach the future, he decided not to let others do it either.
>
> (Korsunsky, 2022)

Looking at the Russo-Ukrainian war in the historical context, it is worth turning to the concise explanation by experts from the Ukrainian Institute of National Memory as to why Ukrainians and Russians historically are not 'brotherly nations' (Why Ukrainians and Russians Are Not Fraternal Nations [infographics], 2023).

As known, in the 9th century, the medieval state of Rus with its centre in Kyiv was formed. Throughout the following centuries, Rus in a broad sense referred to the entire territory where the rule of Kyivan princes was recognised. However, in a narrow sense, Rus denoted the lands of the Middle Dnieper region around Kyiv. The lands in the northeast, where the Moscow Principality later formed, were called Zalesye at that time. Russia's imperial ambitions emerged much later.

Medieval Rus can be considered the source of Ukrainian, Russian, Belarusian, and partially Lithuanian peoples. It's crucial to recognise that despite sharing a common historical origin, the divergent paths taken by these nations over time have resulted in unique identities. The linguistic, cultural, and political differences that evolved over centuries have contributed to the complex relationships among Ukraine, Russia, Belarus, and Lithuania. These divergences have historical roots that extend beyond the medieval period and have shaped the geopolitical landscape of the region.

The 13th century is marked by brutal Mongol invasions on the territories of modern Ukraine and Russia, resulting in the definitive divergence of the historical paths of both countries. Kyiv, along with surrounding towns and villages, was completely devastated. King Danylo Halytskyi "preserved the integrity of the Western Rus lands by not allowing Mongol-Tatar deputies, the baskaks, into the region, buying time necessary to consolidate Russian forces to repel the invaders" (Kotlyar, 2002: 273). Similar views are shared by Avenarius (1984: 856), Holovko (2006: 331), Hrytsak (1958: 98), Zhdan (1968: 12), Kostomarov (1918: 148), Krypyakevych (1999: 127–128), Plokhii (2016: 88), Stasiv (1954: 142), and Tomashivskyi (1993: 341).

The western part of Rus developed in a European direction, characterised by democracy, self-government, European law, religion, and respect for private property. These features persisted in the Cossack state of Hetmanate. The northeastern territories of the former Rus became part of the Mongol Golden Horde. The political culture of the Moscow Principality was significantly influenced by the Tatar norms and traditions, which emphasised the glorification of the ruler, complete submission to him, absolute state dominance, the absence of private land ownership, and communal orders.

Up to this day, scholars engage in debates over the nature of the 'Pereyaslav Agreement', concluded in the city of Pereyaslav 370 years ago (1654) between the hetman of Ukraine at that time, Bohdan Khmelnytskyi, and the Moscow Tsar Alexis Romanov. In the monograph "Key International Treaties of Bohdan Khmelnytskyi, 1648–1657" by Pritzak (2003), it is convincingly argued that "endless discussions about what the so-called Pereyaslav Agreement of 1654 represents – reunification, annexation, military alliance, protectorate, incorporation – lose their meaning because all the treaties of the hetman, including the so-called Pereyaslav one, had the nature of a protectorate" (Pritzak, 2003).

It is pertinent to clarify that in the acts of the 17th century, political agreements were made between monarchs, not individual nations. Since Bohdan Khmelnytskyi was not on the same level as the tsar, he could not act as an equal partner. Khmelnytskyi and his diplomats insisted on a protectorate 'under the high hand' of the tsar, but the Moscow government consistently used the well-known Moscow formula 'under the hand', which implied subordination. Therefore, the 1654 agreement, in its Moscow version, was not ratified by the Ukrainian government (Ogloblyn, 2003). This issue was thoroughly investigated by Mykhailo Hrushevskyi back in 1929. At that time, as the head of the Archaeographic Commission of the Academy of Sciences of Ukraine, he concluded that "the hetman… and the elders did not accept either the articles or the charter" (Hrushevsky, 1997).

Continuing the study of the works of Hrushevskyi, Pritzak (2005) argues that the primary treaty at that time was the Chyhyryn-Moscow Treaty (named after the capitals of the respective states). In Chyhyryn, Bohdan Khmelnytskyi prepared the 'Articles of Khmelnytskyi', and in Moscow, Tsarist and Ukrainian diplomats discussed and adopted the final form of the treaty – the so-called 'Articles of Bohdan Khmelnytskyi'. Representatives of the Russian imperial opinion believed that it was safer to focus on the religious ceremony at the Pereyaslav Rada, distorting it as an expression of the popular will, rather than dealing with the legal aspects of the treaty. This was because it would have become clear that the Moscow state did not adhere to the provisions of the so-called Pereyaslav Treaty from the very beginning (Pritzak, 2005).

So, having provided the imperial guarantee to preserve the state rights of the Hetmanate, for 120 years, they violated them repeatedly, leading to the complete loss of autonomy for Ukrainian lands.

Russian historians are willing to recognise the Ukrainian, or 'Little Russian', subethnos only from the modern era, attributing its formation to the 15th and 16th centuries. According to their perspective, Kievan Rus has a direct continuation in the Moscow state and the Russian Empire, having nothing in common with contemporary Ukraine. Consequently, Prince Volodymyr is depicted as a 'Russian' prince and the baptiser of 'Russia', while the French queen Anne Yaroslavna becomes a 'Russian princess' (Parakhonskyi & Yavorska, 2019: 255). This way, Russians seek to expand the spatial and temporal boundaries of Russian identity while narrowing the boundaries of Ukrainian identity, even declaring the Ukrainian nation non-existent.

Antoniuk and Mytsenko (2022: 11) argue that.

> The only thing Russia lacks without Ukraine is a thousand-year history to shape and justify its greatness and future Eurasian Empire. Ancient Kievan Rus was already forming in the 9th century, and in the 10th century, the Christianization of Kievan Rus took place. The Moscow Principality began to form in the 13th century. After the conclusion of the military-political union between the Cossack State and Muscovy in 1654 by Bohdan Khmelnytsky, the latter began to subjugate and colonize Ukrainian lands and claim the historical heritage of Kievan Rus. It was based on the colonization of the territory of present-day Ukraine and the appropriation of its history that the name of the Russian Empire arose, which began to keep its chronicle from the founding of the Kievan Principality.

The constant interference of Moscow in the internal affairs of the Ukrainian state eventually led to the Russo-Ukrainian War of 1658–1659, which ended in defeat and caused the liquidation of Ukraine's independence.

It is relevant to note that

> since the Hetman governments swore allegiance to the tsars, all agreements between Hetmanate and the Moscow Kingdom, despite the legitimacy of each individually taken, finally lost their validity in February 1917 with the overthrow of the Romanov dynasty represented by the Russian Emperor Nicholas II. This fact, as well as the right to self-determination of Ukraine, were recognized by the world community on the eve of signing the peace treaty in Brest on February 9, 1918. Therefore, the subsequent 'formal cancellations' of the decisions of the Pereyaslav Rada regarding the union of Hetmanate and the Moscow Kingdom, which took place on July 15, 1919, and June 21, 1992, were only symbolic acts and had no legal significance.
>
> (Buket, 2022)

The Soviet occupation of Ukraine, known as the 'Russian elder brother', continued. "The so-called 300th anniversary of the Pereyaslav Rada was so widely celebrated by the Soviet authorities in 1954 that they 'returned' the Crimean Peninsula to Ukraine" (Buket, 2022).

During the existence of the Soviet Union, Ukraine had the status of a Soviet republic but lacked political, economic, and cultural independence. There was a constant suppression of everything Ukrainian and active promotion of the Russian language and culture. Throughout the Soviet period, the Ukrainian people fought through various means for national independence. Therefore, the declaration of Ukraine's independence in 1991 is the result of the Ukrainian people's long struggle for freedom and self-determination.

Instead, for Russia, Ukraine's declaration of independence and its withdrawal from the Soviet Union, of which Russia is the successor, "undermines the legitimacy of Russia's thousand-year history, which it cannot allow" (Antoniuk & Mytsenko, 2022: 11). Most scholars, experts, and other researchers consider this the main reason for the current war between Russia and Ukraine. Undoubtedly, the assertion that

> NATO, Eurointegration, mythical Nazis in the Ukrainian government are only pretexts for Russia's aggression today. The global reason is the impermissibility for the metropolis to lose control over the territories crucial for the empire. For the Moscow mentality, Ukraine is not only key but also sacred, and Ukrainian identity has always been perceived as a threat to the Russian state.
>
> (Sydorovych, 2022) is valid

Dickinson (2022), a research fellow at the Atlantic Council, aptly points out:

For centuries, successive Russian regimes ruthlessly suppressed Ukraine's independence aspirations while imposing wave upon wave of russification. Generations of Ukrainians were robbed of their past and banned from using their own language. The nadir was reached in the earlier 1930s when millions were starved to death in a genocidal famine engineered by Soviet dictator Josef Stalin to eradicate Ukrainian national identity in its rural heartlands.

While Ukraine officially achieved independence in 1991, Russia never came to terms with this separation. Instead, Moscow sought to keep independent Ukraine firmly within the Kremlin orbit and viewed Ukrainian efforts to embrace a democratic European future as an existential threat to authoritarian Russia that must be prevented at almost any cost.

> Throughout his reign, the need to either control or crush Ukraine has dominated Vladimir Putin's foreign policy thinking. His pivot from early cooperation with the West to Cold War-style confrontation came about as a direct response to Ukraine's 2004 Orange Revolution. Ten years later when millions of Ukrainians took to the streets once again in defense of their European choice and fledgling democracy, Putin went one step further and ordered his military to intervene. The 2014 seizure of Crimea and occupation of eastern Ukraine set the stage for this year's full-scale invasion and illustrated Putin's readiness to make remarkable sacrifices in order to resolve the Ukrainian question.
>
> As the outbreak of hostilities drew closer, Putin's obsession with the destruction of Ukraine became increasingly obvious. He proclaimed Ukraine an inalienable part of Russia's own history, culture, and spiritual space, while

> at the same time denouncing the present Ukrainian state as an illegitimate "anti-Russia" that could no longer be tolerated.
>
> (Dickinson, 2022)

Starting the war, Russia did not expect such strong resistance from Ukraine. Ideology, means, and events demonstrate that it is a war between two civilisations built on different principles:

- Ukrainian, characterised by freedom, democracy, and respect for human values.
- Russian, characterised by authoritarianism, aggressive imperial chauvinism, and disregard for human rights and norms of human life.

Despite the fact that Russian aggression is dangerous for the Ukrainian state, destroying its economy, ecology, and human lives, it poses a significant risk to the entire world. Such an aggressive military strategy becomes an enemy to democratic systems and stable development in other countries. It contributes to increasing military expenses, reducing social expenditures, involving more countries in armed conflict, exacerbating food supply problems in different countries, and provoking mass migration.

1.3 Economic Reasons for Russia's War with Ukraine and Their Impact on Geopolitics

Ukraine is a country rich in natural resources with a strategically advantageous geographical location. Increasingly, among analysts and experts from developed countries, discussions arise regarding the world order after Russia's war in Ukraine. Most of them agree that geopolitics is a tool for understanding the true interests driving the war in Ukraine. To gain control over Ukrainian territory, the aggressor country, Russia, is taking the simplest and proven path – waging war.

> Geopolitical interests are the driving force behind the aggressor's actions of brutal hostilities, killing of people, and atrocities in captured territories. Russia needs to ensure its control over space and territories – objects of its genuine interest. According to the aggressor, such a space should be under control in all dimensions, including underground, where Ukraine holds deposits of natural resources. These resources are believed to ensure the existence, economic advantages, and prosperity of the aggressor country.
>
> (Polyovyk, 2023)

Correspondent of the German publication Berliner Zeitung, Maximilian Beer (2023), analyses in detail the probable reasons for Russia's aggressive war in Ukraine. Among them is "Ukraine's natural resources, which represent real value and necessity for ensuring the existence of the Putinist empire". Beer (2023) emphasises that Ukraine has vast reserves of raw materials, including natural gas, oil, lithium, and more. In this sense, Berliner Zeitung notes that Ukraine is a wealthy country.

> At the same time, since 2014, Russia has controlled numerous deposits in the east of the country. These are the economic reasons for the invasion of regular Russian troops into Donbas and the establishment of pro-Russian puppet regimes with capitals in Donetsk and Luhansk.
>
> (Polyovyk, 2023)

Renowned writer E. Topol (October 5, 2022) also asserts the presence of economic reasons for Russia's military invasion in Ukraine. He refutes quite common claims that V. Putin seeks to prove his significance to world leaders, dreams of entering history as a 'gatherer of Russian lands', or is irritated by the possibility of Ukraine joining NATO. In an article published by Russian generals Ovchinsky and Zhdanov titled "Lithium and Death" (2022), attention is drawn to the fact that "Ukraine has a huge amount of mountainous rocks and minerals with different distribution across the territory. There are about 800 deposits discovered here, where 94 types of useful minerals are extracted".

Furthermore, Ukrainian deposits are described in detail (Ovchinsky & Zhdanov, 2022):

1 Ukraine has large deposits of oil and natural gas, coal (i.e. bituminous and brown), peat, and oil shale. Oil and gas extraction is carried out in the Black Sea-Crimean region, in the Carpathian region, and in the Dnicper-Donetsk region. As for coal, it is extracted in the Lviv-Volyn basin, and in the Dnieper and Donetsk basins.
2 Ore minerals: manganese ore (Nikopol basin and Velikotokmatske deposit); iron (Kryvyi Rih and Crimean basins, Bilozerka and Mariupol deposits); nickel ore; titanium (Malyshevske, Stremigorodske, Irshanske deposits); chrome; mercury (Mykytivske deposit); uranium (Zovtorichenske deposit and Kirovohrad region); gold (Sergiivske, Travneve, Muzhiivske, Klyntsiivske deposits).
3 Non-metallic minerals: Deposits of ozokerite and sulfur are located in the Carpathians. Rock salt is extracted in the Solotvynsk, Artemivsk, and Slovyansk deposits, as well as in the Sivash lake. Labradorite and granite are mainly extracted in the Zhytomyr region. Deposits of semi-precious and precious stones, such as mountain crystal and amethyst, amber and beryl, jade, are mined in Zakarpattia, Crimea, Kryvyi Rih, and Pryazovye.

Canadian experts from the Ottawa-based SecDev think tank have assessed geopolitical risks (Faiola & Bennett, 2022, August 10) and claim that Russia has taken control of Ukrainian territories with energy, metals and mineral deposits worth \$12.4 trillion. This is only half the dollar value of the 2,209 deposits that the Canadian firm examined. In addition to 63% of Ukraine's coal deposits, Russia has seized 11% of oil, 20% of gas, 42% of metals, and 33% of rare earths and other important minerals, including lithium (Kishchak, 2022).

If oil is traditionally called 'black gold' due to its significance, then lithium, according to global experts, becomes the 'white gold' of the current century. It is forecasted that by 2030, global demand for lithium will increase five to ten times. Lithium is the lightest metal in the world. In metallurgy, it is used for desulfurisation and to increase the plasticity and strength of alloys. In optics, it is used to make glasses that protect against ultraviolet rays. In addition, in atomic energy and nuclear technology, it is used to obtain the radioactive isotope of hydrogen – tritium. But the lion's share of lithium goes into the production of lithium-ion batteries. The growth in demand for electric vehicles led to a 400% surge in lithium prices in 2021. By 2040, two-thirds of global car sales will be electric vehicles.

According to the United States Geological Survey (USGS), the largest predicted lithium resources in the world as of 2021 were in Bolivia, estimated at 21 million tons, followed by Argentina (19 million tons), Chile (9.8 million tons), the United States (9.1 million tons), Australia (7.3 million tons), and China (5.1 million tons). The USGS estimates the predicted lithium reserves in Russia at 1 million tons (Ovchinsky & Zhdanov, 2022). According to the National Academy of Sciences of Ukraine, the lithium reserves in the country are approximately 500,000 tons. With this figure, they are among the largest in the world (Beer, 2023).

In 2016, Forbes-Ukraine reported that Mkango Resource, headquartered in Canada, was exploring the potential of Ukrainian lithium. Currently, international companies are acquiring inexpensive licenses and rights for the development of lithium deposits in countries where there are reserves but no extraction. This situation also applies to Ukraine, where lithium deposits, according to geological exploration data, amount to 500 million tons (the largest in Europe) and are located in Donetsk, Zakarpattia, and Kirovohrad Oblasts. However, Ukraine does not extract lithium on an industrial scale, making prospective deposits attractive to investors (Ovchinsky & Zhdanov, 2022).

This situation is cited by Topol (2022, October 5) as one of the reasons for Russia's invasion of Ukraine.

> In late 2021, Ukraine began auctioning permits for the exploration of its lithium reserves, as well as copper, cobalt, and nickel [...] The potential for lithium extraction in Ukraine began to attract global attention. In November 2021, the Australian company, European Lithium, announced that it was in the process of obtaining rights to two promising deposits in Donetsk Oblast in eastern Ukraine and in Kirovohrad in the central part of the country [...] In the same month, the Chinese company, Chengxin Lithium, also applied for the rights to lithium deposits in Donetsk and Kirovohrad [...] In mid-February 2022, 17, American military experts wrote a letter to U.S. Secretary of Defense Lloyd Austin, emphasizing the need to expand U.S. access to strategic minerals.
>
> (Ovchinskiy & Zhdanov, 2022)

Topol (October 5, 2022) concludes that

> immediately after Australia and China applied for the right to develop Ukrainian lithium, Putin began gathering troops along the Ukrainian border,

> and as soon as American experts mentioned the 'need for U.S. access to strategic minerals', he immediately ordered the invasion.

According to a document from the Scientific Service of the Bundestag, Ukraine is considered a "potential superpower in the production of important industrial metals" (Beer, 2023). Based on publicly available data, Ukraine possesses

> commercially significant volumes of 117 out of 120 of the most demanded industrial minerals in more than 8,700 surveyed deposits [...] The total value of these deposits, including titanium, iron, neon, nickel, lithium, may range from 3 to 11.5 trillion US dollars.
>
> (Polyovyk, 2023)

It's worth recalling that in January 2023, when Russians captured the city of Soledar, rich in rock salt near Bakhmut, there were speculations regarding the interest in valuable minerals. There were reports suggesting that the leader of the Wagner Private Military Company (PMC), Yevgenyi Prigozhin, might be interested in Ukrainian salt and gypsum deposits. Reuters also reported on the possible interest in Ukrainian salt and gypsum, citing a representative from the U.S. administration (Dorosh, 2023).

The significant reserves of valuable minerals in the regions occupied by Russia are acknowledged by Russian state media as they discuss the prospects of these territories with experts. Scientists confirm the opinion from the German publication (Beer, 2023), stating that Ukraine concentrates approximately 120 types of valuable minerals with industrial significance. Despite this, there are deposits of the 21st rare earth element from the list of 30 substances identified by the European Union as 'critical raw materials'. These are essential for the development of 'green' energy. This includes lithium, cobalt, scandium, graphite, tantalum, niobium, and others. Thus, around 5% of the world's reserves of 'critical raw materials' are located in Ukraine, as mentioned by the deputy minister of Environmental Protection and Natural Resources, Svitlana Hrynchuk, at the meeting of the United Nations Economic Commission for Europe (Dorosh, 2023).

Despite Russia's strong interest in Ukraine's valuable minerals, another economic reason for the Russian invasion becomes apparent during the war – the issue of food security in the Black Sea region. Russia focused significant attention on this matter as it seized the southern Ukrainian ports in Mariupol and Berdiansk. Russia attempted to sell the stolen grain from Ukraine to Egypt.

At that time, the data on prices in the region were quite alarming. While Ukrainian exporters planned to sell wheat for around $300 per ton at the beginning of 2022, during the war in Ukraine, prices soared to $450–500 per ton. This situation had a severe impact on Middle Eastern countries, as there was a drought and poor harvest in the region in 2021. Wheat and barley yields in Syria fell by more than 25%, and in Iraq and Iran, wheat yields decreased by 14% and 16%, respectively (Shapran, 2022).

The mentioned countries missed the planned replenishment of their grain reserves at the beginning of 2022. Prices remained high for quite a long time.

Drought and high wheat prices in the Mediterranean region posed threats of famine (in Yemen, Iraq, Iran, Syria).

> Hungry riots took place in large cities of Iran in May and June. Food prices in Iran significantly increased. The cost of vegetable oil, poultry, eggs, and milk increased fourfold, while bread and flour tripled [...] There is a likelihood that the Iranian government deliberately stopped subsidizing basic food products for the population, knowing that it would affect not only Iran but also other countries in the region [...] It is well known that the current leader of Iran, Ali Khamenei, is a native of the Azerbaijan Soviet Republic. In 2013, Russia commissioned the Bushehr Nuclear Power Plant in Iran and implements a whole range of economic projects [...] Recent evidence of smuggling Brazilian weapons from Iraq to Russia through Iran for the war in Ukraine, reported by *The Guardian*, confirms the warm Russian-Iranian relations.
>
> (Shapran, 2022)

Thus, Russia's efforts to significantly increase the cost of food for certain countries in the Middle East have proven successful:

- drought in Canada, the Middle East, South America, and the USA intensified the strain on global food reserves due to the war
- blockade of southern Ukrainian ports
- official cessation of Russia's participation in the grain deal (since July 2022, it has been carried out through Turkey and the UN to export Ukrainian products via the Black Sea)
- significant increase in grain prices in the Black Sea region

V. Shapran's statement (2022) that "among the goals of the war in Ukraine may well be the provocation of unrest and war in the Middle East. This scenario is beneficial to the Russian Federation because any war in the Middle East always means price highs for oil and its derivatives. As a bonus, there is a revision of geopolitical influence in the Middle East" is reasonable.

1.4 Economic Consequences of Russia's Full-Scale Invasion of Ukraine

First and foremost, it is crucial to note that throughout the entire war, Russia's genocidal intentions only intensified. These horrific words were more than confirmed by actions. The advancing Russian army employed massive artillery shelling to destroy Ukrainian cities along with the civilian population. In regions under Russian occupation, Putin's forces systematically carried out mass killings. Groups of victims with bound hands and signs of torture were repeatedly found in liberated territories. Millions of peaceful Ukrainian citizens were forcibly deported to Russia. Those who remained are subjected to terror, including abductions and hostage-taking. Since the beginning of Russia's full-scale invasion of Ukraine, over 195,000 Ukrainian children have been abducted (Children of War, 2024). According to the European Parliament, the number of illegally deported Ukrainian children to Russia since 2014 may range from 16,000 to 300,000 (Perun, 2023).

Russia's invasion of Ukraine was preceded by the declaration of war goals that did not encompass any economic objectives. However, from the occupied territories, Russians actively loot not only agricultural products and liquid metal products but also agricultural machinery and even entire factories.

Throughout the years of war and the annexation of Crimea, starting from 2014, Russia seized hundreds of Ukrainian deposits. "By the most conservative estimates, their value may range from 12.5 trillion to 15 trillion dollars" (Dorosh, 2023).

Ukraine is losing access to coal, oil, gas, iron and titanium ores, gold, uranium, granite, manganese, lithium, and salt. According to the Institute of Geological Sciences of the National Academy of Sciences of Ukraine, control has been lost over more than 700 deposits out of 2,160 (Dorosh, 2023). In other words, almost one-third of the deposits are located in the occupied territories or near the front line.

Experts from the Institute also assessed Ukraine's losses starting from the annexation of Crimea by Russia in 2014 – in the peninsula and its waters, there are deposits of hydrocarbons, iron ores, and limestone for soda production. Ukraine had just begun to develop natural gas reserves in Crimea and southern regions. These reserves are estimated at a minimum of 2–3 trillion cubic metres of gas, and the reserves of oil with condensate are estimated at another trillion tons. The director of the mentioned institute, academician Stella Shekhunova, suggests that Ukraine could have become the second-largest exporter of natural gas in Europe (Dorosh, 2023). These resources could have ensured the country's energy independence and even created new export positions.

Russia seized not only the water areas of deposits and wells but also the infrastructure: storages, ships, underwater pipelines, drilling rigs, such as 'Tavryda' and 'Syvash', platforms like 'Petro Hodovanets', and 'Nezalezhnist' (i.e. Independence). "The biggest losses suffered by Ukraine are in the deposits of combustible minerals: hydrocarbons and coal", states S. Shekhunova (Dorosh, 2023). Ukraine does not control 80% of its coal deposits. According to the Minister of Energy of Ukraine, Herman Halushchenko, among the captured are a quarter of state-owned coal mines.

Shekhunova asserts that Ukraine has the world's largest deposits of iron ore. In 2014, Crimea seized the deposits of the Kerch iron ore basin, where the Kerch iron ore combine operated. In 2022, Russia also seized deposits in the Bilozerskyi and Priazovskyi iron ore districts in the Zaporizhzhia and Donetsk regions. The reserves of the Priazovsky district alone are estimated at 3 billion tons. In 2014, Ukraine also lost almost 100% of dolomites for metallurgy, 100% of carbonate raw materials for sodium carbonate production, 90% of powdered stone, over 80% of flux raw material deposits, over 95% of refractory clay deposits, as well as the raw material base and the complex for the production of bromine, magnesium oxide, soda, hafnium, and more (Dorosh, 2023)

Various gold deposits with different levels of development and origin are located in the occupied territories. These include the Bobrykivsk deposit in Luhansk, the

Surozhsk deposit near Berdiansk (Zaporizhzhia region), and several deposits in the Donetsk region.

The situation with salt is critical. There are a total of 15 deposits, one-third of which are licensed. However, for the past ten years, almost all needs have been met only by the Artemivsk deposit in Soledar. Today, Soledar is completely destroyed (Labiak, 2024). Currently, only the Drohobych deposit (Lviv region) supplies salt to the domestic market.

Ukraine is also rich in manganese reserves, crucial for metallurgy development. Russia occupied the Veliko-Tokmatsk deposit of manganese ores in the Zaporizhzhia region. Nikopol and Marganets (Dnipropetrovsk region), where manganese is extracted, are constantly under fire.

Regarding lithium reserves in Ukraine, government data suggests they are around 500,000 tons. Although the extraction has not been fully established yet, plans were in place (Ehrman, 2021). Russia occupied at least two deposits: in Shevchenkivsk (Donetsk region) and the deposit of complex ores, Kruta Balka, near Berdyansk. Russia does not extract lithium. Its official, Vladislav Demidov, called the lithium problem 'gigantic' for Russia since Argentina and Chile stopped exports, leaving Bolivia as the only supplier (Dorosh, 2023). Russia also imports kaolin, and Ukraine was the top supplier before the war. Now, deposits in the Donetsk region are captured.

Before the war, Ukraine was one of the top ten countries in uranium mining. In the occupied territories of Mykolaiv, Kharkiv, Donetsk, and Luhansk regions, there are unexplored uranium deposits. However, the largest deposits are located in the controlled territory in the Kirovohrad region. It is essential not to allow Russia to occupy the largest uranium deposit in Europe, as it would significantly strengthen its position in the nuclear fuel market.

1.5 Assessment of the State of Ukraine's Economy during the War

Despite the occupation of 850 km² of territory (CES Team, 2023) and challenging wartime conditions, the economy is striving to stay afloat. According to experts from the Ministry of Economy of Ukraine, in 2023, the GDP grew by approximately 5% (compared to a 28.8% decline in 2022) (Figure 1.1). The most significant recovery rates are observed in the following economic sectors: public administration and defence, construction, agriculture, domestic trade, and manufacturing. The GDP growth occurred based on a low comparison base in 2022. Therefore, economic recovery has not yet taken place. Each quarter in 2023, the real GDP was lower than the real GDP in the corresponding quarter of 2021. Overall, the GDP for 2023 represents three-fourth of the value of the GDP in 2021.

In challenging periods, maintaining macroeconomic stability in the country is facilitated by trust in monetary policy. Bombardment of Ukraine began on February 24, 2022, at 4 a.m., and by 9:52 a.m., the National Bank of Ukraine (NBU) had already published a list of measures implemented to ensure financial stability (Lepushynskyi, 2023). On the same day, the NBU set the official exchange rate at 29.25 UAH per USD. Five months later (July 21), the NBU adjusted the rate by

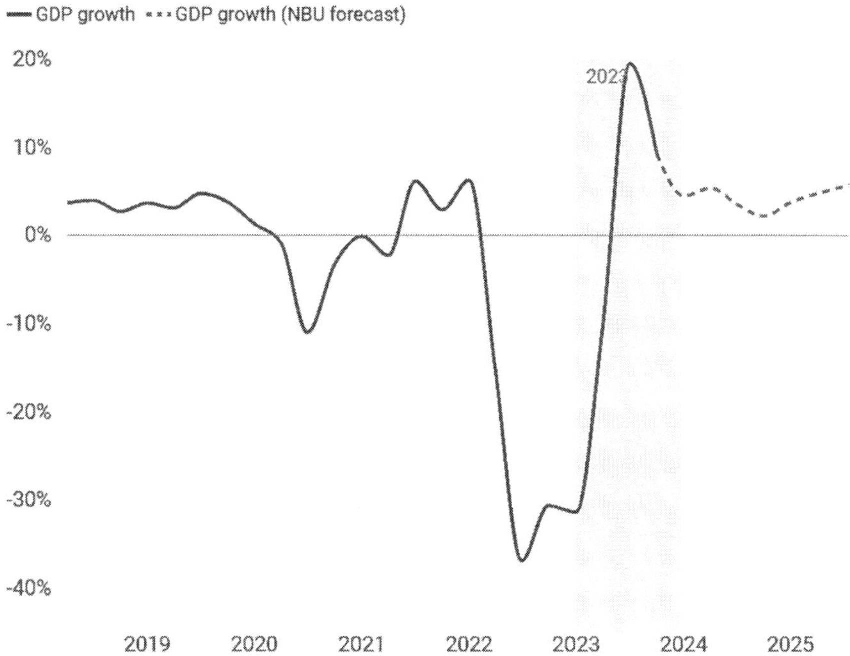

Figure 1.1 GDP growth & GDP growth (NBU forecast)

Source: Own elaboration based on the State Statistics Service of Ukraine (2023); NBU (2023); Ukrainian Economy in 2023: Key figures – Centre for Economic Strategy (2024).

25% to 36.6 UAH per USD, considering the economic consequences of the war and the strengthening of the dollar against other currencies. In the face of uncertainty due to the war, maintaining exchange rate stability for price and financial stabilisation of the economy was a justified decision by the NBU.

It's worth noting that the year 2023 started with a fixed official exchange rate of 36.6 UAH/USD. The cash rate as of January 1 was significantly higher, standing at 40.5 UAH/USD. Expectations varied, with the government budgeting for an average rate of 42.2 UAH/USD in 2023. The NBU maintained the rate at 36.6 for over half a year. The gap with the cash rate gradually narrowed. On October 3, 2023, the NBU transitioned to a managed floating regime. Due to substantial currency interventions, the hryvnia slightly strengthened. In December 2023, the dollar rate increased, reaching 38 UAH/USD in January 2024. This trend is clearly visible in Figure 1.2.

At the beginning of 2023, Ukraine experienced a relatively high level of inflation. Primarily, this was a consequence of printing hryvnias to cover war expenses.

The positive aspect is that inflation was subsequently contained: assistance from other countries allowed the halt of hryvnia printing. Additionally, a good harvest contributed to a reduction in food prices. By the end of 2023, the inflation rate was 5.1%, returning to the pre-war level of 5% (CES Team, 2023; Minfin, 2024).

Figure 1.2 Cash and official exchange rate in Ukraine, UAH/USD, 2022–2023

Source: Own elaboration based on the Minfin (2024); CES Team (2023).

Sound monetary policy relies on forecasting inflation and considering potential risks. Interest rates play a crucial role in aligning inflation forecasts with the medium-term target. Following Russia's invasion, a significant increase in the central bank's policy rate occurred in 2022. This was done to enhance the attractiveness of hryvnia assets and support the exchange rate. In Figure 1.3, we can observe that in 2023, the policy rate was reduced from 25 to 15%. This reduction became possible due to a faster-than-expected decline in inflation and the adaptation of the currency market to the new exchange rate. The yield on one-year hryvnia military bonds decreased from 18.5 to 16.9% in 2023. Throughout the year, the average deposit rates for individuals (UIRD) remained in the range of 13–14%, significantly exceeding the inflation rate.

On January 25, 2024, the NBU board decided to maintain the policy rate at 15% (National Bank of Ukraine, 2024). This decision helped sustain exchange rate stability and maintain moderate inflation levels within the target range of 5% ± 1 percentage point.

Foreign financial assistance played a crucial role in achieving historical maximum by the Ukrainian foreign exchange reserves in 2023. Thus, at the end of the year, Ukraine's international reserves reached $40.5 billion (Figure 1.4). This remarkable situation during wartime became possible due to substantial international financial support for Ukraine. In December 2023, foreign exchange reserves increased by 4.4% compared to November, driven by currency inflows from

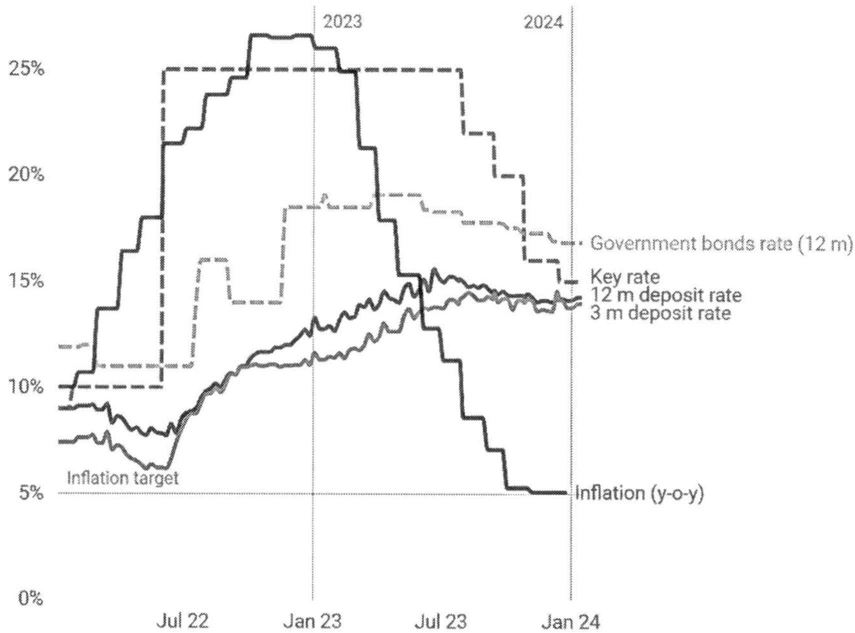

Figure 1.3 Deposit rate and inflation (y-o-y) in Ukraine, 2022–2023, %

Source: Own elaboration based on the Minfin (2024); CES Team (2023).

international partners that exceeded the NBU's net currency sales and Ukraine's foreign debt repayments.

Throughout 2023, the NBU eased currency restrictions for businesses and households, transitioning to a managed floating exchange rate regime in October. The new historical minimum was reached on January 10, 2024, with the official exchange rate standing at 38.2 UAH/USD. Currency fluctuations in Ukraine are likely to become more frequent, but the international reserves are currently at a sufficient level to manage currency expectations and maintain relative currency stability.

In 2023, there was a noticeable increase in the volumes of term deposits and demand deposits in UAH compared to 2022. Foreign currency deposits, after a significant decline, started to recover. The dollarisation of clients' funds decreased as UAH deposits became more attractive, offering higher returns to compensate for devaluation risks compared to less appealing deposits in foreign currencies (Figure 1.5). A certain recovery in economic activity contributed to the growing demand for loans, particularly from businesses, including trade and agricultural enterprises, in the last months of 2023. In contrast to lending in UAH, foreign currency lending remained stagnant. Since the beginning of the full-scale war, the foreign currency loan portfolio decreased by one-third in dollar equivalent (Figure 1.6).

In 2022, due to reduced demand for loans and other banking services, as well as the impact of wartime activities, banks experienced a decrease in profits. However, 2023 proved to be a more successful year for banks. This was facilitated by the

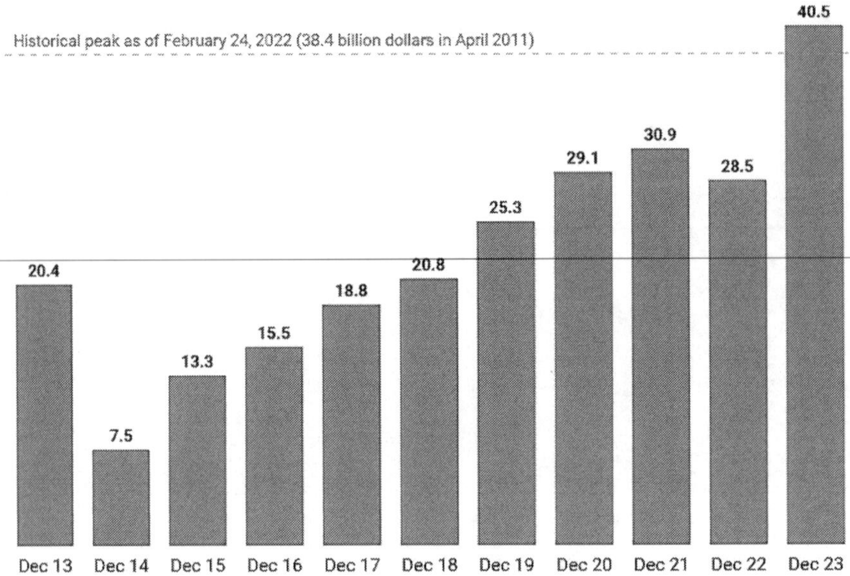

Figure 1.4 Ukraine's foreign exchange reserves, 2013–2023, billion USD

Source: Own elaboration based on *International reserves* (2024); Samoylyuk and Levchenko (2024).

monetary policy, particularly the increase in interest rates on deposit certificates. To fund state defence expenditures, a temporary increase in the corporate income tax on banks was introduced: 50% in 2023 and 25% in 2024–2025 (Samoiliuk & Levchenko, 2024).

The stability of Ukraine heavily relies on foreign aid. In 2023, Ukraine received $11.4 billion more in financial assistance than in 2022 ($42.5 billion compared to $31.1 billion) (CES Team, 2023: 18). Nearly 63% of the financial aid consisted of concessional loans, allowing the financing of crucial budgetary needs.

In 2023, the state budget's need for additional funding totalled $59.9 billion. This included $47.9 billion to cover the budget deficit and $11.9 billion for debt repayment. The financial assistance from various countries allowed covering 71% of these needs (Figure 1.7). The rest was financed mainly through the issuance of Ukraine's domestic government bonds (OVDP).

In December 2023, Ukraine received approximately $2.2 billion in foreign financial assistance from Japan ($0.2 billion in grants); $1.6 billion in loans from the European Union; $0.9 billion in loans from the International Monetary Fund (IMF); $0.3 billion in grants from Norway, Germany, the United States, and Switzerland; $8 million from the World Bank (Figure 1.8).

As of November 2023, the balance of goods and services for Ukraine was −$2.7 billion, with the import of goods exceeded the export by $2.2 billion, while the import of services exceeded the export by $0.6 billion (Figure 1.9). The trade of services has maintained a consistent trend in recent months, whereas the trade of

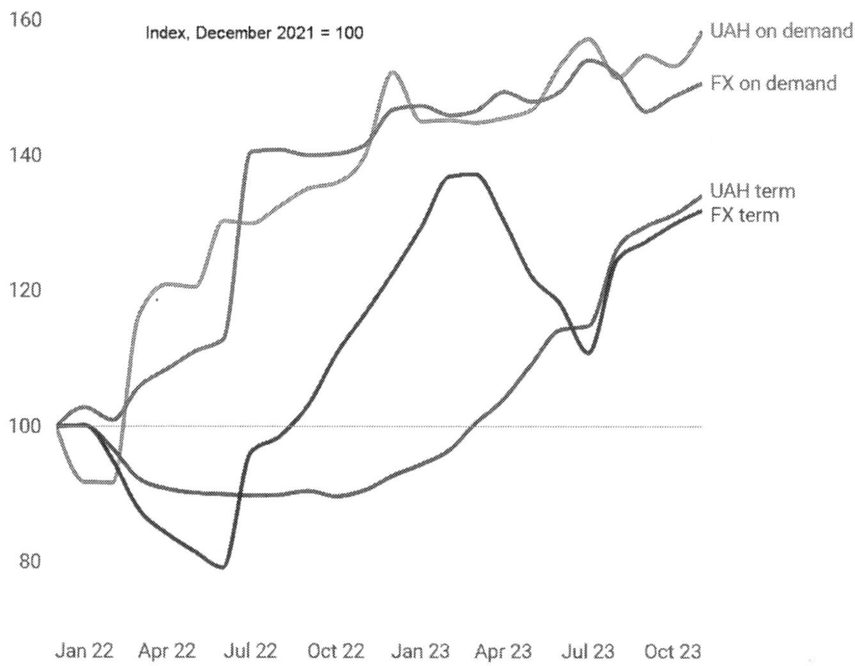

Figure 1.5 Household deposits by currency and maturity, 2022–2023 (index, December 2021 = 100)

Source: Own elaboration based on 3.2-Deposits (2023).

goods has undergone noticeable transformations. The export of goods in November 2023 increased by 8% compared to the previous month, while the import of goods decreased by 10%. It's worth noting that the export of goods has been declining for the second consecutive year. In 2021, the export of goods amounted to $68.2 billion, and in 2022, it decreased to $44.2 billion. The composition of Ukraine's goods exports is dominated by food products and metals.

In response to Russia's disregard for agreements within the Grain Trade Agreement, Ukraine established its own maritime corridor to the Black Sea ports in the Odessa region in 2023. This move not only increased the export of grains but also facilitated the recovery of maritime exports and imports for various goods. However, Ukraine faced challenges in 2023 due to the Polish blockade of the land border, negatively impacting Ukrainian exports and tax revenues from imported goods. It had notable effects on the flow of goods and economic activities between the two countries.

Meanwhile, the metallurgical sector of Ukraine is gradually recovering (Figure 1.10), with metallurgical plants operating at approximately 70% of their capacity. By the end of 2023, the restoration of maritime exports through the Ukrainian maritime corridor expanded the opportunities for exporting black metals. Before the full-scale war, 4/5 of metallurgical production was sold abroad. In December

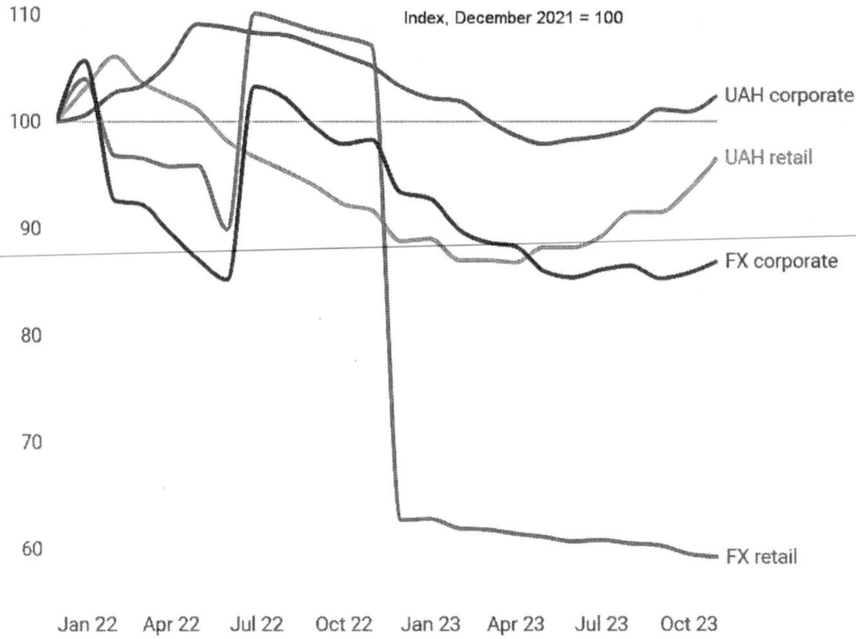

Figure 1.6 Loans for residents by sectors and types of currencies, 2022–2023 (index, December 2021 = 100).

Source: Own elaboration based on 3.3-Loans (2023).

2023, steel production declined by 5% (to 521,000 tons), while pig iron and rolled products increased by 2% and 3% (to 556,000 tons and 508,000 tons, respectively). The overall steel production in 2023 decreased by 0.6% (to 6.23 million tons) (Samoiliuk & Levchenko, 2024).

The Ukrainian Danube Shipping Company anticipates an increase in its share of metal product transportation from 23 to 50% in 2024. The highest loading in 2023 was observed at metallurgical plants such as 'Zaporizhstal' and 'Kametstal', reaching 65–75%. This indicates a positive trend in the recovery of the metallurgical sector and associated transportation activities.

Ukrainian metallurgical enterprises face significant risks due to their proximity to the conflict zone, with the primary threat being the consequences of shelling. This poses a danger to both production assets and the personnel of these enterprises. At the beginning of 2023, a major challenge for metallurgical enterprises was the power outages resulting from shelling of Ukraine's energy infrastructure. Blackouts significantly restricted the operation of metallurgical plants. Emergency power outages led to accelerated equipment wear and increased investments in repairs. The stabilisation of power supply in spring 2023 allowed metallurgical enterprises to increase their capacity utilisation.

In 2023, weather conditions favoured agriculture in Ukraine. The crop yield for cereals increased to 54.7 c/ha, surpassing the figure in 2021 when the yield was

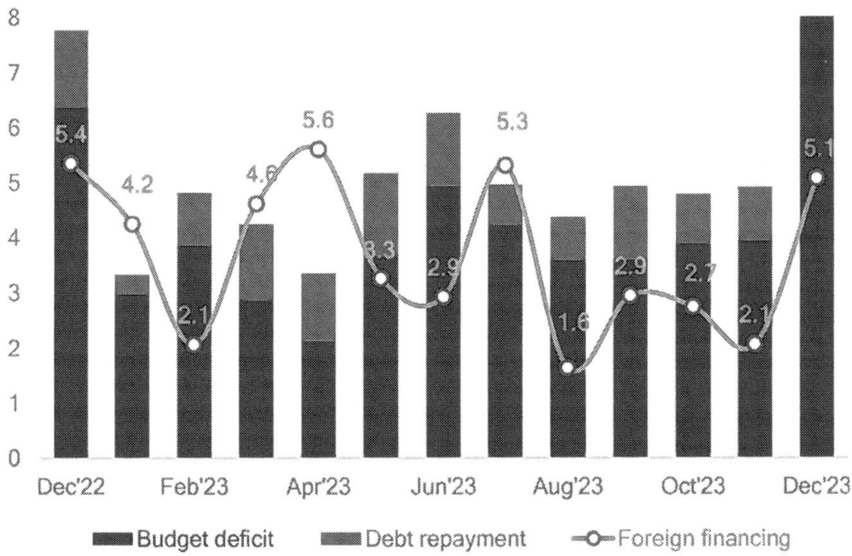

Figure 1.7 Financing Ukraine's budget needs in 2023: foreign financing, state budget deficit, debt repayment, billion USD

Source: Own elaboration based on the Minfin (2024); CES Team (2023).

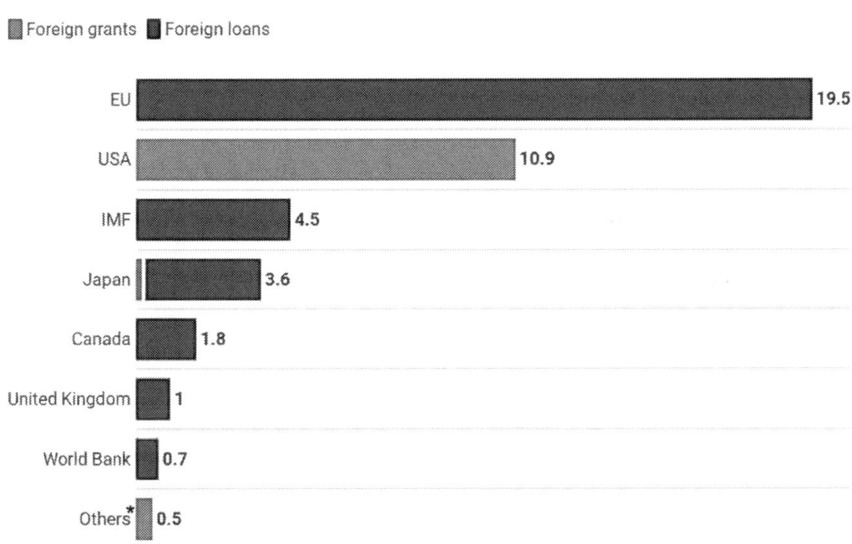

Figure 1.8 Foreign financing of Ukraine's budget needs, 2023, billion USD

Source: Own elaboration based on the Ministry of Finance of Ukraine (2023); CES Team (2023).

*Others – Belgium, Estonia, Finland, Germany, Iceland, Ireland, Norway, Spain, Switzerland.

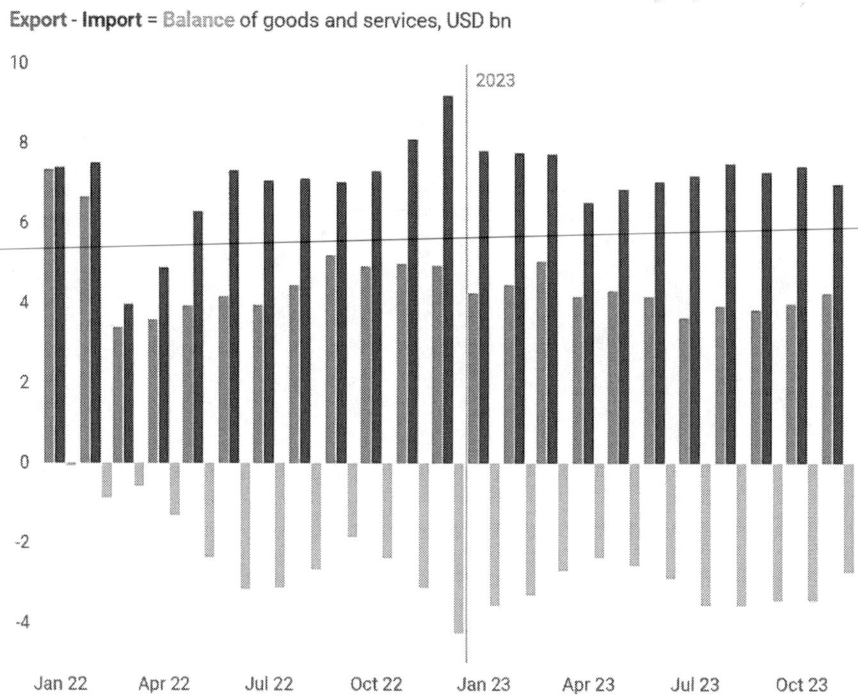

Figure 1.9 Dynamics of Ukraine's balance of payments: exports of goods and services, imports of goods and services, balance of goods and services, 2022–2023, billion USD

Source: Own elaboration based on BOP_m (2023).

53.6 c/ha. Despite substantial losses of agricultural territories under occupation or deemed unsafe, successful yields were observed for various crops. The export of agricultural products by sea transport saw a significant increase in December 2023, reaching 4 million tons, the highest during the war. The overall volume of agricultural product exports grew to 6 million tons, which is 9% lower than in 2021. However, the export of grain by trucks decreased to 60,000 tons in December due to problems at the Polish border (Figure 1.11).

The abundance of high yields underscores the importance of preserving and enhancing logistic capabilities for the export of agricultural products. Maintaining the Ukrainian maritime corridor is crucial for sustaining food exports. Additionally, efforts should be directed towards negotiating with Poland to lift the blockade on Ukraine's western border, facilitating smoother logistics.

Regarding Ukraine's fiscal policy, tax revenues to the general state budget totalled 97.7 billion UAH in December 2023 (Figure 1.12). The fiscal stability and revenue generation are vital components for sustaining economic activities, especially during challenging times.

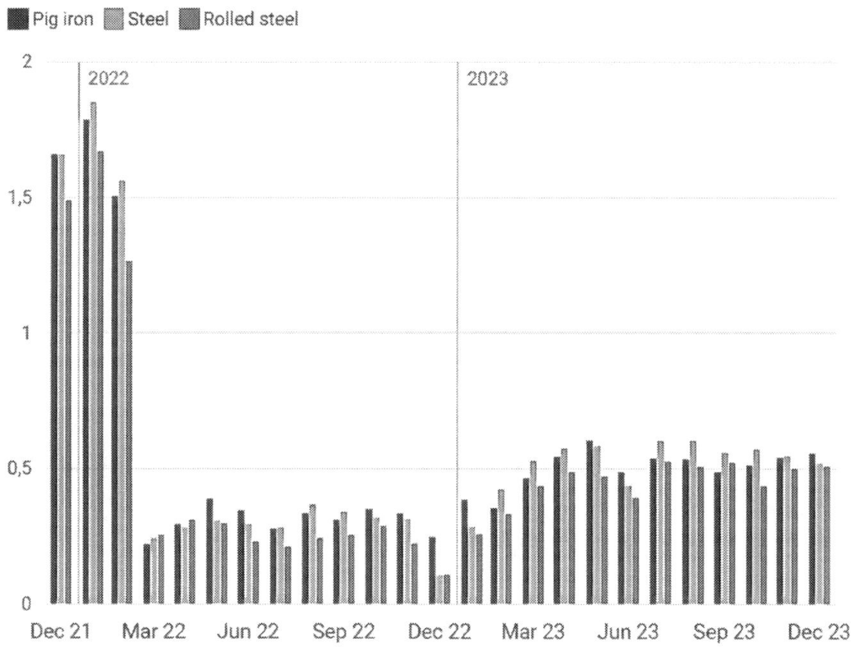

Figure 1.10 Metallurgical production in Ukraine by main categories, 2021–2023, million tons

Source: Own elaboration based on Glushchenko (2024).

For the first time, monthly revenues from the Personal Income Tax (PIT) exceeded 20 billion UAH, indicating a significant contribution from individual taxpayers. Internal VAT revenues have maintained a level of 22.5 billion UAH for the third consecutive month.

Import VAT revenues have recovered to the levels of August–September 2023 (35.7 billion UAH) (CES Team, 2023). The overall tax revenues to the state budget reached 18.2% of GDP in 2023, compared to 18.3% in 2022. Calculated tax revenues to local budgets constituted 6.6% of GDP in 2023, compared to 7.6% in 2022.

The Business Activity Expectations Index dropped to 45.7 points in December 2023, down from 49.1 points in November (National Bank of Ukraine, 2024a). This decline signifies prevailing negative expectations among surveyed business owners. The reasons are evident: the ongoing conflict and war-related challenges, logistical constraints, workforce shortages, and uncertainty regarding international financial assistance in 2024. The Business Activity Expectations Index is an important subjective indicator of the economic situation (Figure 1.13).

It is noteworthy that the Consumer Sentiment Index, as assessed by Info Sapiens, in December 2023, exhibited a value of 77.1, reflecting a decline in comparison to the preceding month. When the Index falls below 100, it indicates a prevalence of adverse consumer sentiments.

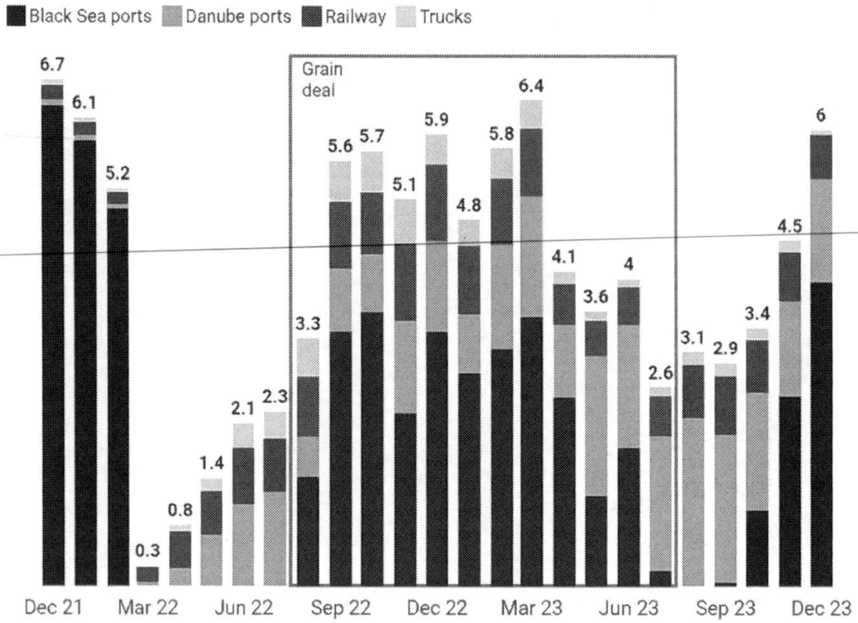

Figure 1.11 Dynamics of Ukraine's exports of grains and oilseeds by transport modes, 2021–2023, million tons

Source: Own elaboration based on Samoiluk (2024).

The constituent elements of the Consumer Sentiment Index encompass the Economic Expectations Index (92.1 in December) and the Current Situation Index (54.7 in December) (Consumer Sentiment Index, 2024). The trajectory of economic expectations displays a more discernible negative inclination than the appraisal of the prevailing situation. Consequently, there is a month-to-month escalation in pessimism concerning the economic future among the surveyed Ukrainian population (Figure 1.14).

In December, the Economic Expectations Index declined by 5.6 points, reaching a value of 92.1. The dynamics of its components are as follows:

- the index reflecting anticipated changes in personal financial status stood at 92.1, registering a 0.8 point decrease compared to the November level,
- the index gauging expected economic development in the country over the next year decreased by 2.8 points, amounting to 80.2,
- the index forecasting the country's economic development over the next five years declined by 13.2 points compared to the previous month, totalling 103.9.

In December, the index measuring anticipated unemployment dynamics remained unchanged at the level of 122. The Inflation Expectations Index decreased by 2.2 points, settling at 182.1. Simultaneously, the Devaluation Expectations Index decreased by 0.3 points, reaching 150.2 (Consumer Sentiment Index, 2024).

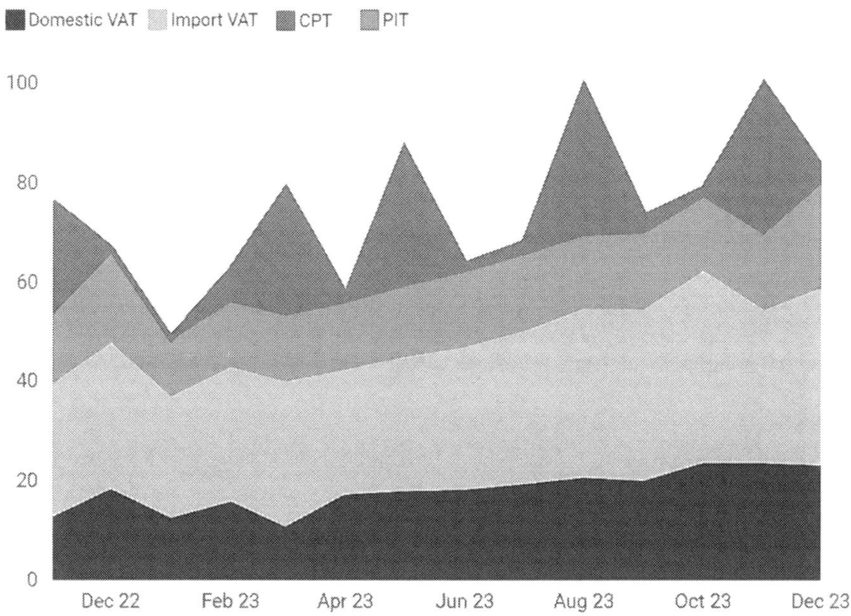

Figure 1.12 Main tax inflows to the general fund of the budget of Ukraine, 2023, UAH billion

Source: Own elaboration based on CES Team (2023).

As official unemployment data in Ukraine has been unavailable since the onset of the war, attention is directed towards the estimation of unemployment levels by the research agency Info Sapiens. According to their assertions, the unemployment rate in Ukraine was 16.1% in December 2023. This signifies a reduction in unemployment after three consecutive months of increase. The poverty rate indicator (the proportion of surveyed individuals compelled to economise on food) in December 2023 was 23.1% (Figure 1.15).

In 2023, the number of job vacancies in the labour market was recovering but had not yet reached the level of 2021. The dynamics of those seeking employment were characterised by a negative trend. The shortage of labour proved to be a significant obstacle to entrepreneurial activities.

At the onset of the full-scale war, marked by mass layoffs and a slowdown in business activities, there was a surplus of job applications from new job seekers compared to the capacity of employers to hire. Throughout 2022, the labour market dynamics stabilised, and in 2023, we observe the ratio of new job seekers to new vacancies at a level similar to that of 2021 (Figures 1.16 and 1.17).

In general, there are more job vacancies in the market, but the number of individuals willing to fill these vacancies has decreased. The market has stabilised after the initial shock of Russia's full-scale invasion and is gradually adapting to structural changes in the economy. Despite this, the pool of available potential workers in Ukraine is diminishing. A significant portion of Ukrainians are abroad, and

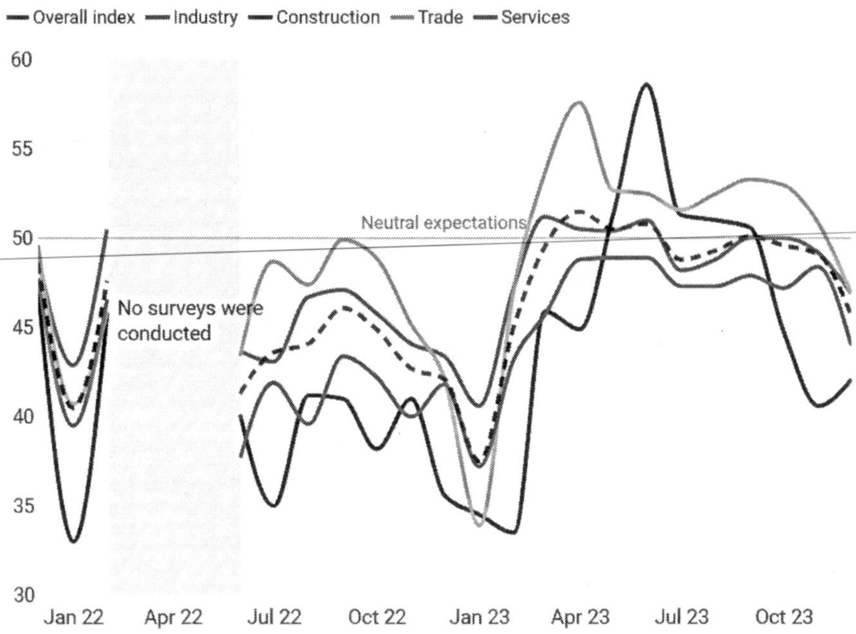

Figure 1.13 Index of Business Confidence in Ukraine, 2022–2023, points (data in March–May 2022 are not available)

Source: Own elaboration based on the National Bank of Ukraine, 2024a; CES Team (2023).

approximately a million men and women are defending the country in the ranks of the defence forces.

Conclusion

Having conducted a comprehensive study of the impact of the war waged by Russia on the Ukrainian economy, the following conclusions have been drawn.

The causes of the war between Russia and Ukraine are multifaceted and deeply rooted in historical complexities. The historical narrative presented here emphasises the divergence of paths between Ukrainians and Russians, debunking the notion of 'brotherly peoples'. The medieval state of Rus, with its centre in Kyiv, is recognised as a common historical origin for the Ukrainian, Russian, Belarusian, and partly Lithuanian peoples. However, over the centuries, linguistic, cultural, and political differences have shaped unique identities, contributing to complex relations in the region.

The Mongol invasion in the 13th century was a turning point that led to the final divergence of the historical paths of Ukraine and Russia. The western part of Rus developed in a European direction, characterised by democracy and self-government, while the northeastern territories became part of the Mongol Golden Horde, which significantly influenced the political culture of the Moscow principality.

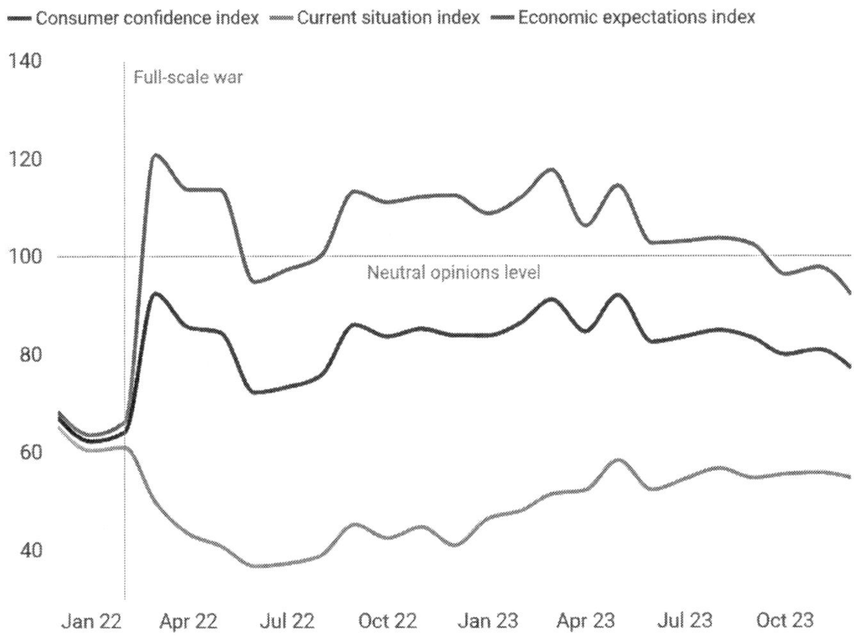

Figure 1.14 Consumer Confidence Indices in Ukraine (16+), 2022–2023, points: 0 – min, 200 – max, 100 – neutral

Source: Own elaboration based on the Consumer Sentiment Index (2024).

The chapter delves into the intricacies of the 1654 Pereyaslav Agreement, emphasising its character as a protectorate rather than a clearly defined union. The subsequent violation of state rights by Moscow led to the loss of autonomy of the Ukrainian lands. Moscow's constant interference in Ukrainian affairs, including the Russian-Ukrainian war of 1658–1659, eventually led to the complete loss of Ukraine's independence.

Soviet occupation further marginalised Ukrainian autonomy, and despite symbolic acts, such as the return of Crimea in 1954, the suppression of Ukrainian identity continued. Ukraine's declaration of independence in 1991 was the culmination of a long struggle for freedom and self-determination.

The main cause of the current war is seen as Russia's inability to accept Ukraine's independence, which calls into question the legitimacy of the Russian historical narrative. The imposition of Russification, suppression of Ukrainian identity, and attempts to keep Ukraine in the Kremlin's orbit have fuelled tensions. The seizure of Crimea in 2014 and the subsequent invasion of eastern Ukraine paved the way for a full-scale invasion in 2022.

Despite the significant risks and destruction that have occurred in Ukraine, the war also poses a wider global risk, affecting democratic systems, increasing military spending, provoking mass migration, and contributing to instability. The aggressive military strategy pursued by Russia is seen as a threat to stable development around the world.

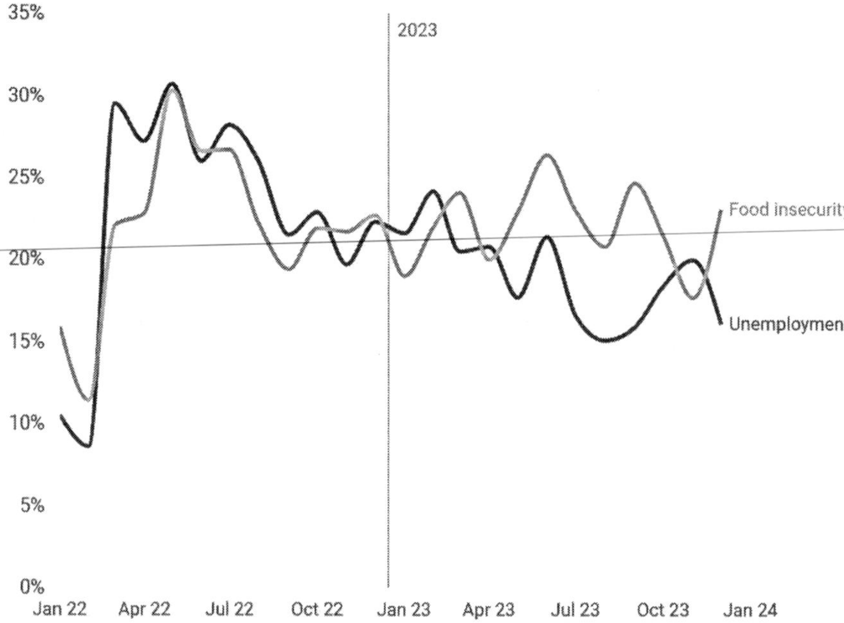

Figure 1.15 Unemployment rate (% of the labour force) and the share of food insecurity, %, data collected by phone interview in Ukraine, 2022–2023

Source: Own elaboration based on the Consumer Sentiment Index (2024).

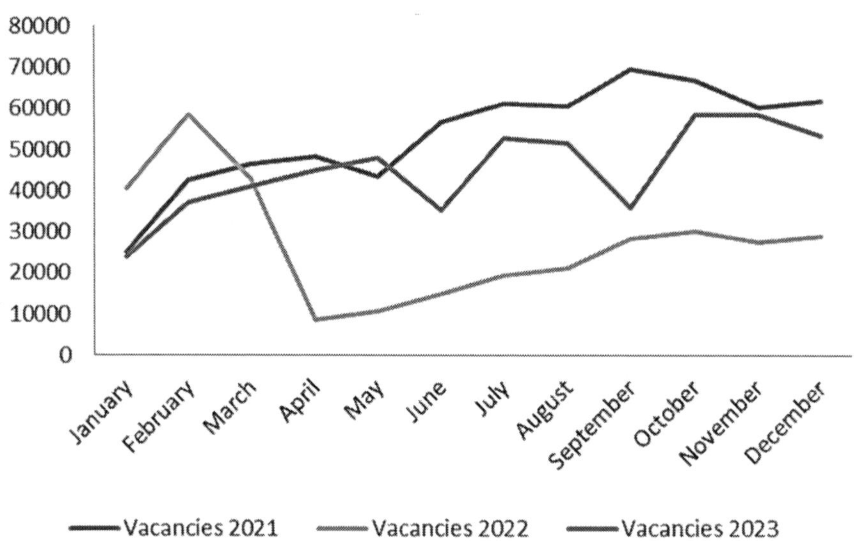

Figure 1.16 The number of vacancies in Ukraine, 2021–2023

Source: Own elaboration based on salary statistics (2024).

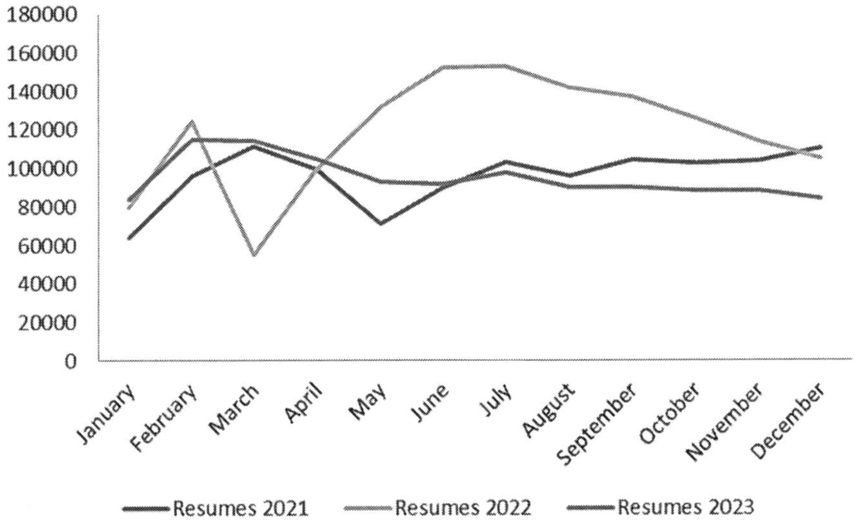

Figure 1.17 The number of résumés in Ukraine, 2021–2023

Source: Own elaboration based on salary statistics (2024).

Many analysts and experts believe that the war in Ukraine is driven by geopolitical interests, in particular, Russia's desire to establish control over Ukrainian territory and its rich natural resources. The invasion is believed to be motivated by economic factors, with a focus on Ukraine's vast reserves of raw materials, including natural gas, oil, lithium, and other valuable minerals. The strategic importance of these resources, especially lithium, in the context of global demand for electric vehicles and green energy, adds another layer to the economic rationale for war.

The analysis suggests that the invasion is not only linked to geopolitical dominance or historical grievances but is also closely intertwined with securing access to valuable resources that make Ukraine a potential "superpower" in the production of important industrial metals. Control over these resources is considered crucial for the economic advantage and prosperity of the aggressor country, Russia.

In addition, the impact of the war on food security in the Black Sea region is becoming apparent as Russia seizes southern Ukrainian ports and attempts to control the grain trade. Disruptions in grain supplies lead to higher prices, which affects countries in the Middle East that are heavily dependent on these imports. This economic aspect underscores Russia's attempts to use the war to its advantage, potentially provoking unrest in the Middle East and affecting global food prices.

In essence, Russia's war in Ukraine is a multifaceted struggle that involves not only geopolitical considerations but also a complex interplay of economic interests, access to critical resources, and manipulation of global markets.

References

Antoniuk, V. P., & Mytsenko, I. M. (2022). War in Ukraine as a Global Civilisational Conflict: Causes and Consequences for the Economy and Human Development. *Economics and Management Organisation. 3*(47): 4–17. https://doi.org/10.31558/2307-2318.2022.3.1 (in Ukrainian)

Avenarius, A. (1984). Tatári ako problém byzantskej politiky a diplomace. *Historický časopis, ročnik 6*(32): 856–857.

Beer, M. (2023, November 3). Neue Analyse: Russland will sich in der Ukraine die Rohstoffe der Zukunft sichern. Berliner Zeitung. https://www.berliner-zeitung.de/politik-gesellschaft/neue-analyse-russland-will-sich-in-der-ukra i ne-die-rohstoffe- d er-zukunft-sichern-lithium-graphite-seltene-erden-li.2154604

BOP_m. (2023, December 29). Balance of Payments of Ukraine. National Bank of Ukraine. https://bank.gov.ua/files/ES/BOP_m.xlsx

Buket, E. (2022). Pereyaslav Rada as a Starting Point of Moscow's Occupation. ArmyInform. History. URL:https://armyinform.com.ua/2022/01/18/pereyaslavska-rada-yak-vidpravna-tochka-moskovskoyi-okupacziyi/

Center for Countering Disinformation (2022, August 6). Russia's Participation in Armed Conflicts from 1991 to the Full-Scale Invasion of Ukraine. NSDC of Ukraine. https://cpd.gov.ua/en/articles-en/russias-participation-in-armed-conflicts-from-1991-to-the-full-scale-invasion-of-ukraine/

CES Team. (2023, January 11). Ukrainian Economy in 2023: Key Figures. Centre for Economic Strategy. https://ces.org.ua/wp-content/uploads/2024/01/ukrainian-economy-in-war-times-2023-1.pdf

Children of war. (2024, January 28). Children of War. https://childrenofwar.gov.ua/

Consumer confidence Index (2024, January 12). In December 2023, the Consumer Confidence Index equals 77.1 points. Info Sapiens. https://www.sapiens.com.ua/ua/publication-single-page?id=300

Dickinson, P. (2022). There Can Be No Compromise between Russian Genocide and Ukrainian Freedom. Atlantic Council. September 8. https://www.atlanticcouncil.org/blogs/ukrainealert/there-can-be-no-compromise-between-russian-genocide-and-ukrainian-freedom/

Dorosh, S. (2023, May 31). Ukraine's Underground Wealth. How Much of It Has Been Seized by Russia and Why It could be Lost Forever. *BBC News Ukraine*. https://www.bbc.com/ukrainian/articles/cqv0v18x2d3o

Ehrman, G. (2021, April 21). "White oil" of Ukraine. Will Zelenskyy Manage to Attract Musk's Money. *BBC News Ukraine*. https://www.bbc.com/ukrainian/features-56604233

Faiola, A., & Bennett, D. (2022, August 10). In the Ukraine War, a Battle for the Nation's Mineral and Energy Wealth. *Washington Post*. https://www.washingtonpost.com/world/2022/08/10/ukraine-russia-energy-mineral-wealth/

Glushchenko, A. (2024, January 17). How the Ukrainian Steel Industry Passed the Test of Strength in 2023 - Posts - GMK Centre. GMK. https://gmk.center/en/posts/how-the-ukrainian-steel-industry-passed-the-test-of-strength-in-2023/

Holovko, O. B. (2006). *The Crown of Danylo Halytskyi: Volhynia and Galicia in the State and Political Development of Central and Eastern Europe in the Early and Classical Middle Ages*. Stylos. 575. (in Ukrainian).

Hrushevsky, M. S. (1997). *History of Ukraine-Rus'*. Naukova Dumka. Vol. 9, Book 2. 1631.

Hrytsak, P. (1958). *The Galician-Volynian State*. NTSH. Obnova, 176. (in Ukrainian).

International reserves. (2024). National Bank of Ukraine. https://bank.gov.ua/en/markets/international-reserves-allinfo

Kappeler, A. (1993). *Russland als Vielvölkerreich: Entstehung, Geschichte, Zerfall*. 2nd ed., Munich: C. H. Beck. 395.

Kishchak, V. (2022, August 11). Russia Has Occupied Territories of Ukraine with at Least $12.4 trillion in Natural Resources. Infographic - Forbes.ua. Forbes.ua | Business, Billionaires, News, Finance, Investments, Companies. https://forbes.ua/ru/news/rosiya-okupuvala-teritorii-ukraini-na-yakikh-prirodnikh-resursiv-minimum-na-124-trln-infografika-11082022-7630

Korsunsky, S. (2022, March 6). Causes and Consequences of Russia's War against Ukraine: What Will Happen Next? Radio Free Europe / Radio Liberty. https://www.radiosvoboda.org/a/rosiya-viyna-ukrayina-shcho-dali/31739012.html

Kostomarov, M. (1918). *History of Ukraine in the Biographies of Its Prominent Figures*, translated by O. Barvinsky. NTSh. 493. (in Ukrainian).

Kotlyar, M. F. (2002). *Danylo Halytskyi: A Biographical Sketch*. Alternatyvy. 328. (in Ukrainian).

Krypyakevych, I. P. (1999). *Galicia-Volyn Principality*. 2nd ed. with changes and additions. Krypyakevych Institute of Ukrainian Studies of the National Academy of Sciences of Ukraine. 220. (in Ukrainian).

Labiak, I. (2024, January 7). Soledar Destroyed to the Ground: Depressing Video from the Occupied City. TSN.ua. https://tsn.ua/ato/soledar-zruynovaniy-vschent-gnityuche-video-z-okupovanogo-mista-2485735.html

Lepushynskyi, V. (2023, May 12). The Role of Monetary Policy during the War and in the post-War Recovery. National Bank of Ukraine. https://bank.gov.ua/admin_uploads/article/Volodymyr_Lepushynskyi_Role_monetary_policy_in_wartime_and_post-war_recovery_pr_2023-05-12.pdf?v=4

Ministry of Finance (2024). Average in Ukraine - USD (US dollar). Rates, indices, tariffs. https://index.minfin.com.ua/ua/exchange/bank/exch/usd/

Ministry of Finance of Ukraine (2023, December 29). Financing of the State Budget of Ukraine since the Beginning of the Full-Scale War. https://mof.gov.ua/uk/news/ukraines_state_budget_financing_since_the_beginning_of_the_full-scale_war-3435

National Bank of Ukraine (2024, January 25). The National Bank of Ukraine Has kept the Key Policy Rate at 15%. https://bank.gov.ua/ua/news/all/natsionalniy-bank-ukrayini-zberig-oblikovu-stavku-na-rivni-15

National Bank of Ukraine (2024a, January 16). Business Expectations of Enterprises, Q4 2023. https://bank.gov.ua/ua/news/all/dilovi-ochikuvannya-pidpriyemstv-iv-kvartal-2023-roku

NBU. (2023). Macroeconomic_Forecast_table_2023_Q2. https://bank.gov.ua/admin_uploads/article/Macroeconomic_Forecast_table_2023_Q2.xlsx?v=4

Ogloblyn, O. (2003). Ukrainian-Moscow Agreement of 1654. Pereyaslav Rada of 1654 (Historiography and Research). Smoloskyp. 201.

Ovchinsky, V., & Zhdanov, Y. (2022, September 7). LITHIUM AND DEATH - The Foreign and Defence Policy Council. The Foreign and Defence Policy Council. https://svop.ru/main/43197/

Parakhonskyi, B. O., & Yavorska, H. M. (2019). Ontology of War and Peace: Security, Strategy, Meaning: A monograph. NISS. 560.

Perun, V. (2023, December 8). The First Meeting of the International Coalition of States on the Return of Deported Ukrainian Children Took Place (video). LB.ua. https://lb.ua/society/2023/12/08/588115_vidbulosya_pershe_zasidannya.html

Plokhii, S. (2016). *Gate of Europe: The History of Ukraine from the Scythian Wars to Independence*. Translated from English. R. Klochko. Kharkiv: Klub simeinoho dozvillia. 496. (in Ukrainian).

Polyovyk, S. (2023, November 8). The War for Ukrainian Subsoil: Russia Is Trying to Secure Its Future with Raw Materials from Ukraine. *Borysfen Intel*. https://bintel.org.ua/analytics/viyna-za-ukrainski-nadra-rosiya-namagaetsya-zabezpechiti-svoe-maybutne-sirovinoyu-z-ukraini/ (in Ukrainian)

Pritzak, L. (2003). The Main International Treaties of Bohdan Khmelnytsky in 1648–1657. National Academy of Sciences of Ukraine. Institute of Ukrainian Archaeography and Source Studies named after M. S.Hrushevsky. Kharkiv: Acta. 493. (in Ukrainian)

Pritzak, L. D. (2005). The so-called Pereyaslav Treaty of 1654 and its problems. *The Eastern World 1*: 75–84. http://nbuv.gov.ua/UJRN/SkhS_2005_1_9 (in Ukrainian).

Salary Statistics. (2024). New Jobs and Resumes in Ukraine. Work.ua - Ukraine's #1 job site. https://www.work.ua/en/stat/count/?time=year2023&setlp=en

Samoiliuk, M., & Levchenko, E. (2024, January 17). Ukraine's Economy in 2023 Overview. Centre for Economic Strategy - Non-Governmental Research Centre on Economic Policy Issues. https://ces.org.ua/en/economy-tracker-special-edition/

Samoiluk, M. (2024, January 25). Ukraine War Economy Tracker - Centre for Economic Strategy. Centre for Economic Strategy - Non-Governmental Research Centre on Economic Policy Issues. https://ces.org.ua/en/tracker-economy-during-the-war/

Shapran, V. (2022, June 10). Economic Causes of the War. Interfax-Ukraine. https://interfax.com.ua/news/blog/838361.html

State Statistics Service of Ukraine (2023). Change in the Volume of Gross Domestic Product. https://ukrstat.gov.ua/operativ/operativ2004/vvp/ind_vvp/ind_vvp_u/arh_indvvp.html (accessed: 27.01.2024).

Stasiv, M. (1954). The Crown of Danylo and the Tatars. *Analecta ordinis S. Basilii Magni*. Romae *2*(8): Fascicle 1–2. 137–153 (in Ukrainian).

Sydorovych, R. (2022). About the Far-Fetched Pretexts and the Real Causes of the War. ZAXID.NET. https://zaxid.net/pro_nadumani_privodi_i_spravzhni_prichini_viyni_n1543648

Tomashivskyi, S. (1993). *Ukrainian History*. Vol. 1: Ancient and Middle Ages. Books 3–4. The Great Unrest: The Second half of the XII–XIII Centuries, compiled and prefaced by V. M. Rychka. 2nd ed. Ukraine. 301–347 (in Ukrainian).

Topol, E. (2022, October 5). Lithium and Death. Eduard Topol on Putin and Ukraine. Radio Liberty. https://www.svoboda.org/a/litiy-i-smertj-eduard-topolj---o-putine-i-ukraine/32060592.html

Why Ukrainians and Russians Are Not Fraternal Nations (infographics). (2023). Ukrainian Institute of National Memory - Official Website. https://uinp.gov.ua/informac and yni-materialy/rosiysko-ukrayinska-viyna-istorichna-kontekst/why-ukrainians-and-russians-are-not-fraternal-nations-infographics

Zhdan, M. (1968). *To the Question of the Dependence of Galicia-Volhynia on the Golden Horde*. Reprint edition. Series: Historical Studies. Part 8. 37. (in Ukrainian).

3.2-Deposits. (2023, December 28). Monetary Statistics. National Bank of Ukraine. https://bank.gov.ua/files/3.2-Deposits.xlsx

3.3-Loans. (2023, December 28). Monetary Statistics. National Bank of Ukraine. https://bank.gov.ua/files/3.3-Loans.xlsx

2 The Effect of the War on European Economy

Oleksandra Struk

Introduction

The geopolitical landscape in Europe underwent significant shifts, marked by the stringent response to Russia's invasion of Ukraine. The ongoing war has resulted in unequal consequences among EU member nations, leading to challenges such as supply shortages, rising inflation, and disruptions in manufacturing and services. Amidst these complexities, this chapter explores the multifaceted responses of the EU, particularly addressing the economic consequences and energy crisis triggered by the war. Emergency regulations, diversification strategies, and a pronounced emphasis on renewable energy underscore the EU's commitment to ensuring energy security and transitioning towards sustainable sources. Additionally, Russia's invasion prompted the EU to extend temporary protection to millions of Ukrainian refugees, presenting a unique interplay of challenges and integration efforts, particularly targeting adult women with higher education. This research delves into the dynamic landscape of geopolitical responses, economic challenges, and humanitarian efforts in the wake of Russia's invasion and the ongoing war in Ukraine.

In order to make a comprehensive analysis of the research problem, the following research questions were formulated:

- What was the EU response to Russia's invasion of Ukraine?
- How has the EU's strategy evolved in response to Russia's invasion, and what role did international cooperation play?
- What are the economic outcomes of wars in light of lessons from history and how do they relate to the situation in Ukraine?
- How did the war in Ukraine impact the economies of EU Member States?
- How did the energy crisis triggered by the war affect the EU economy, and what emergency measures and strategies were implemented in response?
- How successful was the temporary protection programme for Ukrainian refugees, especially in terms of integration, employment, and skills recognition?
- What is the economic impact of Ukrainian refugees on the labour force and GDP growth in host countries?

The study was conducted using a combination of quantitative and qualitative research methods of data analysis, synthesis, and interpretation, as well as

DOI: 10.4324/9781003435433-2

structural-functional approach, and comparative analysis. It contains a comprehensive analysis of scientific studies, statistical data, international reports, and web sources.

2.1 EU Response to Russia's Invasion of Ukraine

Russia's illegal annexation of Crimea and Sevastopol, and its support for a separatist insurgency in eastern Ukraine became the ground for the first set of EU restrictive measures adopted in March 2014. From February 23, 2022, till January 2024, the EU states in cooperation with partners (i.e. the United States, the United Kingdom, Canada, Australia, and Japan) adopted 12 packages of unprecedentedly tough sanctions against Russia (Table 2.1), as well as visa measures (i.e. suspension of visa facilitation agreement between the EU and Russia and suspension of visa facilitation provisions for Russian diplomats and businessmen). Additionally, the EU adopted suspension of broadcasting activities of some Russian media channels, such as Sputnik and subsidiaries, Russia Today, Rossiya RTR / RTR Planeta, Rossiya 24 / Russia 24, REN TV, Rossiya 1, TV Centre International, NTV, Pervyi Kanal, Tsargrad TV Channel, and Spas TV Channel. Besides, the sanctions were adopted against Belarus, such as SWIFT ban for Belarusian banks, ban on transactions with the Central Bank of Belarus, limits in financial inflows from Belarus to the EU, ban on supply of euro-denominated banknotes to Belarus, sanctions on Belarusian military personnel, ban on Belarusian road transport operators, trade restrictions. Experts emphasise that the implementation of sanctions has achieved several significant goals, including sending a clear message of determination and solidarity from the Western countries and causing lasting damage to Russia's military capabilities. Furthermore, the Russian economy and energy sector have been suffocated with enduring outcomes, while the country's elite has also experienced the consequences of economic strains. Meanwhile, the nature of sanctions has revealed new challenges for the EU in terms of implementation. Thus,

> Member States and EU institutions have renewed efforts to make alignment truly global, and to close loopholes to prevent circumvention. In November 2022, the violation of 'restrictive measures' (sanctions) was added to the list of 'EU crimes' included in the Treaties.
>
> (Caprile & Delivorias, 2023).

However, the majority of experts have warned that the effect of sanctions will not be sufficiently severe to limit Russia's ability to conduct a war in the near future. The lack of alignment by a notable group of countries is also indicative of divergent global perceptions of stakes and priorities.

In light of Russia's escalation of missile and drone attacks on Ukrainian cities, the European Commission, on May 9, 2023, has proposed a new, 11th set of sanctions (Table 2.1). As to S. Taran (2023), it focuses on combating the circumvention of pre-existing trade sanctions rather than introducing new bans on still-unsanctioned Russian products and sectors. Among the measures included in the approved package are actions aimed at strengthening both bilateral and multilateral cooperation with third-party countries in order to impede the circumvention of sanctions; prohibiting the passage of goods and technology through Russia; and enhancing export controls. The EU has also imposed additional sanctions against 71 individuals and 33 entities. Despite Ukraine's expectations, according to the International Working Group on Russian Sanctions (2023), it did not cover a ban on imports of diamonds, natural gas, LNG, cast iron and ferroalloys, and nuclear energy cooperation, as Member States were facing difficulties in reaching consensus in these fields. Researcher also underlined that the effectiveness of sanctions has been undermined by the abuse of transit rules (false transit) or the use of third countries of Central Asia and the Caucasus, China, Türkiye, and the United Arab Emirates. Meanwhile,

> for the first time, the European Commission has proposed blacklisting seven Chinese companies accused of supplying banned components to Russia's military sector, although the list has not yet been officially confirmed. They could be subject to an asset freeze in the EU.
>
> (Baczynska, 2023)

The Russian economy's most valuable sectors are the focus of the 12th round of sanctions, which were imposed by the EU on December 18, 2023, in an effort to prevent evasion of the sanctions (Table 2.1). As of December 2023, EU exporters are subject to a new clause that forbids them from re-exporting a limited selection of goods to Russia or for use within Russia, when selling, supplying, transferring, or exporting to a third country, with the exception of partner countries. The clause covers prohibited dual-use goods; advanced technology items used in Russian military systems found on the battlefield in Ukraine or critical to their development; production or use of those Russian military systems; aviation goods and weapons (European Council, 2023a). The bloc adds to its sanctions list roughly 140 individuals and entities, including more than 40 companies involved in the Russian military industrial complex, seven Russian private military companies and one of their founders, 12 Belarusian individuals and further Russian officials and businesspeople in the defence sector.

The Council also unanimously passed a decision on November 28, to include infringement of restrictive measures in the list of 'EU crimes' under the Treaty on the Functioning of the EU. The implementation of this decision will lead to cohesive enforcement of sanctions across the EU and discourage any attempts to evade or violate them. The Council reached a consensus on June 9, 2023, regarding the harmonisation of criminal offenses and penalties for EU sanctions violations at the Member State level. The proposed legislation outlines the actions that would be considered a criminal offense and the corresponding punishments:

- **criminal offences**: include assisting individuals in circumventing an EU travel prohibition, exchanging restricted goods, or conducting transactions with those affected by EU restrictive actions

- **dissuasive penalties:** should vary according to offences but be effective, proportionate, and dissuasive
- **stricter enforcement:** EU Member States must increase their efforts to ensure compliance with sanctions

New regulations have been established by the Council and the European Parliament on December 12, 2023, to address the criminalisation of violating restrictive measures.

Thus, in response to Russia's invasion of Ukraine, a number of countries have imposed escalated sanctions in finance, transport, energy, defence, as well as related to raw materials, other goods and services (Tables 2.1 and 2.2). The United States, the European Union, and other countries have imposed blocking sanctions on the Central Bank of the Russian Federation that prevents the Russian authorities from accessing foreign exchange reserves in the custody of institutions in sanctioning countries. Besides, these countries have enacted a growing list of export bans, import restrictions, and other trade sanctions on Russia. Restrictions on exports to Russia have focused on 'dual-use' technologies, including semiconductors, goods and services related to aviation, aerospace and oil and gas production, and luxury goods (Guenette et al., 2022). In addition, in 2022, more than 150 multinational companies have announced complete withdrawals from Russia, while a further 250-plus have suspended operations or new investments (Guenette et al., 2022). The EU also actively attempted to cut off Russian oil supplies, while Lithuania has become the first European country to cease Russian gas purchases. Moreover, the US, EU, and UK have closed their airspace to Russian flights. Entities and persons in Belarus associated with Russia's invasion, including financial institutions as well as defence and security sector companies, are subject to various travel bans, asset freezes, and export bans.

Table 2.1 Overview of the EU's restrictive measures against Russia

Stages	*Date*	*Restrictive measures*	*The type of sanctions*
First package	February 23 2022	• individual sanctions against members of the Russian State Duma who voted in favour of the recognition of the non-government-controlled areas of the Donetsk and Luhansk oblasts • restrictions on economic relations with the non-government-controlled areas of the Donetsk and Luhansk oblasts • restrictions on Russia's access to the EU's capital and financial markets and services	• economic • financial • individual
Second package	February 25, 2022	• individual sanctions against Vladimir Putin, Sergey Lavrov, and members of the Russian State Duma and National Security Council, among others • economic sanctions covering the finance, energy, transport, and technology sectors • suspension of visa facilitation provisions for Russian diplomats and other Russian officials and businesspeople	• diplomatic • energy • financial • individual • transportation

(*Continued*)

Table 2.1 (Continued)

Stages	*Date*	*Restrictive measures*	*The type of sanctions*
Third package	February 28 and March 2, 2022	• closure of EU airspace to all Russian aircraft • prohibition on transactions with the Russian Central Bank • SWIFT ban for seven Russian banks • prohibition on the provision of euro-denominated banknotes to Russia • suspension of broadcasting in the EU of state-owned outlets Russia Today and Sputnik • individual sanctions against Belarusians in response to Belarus' involvement in Russia's military invasion	• financial • individual • information • transportation
Fourth package	March 15, 2022	• individual sanctions against Roman Abramovich and German Khan, among others • prohibition on all transactions with certain state-owned enterprises • prohibition on the provision of credit-rating services to any Russian person or entity • prohibition on new investments in the Russian energy sector • prohibition on exports to Russia of luxury goods • prohibition on imports from Russia to the EU of iron and steel	• energy • financial • individual • trade • raw materials • luxury goods
Fifth package	April 8, 2022	• prohibition on imports from Russia of coal and other solid fossil fuels • closure of EU ports to all Russian vessels • prohibition on Russian and Belarusian road transport operators from entering the EU • prohibition on imports from Russia of wood, cement, seafood, and liquor • prohibition on exports to Russia of jet fuel and other goods • a series of targeted economic measures • sanctions against 217 individuals and 18 entities	• economic • individual • trade • raw materials and other goods • transportation • travel
Sixth package	June 3, 2022	• prohibition on imports from Russia of crude oil and refined petroleum products (with limited exceptions) • SWIFT ban for an additional three Russian banks and one Belarusian bank • suspension of broadcasting in the EU for Rossiya RTR / RTR Planeta, Rossiya 24 / Russia 24, and TV Centre International • sanctions against 18 entities and 65 individuals, including individuals responsible for the atrocities committed in Bucha and Mariupol	• financial • individual • raw materials • services • trade

(*Continued*)

Table 2.1 (Continued)

Stages	*Date*	*Restrictive measures*	*The type of sanctions*
"Maintenance and alignment" package	July 21, 2022	• prohibition on imports of Russian-origin gold • reinforcement of export controls of dual-use goods • extension of the port access ban to locks • clarification of existing measures (in the field of public procurement, aviation, and justice) • sanctions against 54 individuals and 10 entities, including the mayor of Moscow and Sberbank, a major financial institution	• defence • financial • individual • trade • transportation
Eighth package	October 6, 2022	• a price cap related to the maritime transport of Russian oil for third countries • restrictions on exports of dual-use goods and technology • prohibition on provision of crypto-wallets to Russian persons • prohibition on trade in arms, civilian firearms, ammunition, military vehicles, and paramilitary equipment • prohibition on imports from Russia of steel products • prohibition to provide architectural and engineering services, IT consultancy services, and legal advisory services to Russia • sanctions against 30 persons and 7 entities	• defence • financial • individual • military • raw materials • services • trade • transportation
Ninth package	December 16, 2022	• prohibition on exports of drone engines • restrictions on exports of dual-use goods and technology • prohibition on investments in the mining sector • prohibition on transactions with the Russian Regional Development Bank • prohibition on the provision of advertising, market research, and public opinion polling services • suspension of the broadcasting licenses of four additional Russian media outlets • sanctions against an additional 141 individuals and 49 entities	• defence • financial • individual • information • services • technology • trade
Tenth package	February 25, 2023	• prohibition on exports of critical technology and industrial goods • prohibition on imports of asphalt and synthetic rubber • prohibition on provision of gas storage capacity to Russians • suspension of broadcasting licenses of RT Arabic and Sputnik Arabic • restrictions for Russian nationals to hold any position in the governing bodies of EU critical infrastructures and entities • reporting obligations to ensure the effectiveness of sanctions • additional sanctions against 87 individuals and 34 entities	• diplomatic • defence • individual • raw materials • services • trade

(*Continued*)

Table 2.1 (Continued)

Stages	*Date*	*Restrictive measures*	*The type of sanctions*
Eleventh package	June 23, 2023	• new anti-circumvention tool to restrict the sale, transfer, or export of specified sanctioned goods and technology to third countries • strengthening bilateral and multilateral cooperation with third countries to impede sanctions' circumvention • extension of the transit prohibition for certain sensitive goods • addition of 87 new entities to the list of those directly supporting Russia's military and industrial complex • transport measures (prohibition to transport goods into the EU by road to trailers and semi-trailers registered in Russia) • prohibition on import Russian oil by pipeline for Germany and Poland • insertions of strict derogations to the export bans to enable the maintenance of the Caspian Pipeline Consortium which transports Kazakh oil to the EU through Russia • over 100 additional individuals and entities subject to asset freezes • extension of the media ban to five additional channels	• energy • individual • media • technology • trade • transport
Twelfth package	December 18, 2023	• prohibition on the direct or indirect import, purchase or transfer of diamonds, including jewellery, from Russia • no Russia clause (a new clause which applies to EU exporters and bans the re-exportation to Russia and re-exportation for use in Russia of certain goods) • strengthening bilateral and multilateral cooperation with third countries to impede sanctions' circumvention • tighter export restrictions concerning dual use goods and technologies • enforcement of oil price cap • further restrictions on imports of goods which generate significant revenues for Russia such as; pig iron, copper and aluminium wires, foil, tubes, and pipes • prohibition on the import of liquefied propane	• trade • raw materials • technology

Source: Own elaboration based on European Council (2023a; 2023b); European Commission (2023d); Ashurst (2024).

Table 2.2 Synthesis of the EU economic sanctions within sphere of influence

Sphere of influence	*Restrictive measures*
Finance	• SWIFT ban for ten Russian banks • Restrictions on Russia's access to the EU's capital and financial markets • Ban on transactions with the Russian Central Bank • Bank on supply of euro-denominated banknotes to Russia • Ban on provision of crypto-wallets
Transport	• Closure of EU airspace to all Russian-owned aircrafts • Closure of EU ports to Russian vessels • Ban on Russian road transport operators • Ban on maritime transport of Russian oil to third countries • Ban on exports to Russia of goods and technology in the aviation, maritime, and space sectors • ban on re-exportation to Russia and re-exportation for use in Russia of certain goods • prohibition to transport goods into the EU by road to trailers and semi-trailers registered in Russia • prohibition on import Russian oil by pipeline for Germany and Poland
Energy	• Ban on imports from Russia of oil and coal • Price cap related to the maritime transport of Russian oil • Ban on exports to Russia of goods and technologies in the oil refining sector • Ban on new investments in the Russian energy and mining sector • Ban on providing gas storage capacity to Russian nationals
Defence and technology	• Ban on export to Russia of dual-use goods and technology for military use, drone engines, arms and civilian firearms, ammunition, military vehicles, and paramilitary equipment
Raw materials and other goods	• Ban on imports from Russia of luxury goods, as well as steel, iron, cement, and asphalt; wood, paper, synthetic rubber, and plastic; seafood, spirits, cigarettes, and cosmetics; gold including jewellery; pig iron, copper and aluminium wires, foil, tubes, and pipes; purchase or transfer of diamonds, including jewellery, from Russia
Services	• Ban to provide Russia or Russian persons architectural and engineering services, IT consultancy and legal advisory services, advertising, market research, and public opinion polling services

Source: Own elaboration based on European Council (2023a; 2023b); European Commission (2023); Ashurst (2024).

2.2 Effects of War in Academic Discourse: Lessons from the History

The scientific literature contains a range of studies concerning effects of war, mainly focused on the depletion of human and physical capital, disruption to production processes, and growing uncertainty among consumers and producers (see:

Abadie & Gardeazabal, 2003; Cappelen et al., 1984; Cerra & Saxena, 2008). For instance, Chupilkin and Kóczán (2022), economists from the EBRD, created a dataset to define the economic consequences (shown as changes in GDP per capita) of 400 wars that have taken place during the last centuries. They visualised the data in the form of graphs representing the change in GDP per capita in the period before the war, during the war and after the war for particular countries. They proved that wars cause a substantial reduction in GDP per capita by more than 7 pp. in comparison to the year following the war's end, whereas the most destructive conflicts have resulted in GDP per capita reduction ranging from 40 to 70%. Considering the data from 400 wars that have occurred in almost two centuries, the projected decrease in GDP per capita in Ukraine by September 2022 was expected to be among the most significant 10–20% in the modern war history. Meanwhile, the actual data is even worse, according to the National Bank of Ukraine, the GDP dropped by 19.1% in the first quarter of 2022 and by 37.2% in the second quarter. From January to September 2022, it fell by 30%.

During times of war, regardless of the severity, economies can undergo significant changes (see: Rasler & Thompson, 1985; Van Raemdonck & Diehi, 1989). During world wars, the United Kingdom and the United States witnessed a 40% GDP spending on the military, while 10% of the population was actively employed in the military. Thus, boosting GDP through military production, higher utilisation rates and higher productivity is possible (Deane, 1975; Olson, 2008; Organski & Kugler, 1980; 1977); however, wars, particularly those fought on the nation's territory, can cause economic activity to be disrupted, create more uncertainty and impose a heavier fiscal cost (Cappelen et al., 1984; Thorp, 1941).

Meanwhile, according to some researches conducted on the drivers of economic growth (by Acemoglu et al., 2005; Barro & Lee 1994), there is no evidence of a meaningful effect of war on growth. In contrast, some have suggested that war can actually have a positive impact on output, resulting from higher military spending, enhanced labour and capital utilisation, or increased total factor productivity (Deane, 1975; Olson, 2008; Organski & Kugler, 1980).

A lot of studies have exclusively concentrated on certain countries or areas within countries (Abadie & Gardeazabal, 2003; Broadberry & Harrison, 2005; Harrison, 1998), while some limited their examination to only internal conflicts (Blattman & Miguel, 2010; Collier, 1999; Hoeffler & Reynal-Querol, 2003) to make certain that a war occurred within the country's own boundaries (Cerra & Saxena, 2008: 439; Collier, 1999: 168). Kuznets underlined the discrepancy between countries that experienced wars on their territories and those that actively took part in wars without military actions on their own ground comparing the post-Second World War economic growth of France, Germany, Japan, and the USSR to that of the UK and US (Kuznets, 1964; 1971). Investigations of interstate wars have usually covered limited data, and typically assess the GDP losses related to estimations based on the nation's prior trends, either in the immediate period prior to the war or based on the total span of time (Organski & Kugler, 1977; Koubi, 2005; Rasler & Thompson, 1985; Wheeler, 1980).

Aside from influencing flows like value added, wars can have a lasting impact on populations, covering casualties, outflows of refugees, and a decrease in births. For example, ten years after the First World War revealed, that populations of France, Germany, and the United Kingdom were fewer than in 1913, while the populations of Denmark, the Netherlands, and Spain increased by 13–24% compared to prewar.

War brings stagnation and decline in years of schooling in contrast to countries not experiencing war, in which years of schooling accumulate. Ichino and Winter-Ebmer (2004: 57) found that "10-year-olds from Austria and Germany during the Second World War had a lower level of schooling than those from countries not involved in the conflict, such as Switzerland and Sweden". Thus, these people faced a significant decline in income up to 40 years after the war, demonstrating the war had long-term consequences.

Furthermore, wars can have a major negative effect on capital stocks due to destruction of existing capital or its removal from the country, while investments in new capital may be greatly diminished. An example of this is Mozambique's railways, which saw more than 90% of its rolling stock destroyed during the civil war of 1977 (Brück, 2001: 64). The 1861 Civil War had a dramatic and lasting result on the US, with capital stocks not fully recovering until two decades later and agricultural investment in the affected areas staying suppressed for an extended period of almost 60 years (Feigenbaum et al., 2018). Subsequent to the war, the capital stocks of France, Germany, and Italy were seen to be 20–40% lower than 1939 and did not return to their pre-war trend for up to 25 years (Alvarez-Cuadrado, 2008).

The Total Factor Productivity may decrease as a result of the disruption of usual manufacturing processes in times of conflict. However, it is possible that technologies initially developed for military objectives might be converted for civilian utilisation, as exemplified by the Internet, nuclear energy, and aircraft construction (Gross & Sampat, 2020; Ruttan, 2006), public investments in military research and development converted to the private investments (Deleidi & Mazzucato, 2021; Moretti et al., 2019; Surico & Antolin-Diaz, 2022) or business could find new solutions out of necessity, for instance, modified process of production because of the lack of labour and capital (Lafond et al., 2022).

Studies suggest that warfare has the potential to prompt economic growth by swelling the government's expenditure on armaments, thus inducing production in the heavy industry sector. This is followed by an upsurge in investment rates, employment, and capital resources. Nevertheless, this growth has no positive effect on people's welfare, since it does not encompass the building of new roads, highways, or improvements in public services (such as health care or education).

Examining the GDP per capita of Germany from 1934 to 1950, it is clear that the period between 1934 and 1944 was marked by an upsurge in the economy as a result of the armament race, with the Third Reich at the forefront. The result of intensive state funding into the armaments industry was a cumulative growth of 40% in the course of ten years, giving an average yearly GDP growth rate of approximately 4%. Nonetheless, Germany's economy encountered an equally remarkable dip in GDP between 1944 and 1946, leading to a decrease in GDP per capita to pre-prosperity figures. In addition, the war had a severe impact on the German population, resulting in a decrease of about 9% between 1942 and 1946. Notably, it was not until 1951 that it recovered its prior population level.

Moreover, the effects of the war on indicators of long-term growth, for instance, population, capital resources, and factor productivity, are also of great importance. Findings suggest that although the economy is restored a few years following the war, the effects on growth factors are extended over a lengthy period of time, mainly in terms of population and capital. Despite productivity reverting to its pre-war level after a mean of five years, population and capital continue to be substantially lower.

2.3 European Economies within War in Ukraine: General Overview, Data Analysis, and Some Forecasts

The overall impact of the war in Ukraine on EU economy as well as its overall economic costs is still difficult to predict. However, it is clear that it has caused asymmetric consequences in EU Member States, depends on trade links, potential costs of energy dependence on Russia as well as vulnerability on financial markets. Undoubtedly, the war triggered a massive shock to energy and food markets, reducing supply and raising prices to historically unprecedented levels. In the meantime, it is evident that the EU economy is coping with the adaptation to the shocks caused by the pandemic and Russia's aggression against Ukraine exceptionally well (see Figure 2.1). After a period of sustained growth, 2020 saw a sharp decline in consumption expenditure by households and NPISHs, falling by 7.1%. However, the following years of 2021 and 2022 showed a recovery with growth rates of 4.0%

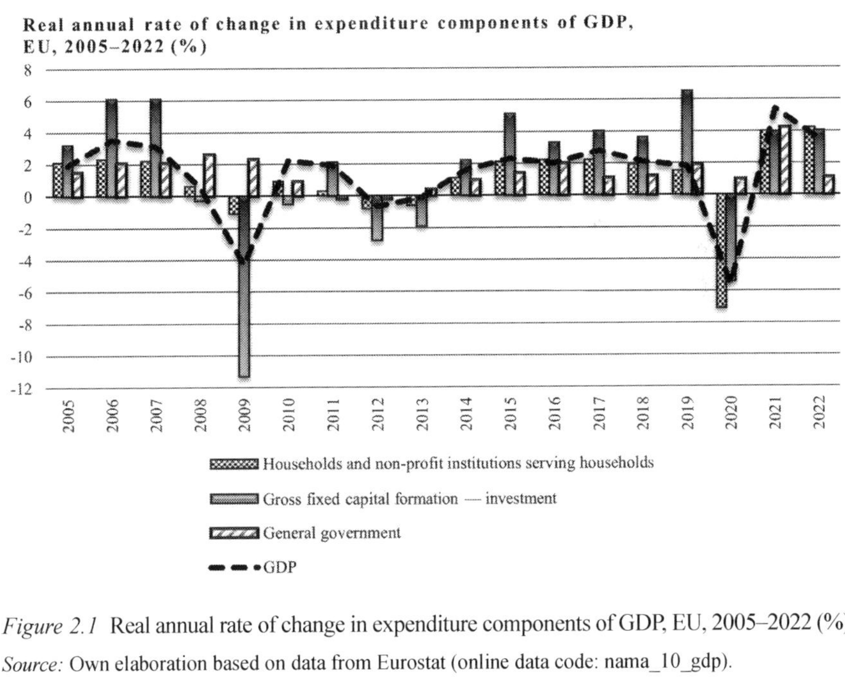

Figure 2.1 Real annual rate of change in expenditure components of GDP, EU, 2005–2022 (%)

Source: Own elaboration based on data from Eurostat (online data code: nama_10_gdp).

and 4.2%, respectively. The increases in investments were observed from 2014 to 2019, rising in the range of 2.2–6.5% each year. The majority of other expenditure measures experienced a sharp decline in 2020, with a 5.4% decrease in investment marking the end of a period of growth. The combined growth of 3.9% in 2021 and 4.0% in 2022 resulted in the recovery of 2020's losses. In 2022, Eurostat reported that household and non-profit institution spending made up 52.3% of the EU's GDP in current prices. Gross capital formation and general government expenditure accounted for 24.7% and 21.4%, respectively. The external balance of goods and services comprised 1.5%. The EU has successfully managed to wean itself off Russian gas in 2022. It noted moderate growth in the first quarter of 2023, dispelling fears of a winter recession that seemed unavoidable just a few months ago. A better-than-expected start of the year 2023 for the EU economy was driven by declining energy prices. Besides, the EU has dealt well with the energy crisis by prompt diversification of supply and a significant decline in energy consumption. Rapid deterioration of terms of trade in 2021 and 2022, along with an increase in energy (i.e. import) prices, has shifted purchasing power from the EU to the rest of the world. With the rapid decline in energy prices, the expected improvement in terms of trade will lead to benefits for all domestic economic sectors, households, businesses, and governments.

It is worth noting that the war caused inflationary pressure in the euro area during the post-pandemic recovery and pushed up consumer prices, especially for energy and food. Headline inflation increased from 0.3% in 2020 to 5.0% in 2021 and then to 10.6% in 2022. Energy and food inflation accounted for more than two-thirds of this record-high inflation in 2022 (ECB, 2023). According to the European Economic Forecast, the average core inflation in 2023, at 6.9% in the EU, is set to fall to 3.6% in 2024 (European Commission, 2023a). Figure 2.2 also presents that the inflation has concurrently trended down since November 2022.

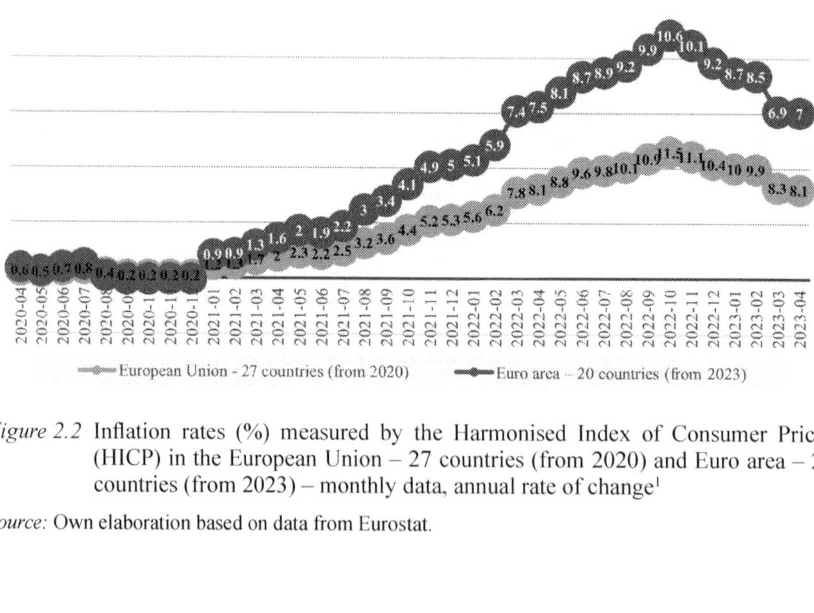

Figure 2.2 Inflation rates (%) measured by the Harmonised Index of Consumer Prices (HICP) in the European Union – 27 countries (from 2020) and Euro area – 20 countries (from 2023) – monthly data, annual rate of change[1]

Source: Own elaboration based on data from Eurostat.

Meanwhile, some experts warn that there is a possibility of increased inflation in the near future caused by potentially rising energy prices. Private consumption in the EU is set to rebound to 1.8% in 2024, while the household saving rate is projected to decrease from 13.2% in 2022 to 12.8% in 2024 (European Commission, 2023a). Considering labour market, experts predict that employment is set to keep growing moderately, while unemployment rate is expected to remain close to its historical low, at around 6% in the EU in 2023 and 2024.

The export dependence and reliance on energy imports from Russia has made Central and Eastern European countries particularly vulnerable. Germany and Italy were heavily dependent on Russian gas but also could be hit by supply shortages in the automotive industries. According to data from Eurostat (2022), the value of exports to Russia fell by 55% between February 2022 and March 2022, while imports from Russia rose by 3% in these months due to a sharp increase of the price of energy products and raw materials. Then, the value of imports from Russia fell by 53%, from €21.8 billion in March 2022 to €10.3 billion in December 2022 (Eurostat, 2023). Russia's share in the extra-EU imports for six key products decreased (it has been gradually replaced by other trade partners) with strong declines visible for coal, natural gas, fertilisers, petroleum oil, and iron and steel. In particular, the highest drops have been recorded for coal (from 45% in 2021 to 22% in 2022), natural gas (from 36 to 21%), fertilisers (from 29 to 22%), petroleum oil (from 28 to 21%), and iron and steel (from 16 to 10%) (Eurostat, 2023). The EU coped with the reduction in gas imports from Russia in 2022 thanks to decreased natural gas consumption by almost 20%. National measures and the REPowerEU initiative are helping to accelerate the transition to green energy and increase the EU's energy independence.

The year 2020 saw a significant decline in industrial production, particularly for durable consumer goods and capital goods, due to the COVID-19 crisis and resulting containment measures like lockdowns. The following months saw a significant recovery. However, in the summer of 2022, there was a shift in the trend of industrial production. During the period of August 2022 to September 2023, it experienced a decline of over 5%. Significant drops were observed specifically in the production of durable consumer goods (−9.4%) and capital goods (−7.6%) (Figure 2.3).

In order to examine the current economic conditions in both manufacturing and service, it is useful to present the Purchasing Managers' Index (hereafter: PMI). The main objective of the PMI is to supply crucial insights on present and upcoming business conditions to company executives, analysts, and shareholders. By summarising the views of purchasing managers, this diffusion index showcases whether market conditions are advancing, remaining constant, or declining. S&P Global gathers information for the HCOB Eurozone Manufacturing PMI by sending out monthly questionnaires to manufacturing companies in Germany, France, Italy, Spain, the Netherlands, Austria, Ireland, and Greece, which make up a total of 3,000 private sector entities. The PMI consists of the following five indices with varying weights: New Orders (30%), Output (25%), Employment (20%), Suppliers' Delivery Times (15%), and Stocks of Purchases (10%). The index ranges from 0 to 100, with a score above 50 indicating a general rise compared to the previous

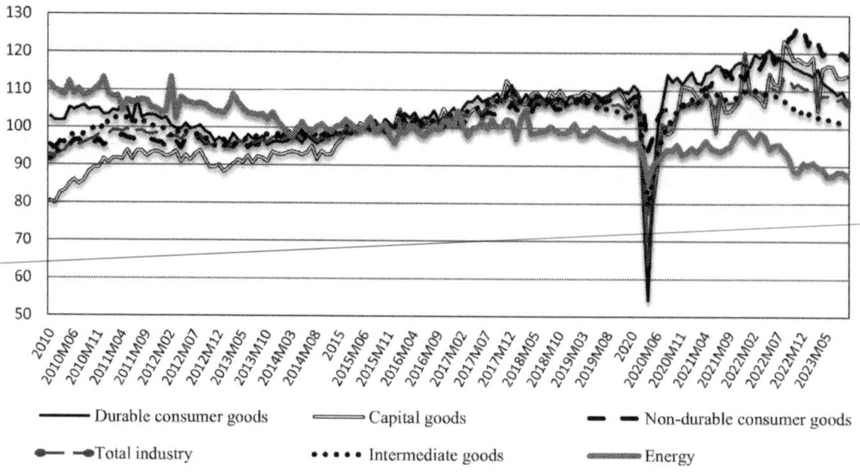

Figure 2.3 Industrial production for total industry and main industrial grouping in EU, 2010–2023

Source: Own elaboration based on data from Eurostat (online data code: sts inpr_m).

month, and a score below 50 indicating a general decline (The Investopedia Team, 2023). The data showed a 44.40 points of manufacturing PMI in the Euro Area in December 2023. The long-term forecast for the Euro Area Manufacturing PMI is expected to be approximately 53.00 points in 2025 and 52.00 points in 2026, according to econometric models presented by Trading Economics.

Meanwhile, the HCOB Eurozone Services PMI is formed by S&P Global using information from questionnaires distributed to a panel of service providers in Germany, France, Italy, Spain, and Ireland. This research focuses on consumer (excluding retail), transportation, information, communication, finance, insurance, real estate, and business services sectors. The HCOB Eurozone Services PMI exhibited a comparable value to the manufacturing PMI, i.e., 48.8 in December 2023 (Trading Economics, 2023b, 2023c). The data reveals a consecutive decrease in services output for the fifth time, reflecting a decrease in demand for eurozone services towards the end of the fiscal year. Additionally, employment growth has decelerated to its second slowest rate since February 2021. Moreover, there was a continued decrease in the backlog of work, which has been observed since July 2023. In terms of prices, there was a decrease in input cost inflation to the lowest level in five months, while output charges increased at a faster rate. In December, business confidence experienced an improvement, reaching its peak level since mid-2023, although expectations for growth continued to be low in comparison to past standards.

The seasonally adjusted HCOB Eurozone Composite PMI Output Index (Figure 2.4), a weighted average of the HCOB Manufacturing PMI Output Index and the HCOB Services PMI Business Activity Index, showed a sub-50.0 reading in December 2023 (S&P Global, 2023; Trading Economics, 2023a). This indicates a continued decrease in private sector output levels throughout the eurozone.

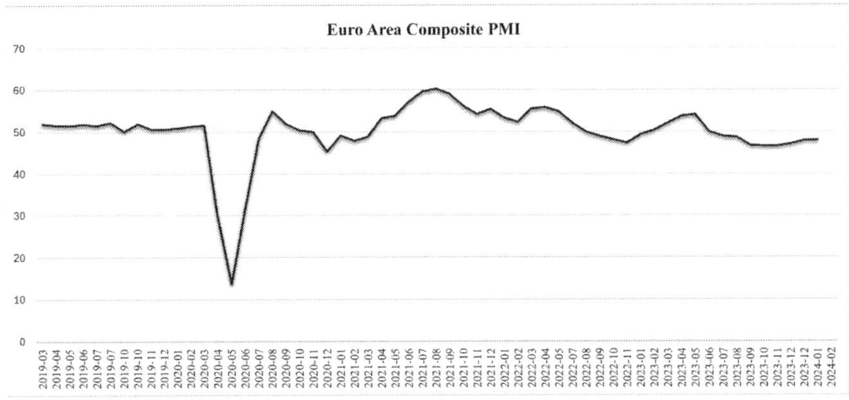

Figure 2.4 Euro Area Composite PMI, 2014–2025

Source: Trading Economics.

Economic activity in the euro area saw a continued weakening in demand for goods and services, with employment levels dropping for the second time in nearly three years. Businesses' expectations for growth have recovered significantly, rising from a low point in September and reaching their strongest level in seven months, though still below historical averages.

In order to gain insight into the influence of war on consumer and business sentiment, it is worthwhile to analyse the indicators of consumer and business confidence (see: OECD, 2024a; 2024b).

The consumer confidence indicator serves as a measure of forthcoming trends in households' expenditure and savings, derived from responses regarding their anticipated financial status and overall economic sentiment, unemployment, and capability of savings. When the indicator rises above 100, it indicates that consumers are more confident about the future economy, causing them to save less and spend more on significant purchases within the next year. When values fall below 100, it reflects a pessimistic perspective on the economy's future trajectory, which may lead individuals to save more and spend less.

The business confidence indicator gathers information from opinion surveys regarding production, orders, and stocks of finished goods, providing insight into potential future changes within the industry sector. The application of this approach allows for the observation of output growth and anticipation of changes in economic activity. Numbers exceeding 100 indicate a higher level of confidence in the upcoming business performance, while numbers below 100 reflect a negative outlook towards future performance.

Thus, Figure 2.5 shows the consumer confidence crunch in European states, even worser than during the pandemic, caused by the collapse in households' expectations about the general economic situation in their country, as well as their assessments of future financial situation, which fell to a historical low. Consumer confidence plummeted in Spain (−14.2), Italy (−13.5), France (−11.1), the Netherlands (−10.6), as well as Germany (−6.9) to levels just slightly above the trough marked in the

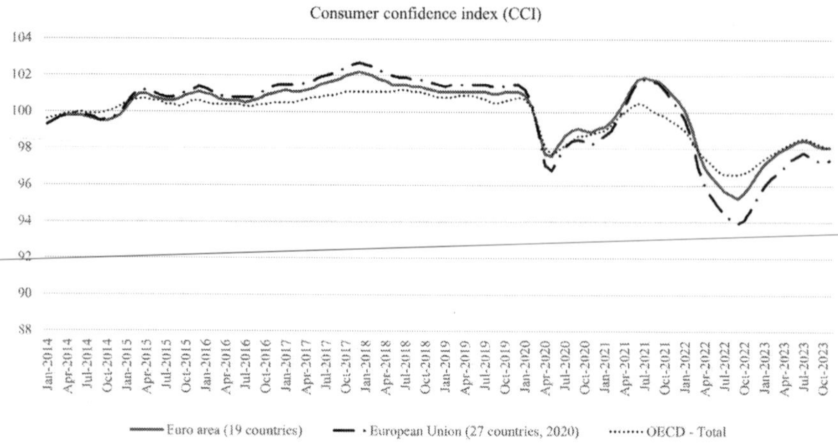

Figure 2.5 Consumer confidence index (CCI) for Euro area and EU with background – OECD, January 2014 – November 2023

Source: OECD (2024b).

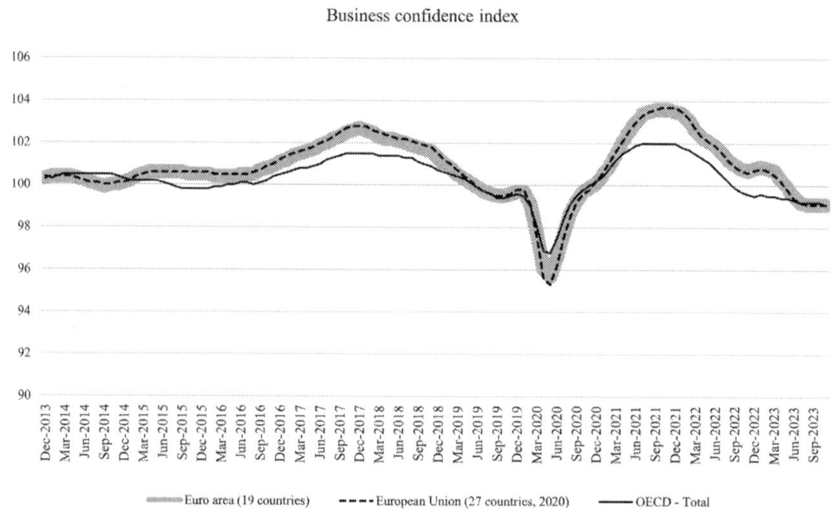

Figure 2.6 Business confidence index for Euro area, EU, and OECD, January 2008–November 2023

Source: OECD (2024a).

first COVID-19 wave (European Commission, 2022). The consumer sentiment in Poland showed a slight drop of −3.9, positioning the indicator in the middle of its pre-pandemic level and its lowest point during the initial wave. Managers' expectations regarding the future business situation collapsed in March 2022 and the business confidence index reflects a similar negative trend in the European states (Figure 2.6).

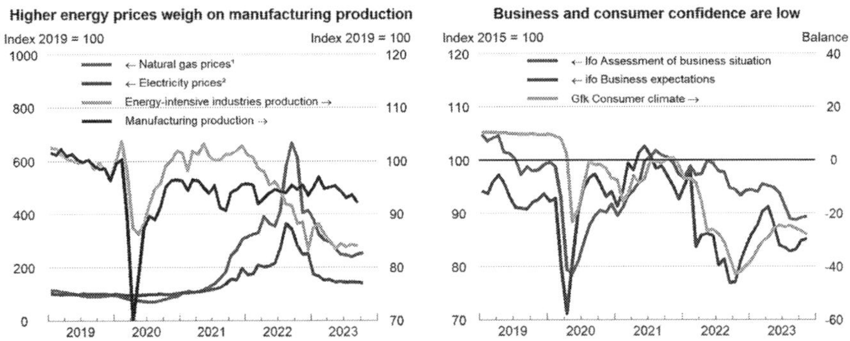

Figure 2.7 Germany: Energy prices, manufacturing, confidence indicators, 2019–2023

Note: 1 – prices of natural gas sold to industry; 2 – Electricity prices, when delivered to special contract customers

Source: OECD (2023).

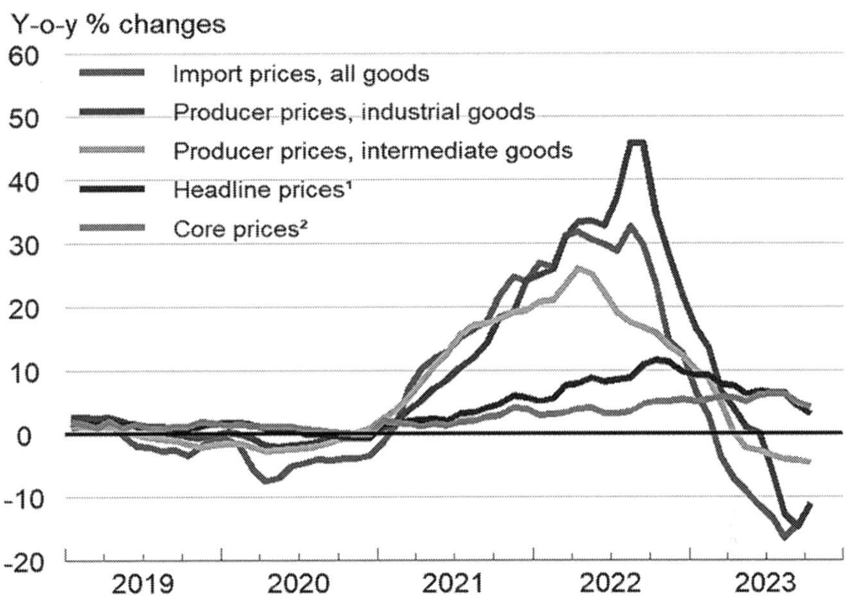

Figure 2.8 Germany: inflation, 2019–2023

Note: 1 – harmonised index of consumer prices; 2 – harmonised index of consumer prices excluding food, energy, alcohol, and tobacco.

Source: OECD (2023).

The impact of war on industry is particularly noticeable when examining a certain country, rather than a whole region. Considering the case of Germany, the data (Figure 2.7) clearly shows a substantial rise in gas and energy prices, resulting in a steep decline in the energy-intensive industries production. This has resulted in a

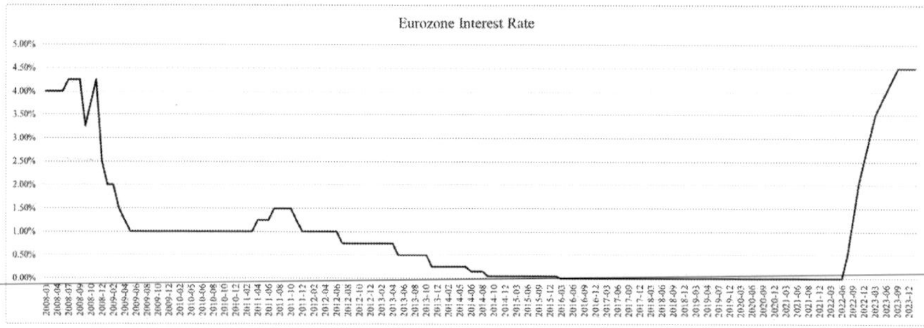

Figure 2.9 The benchmark interest rate in the Euro Area, 2000–2023

Source: Trading Economics.

marked decline in business optimism and consumer confidence. When examining year-over-year percentage changes, it can be seen that prices for industrial goods increased by nearly 50%, while import prices for all goods experienced a 30% rise and intermediate goods saw a 25% increase (Figure 2.8).

The main goal of the European Central Bank's monetary policy is to ensure price stability, specifically to keep inflation below 2% over the medium term. The benchmark interest rate in the Euro Area is determined by the Governing Council of the European Central Bank. The European Central Bank kept interest rates at multi-year highs during its October meeting, marking a significant shift from its 15-month streak of rate hikes and reflecting a more cautious 'wait-and-see' stance among policymakers, influenced by the gradual easing of price pressures and concerns about an impending recession. This decision follows a series of ten consecutive rate increases since July 2022 (Figure 2.9), which elevated the main refinancing operations rate to a 22-year high of 4.5% and the deposit facility rate to an all-time record of 4%. The European Central Bank last hiked its policy interest rates in September, by 25 bps. Reflecting market expectations, the Euribor-3 months futures suggests that, after peaking at 4% in October, euro area short-term nominal interest rates will gradually decrease to 3% by the end of 2025 (European Commission, 2023c).

2.4 EU Energy Dependency

Energy prices in European countries have been experiencing fluctuations since the second half of 2021. The post-COVID-19 economic recovery and the lifting of travel restrictions have led to a greater increase in energy prices than originally anticipated. Several factors have played a role in the increase of prices since 2021. First of all, the global markets have experienced an unprecedented surge in gas prices, with an increase of over 170% in 2021. In the EU, there has been a significant rise of more than 150% between July 2021 and July 2022. Moreover, severe climate circumstances, including intense summer heatwaves in Europe, contribute to increased energy consumption for cooling and put pressure on electricity generation. The demand for liquefied natural gas has risen, causing a significant increase in its price. Besides, the economic recovery in Asia has led to a significant increase in gas consumption. Climate conditions have been partly responsible for the recent shortage of nuclear and hydropower electricity generation. Russia's decision to terminate gas supply to a number of EU countries in 2022 has resulted in supply uncertainty and a considerable increase in gas prices leading to a significant surge in electricity costs (Eurostat, 2023b).

Thus, energy prices have been unsteady since mid-2021, while prices for key goods, for instance, fuels and fertilisers, increased to remarkable level in 2022. Russia's intentional reduction of gas supplies was the key cause of the remarkable increase in gas prices in the EU, which has had an influence on the price of electricity produced in gas-fired power plants and caused electricity prices to rise. In view of the instability in the energy markets, the countries of the EU have consented to measures designed to strengthen solidarity among the EU nations and to facilitate a more unified approach to the joint procurement of gas.

In October of 2022, the European Union implemented emergency regulation to address the high energy prices and provide relief to the citizens and businesses that had been adversely affected by the energy crisis (European Council, 2022).

The regulation contains the following emergency measures:

- reducing electricity use (i.e. a positive effect on the EU electricity rates and, as a result, on consumers' energy bills),
- capping revenues of electricity producers (i.e. enable the member countries to gather financial resources from the extra earnings of the energy industry and allocate them to the most disadvantaged citizens and companies in the EU, thereby offering direct aid to those endeavouring to cover their expenses),
- securing a solidarity contribution from fossil fuel businesses (i.e. these companies contribute their fair share to providing relief to people and business struggling to pay their energy bills).

At the end of March 2022, consensus was reached among EU top officials to discontinue reliance on Russian fossil fuel imports. Moreover, European Union countries are striving together to ensure gas supplies while reducing demand for gas, softening the effects of high energy prices on households and businesses, and accelerating the transition to renewable energy (European Council, 2024).

At the December 2022 meeting of EU leaders, the significance of a heightened level of EU collaboration for the purpose of being ready for cold seasons was articulated, and the Council was asked to finish its proposals for enhanced energy solidarity, expedited deployment of renewables, and a market correction mechanism for gas prices. At their meeting on December 19, 2022, the Council came to a consensus regarding the implementation of a regulatory mechanism to prevent episodes of overly high gas prices (European Council, 2023b). At the end of March 2023, the Council formally adopted 15% gas demand reduction target. At the end of 2023, Council and Parliament reached a deal on the reform of electricity market design, while the Council agreed to extend emergency measures regarding energy prices and security of supply. Thus, as a response to the energy crisis, the EU has been striving to make sure European consumers have access to affordable and competitive energy, to enhance the EU's energy security and readiness in case of emergencies, and to bolster the energy robustness and self-sufficiency of EU countries. With this in mind, EU countries are joining forces to focus on limiting excessively high gas prices, boosting solidarity and sharing supply, cutting energy costs for households, and businesses and reducing the EU's energy dependencies.

Table 2.3 provides a comprehensive chronology of the EU's actions regarding energy prices and supply security since the start of the war.

Table 2.3 What are EU countries doing to address the energy crisis? Timeline – energy prices and security of supply, 2022–2023

Time	*Actions*
19/12/2023	Energy prices and security of supply: Council agrees to extend emergency measures
14/12/2023	Reform of electricity market design: Council and Parliament reach deal
17/10/2023	Reform of electricity market design: Council reaches agreement
19/06/2023	Council reaches agreement on parts of electricity market reform
30/03/2023	Council formally adopts 15% gas demand reduction target
28/03/2023	Member states agree to extend voluntary 15% gas demand reduction target
19/12/2022	Council agrees on market mechanism to limit excessive gas prices
15/12/2022	European Council: more EU coordination is key to face coming winters
14/12/2022	Provisional agreement reached on REPowerEU
13/12/2022	Energy ministers discuss market mechanism for gas prices
03/12/2022	Russian oil: EU agrees on level of price cap
24/11/2022	Council agrees on content of new measures to address the energy crisis
07/11/2022	Eurogroup discusses high energy prices
20-21/10/2022	EU leaders reach a deal on energy
07/10/2022	EU leaders discuss measures to reduce energy demand, ensure security of supply, and guarantee affordable prices
06/10/2022	Council formally adopts emergency measures to reduce energy prices
30/09/2022	Council agrees on emergency measures to reduce energy prices
05/08/2022	Council adopts regulation on reducing gas demand by 15%
26-28/06/2022	G7 leaders commit to immediate action to secure energy supply and reduce prices
27/06/2022	Energy ministers welcome REPowerEU plan
27/06/2022	Council adopts regulation on gas storage
03/06/2022	EU adopts sixth package of sanctions against Russia. The EU decided to prohibit the purchase, import, or transfer of crude oil and certain petroleum products from Russia into the EU
30-31/05/2022	EU leaders agree on oil ban and priorities to strengthen the EU's energy independence
19/05/2022	Gas storage: Council and Parliament reach a provisional agreement
02/05/2022	Energy ministers hold extraordinary meeting to discuss gas supply following Gazprom's delivery suspension
10-11/03/2022	EU leaders agree on how to reduce energy dependencies
28/02/2022	Energy ministers discuss energy market situation following Ukraine crisis
24/02/2022	EU leaders call for emergency measures on energy

Source: Own elaboration based on European Council (2024).

Following a long period of lockdowns and restrictive steps taken to obstruct the spread of the COVID-19 virus in 2020, a large number of EU Member States witnessed a recovery of economic activity in 2021, which further intensified in 2022. Whilst the EU still mostly relies on imported fossil fuels, it is actively endeavouring to diversify its gas suppliers. This process is not without challenges, involving extensive expenditure on infrastructure such as pipelines and LNG terminals, yet the results are already becoming evident. In 2021, the EU obtained 83% of its natural gas from external sources (Eurostat, 2023c). Following Russia's invasion of Ukraine, imports of gas from Russia to the EU have seen a drastic decline. This shortfall has been mainly remedied by a considerable boost in LNG imports, mainly from the United States. As businesses resumed activity and people started to travel again, energy demand rose significantly. This, in turn, led to a dramatic surge in natural gas prices in the second half of 2021. In addition, the summer of 2022 saw extraordinarily high temperatures and dry conditions in a number of EU Member States, which had a bearing on nuclear and hydro power generation. All these elements, along with others, had a considerable effect on energy supply and the changes in specific energy commodities. Meanwhile, following a surge in 2021 in contrast to 2020 for fossil fuels and nuclear energy, nuclear and natural gas experienced a sharp decline (from 155 bcm in 2021 to around 80 bcm in 2022 and to an estimated 40–45 bcm in 2023), yet brown coal and petroleum products persisted to rise (Figure 2.10). Hard coal nearly stayed at the same rate as in 2021, with only a negligible decrease.

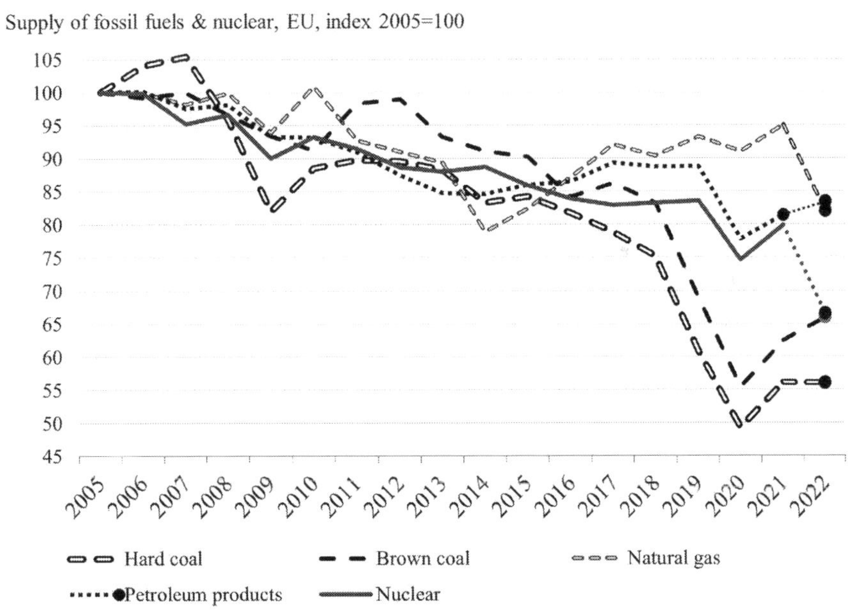

Figure 2.10 Supply of fossil fuels and nuclear, EU, index 2005=100

Source: Own elaboration based on data from Eurostat (online data codes: nrg_cg_sff, nrg_cb_gas, nrg_cb_oil, nrg_ind_pehnf).

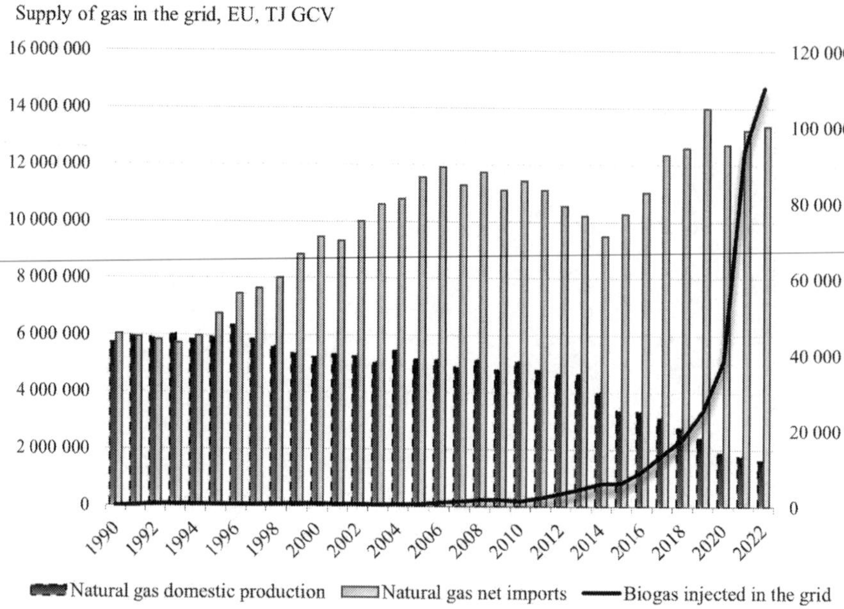

Figure 2.11 Supply of gas in the grid (categorised by natural gas domestic production, net imports, and biogas injected in the grid), EU, 1990–2022

Note: main axis – natural gas domestic production and natural gas net imports; auxiliary axis – biogas in the grid.

Source: Own elaboration based on data from Eurostat (online data code: nrg_cb_gas).

Figure 2.11 reveals the gas supply in the grid from 1990 to 2022, categorised by natural gas domestic production, net imports, and biogas injected in the grid. The EU was clearly turned to imports of natural gas more, while domestic production is diminishing. By the year 2022, imports of gas were estimated to account for as much as 89% of the energy supply in the grid (Eurostat, 2023c). While the utilisation of biogas has seen a gradual increase, it still only makes up a minuscule amount of the overall gas supply in the grid, meaning that it is highly unlikely to be of any consequence in replacing any possible gas shortages in the coming years.

The data from Figure 2.12 displays the share of Russian pipeline gas in total EU natural gas imports from January 2019 to June 2023. Until the second half of 2021, Russia held approximately 40% of the market share. Meanwhile, at an unofficial summit of national leaders in March 2022, the heads of the 27 EU member states jointly agreed to phase out the EU's dependence on Russian fossil fuels by reducing the overall reliance on fossil fuels, diversifying energy supplies and routes, including for liquefied natural gas (LNG), speeding up the development of renewables and hydrogen, improving interconnections between EU energy networks and increasing energy efficiency.

In May 2022, the commission introduced the REPowerEU plan regarding Russian imports that includes the voluntary EU Energy Platform, aimed at facilitating joint

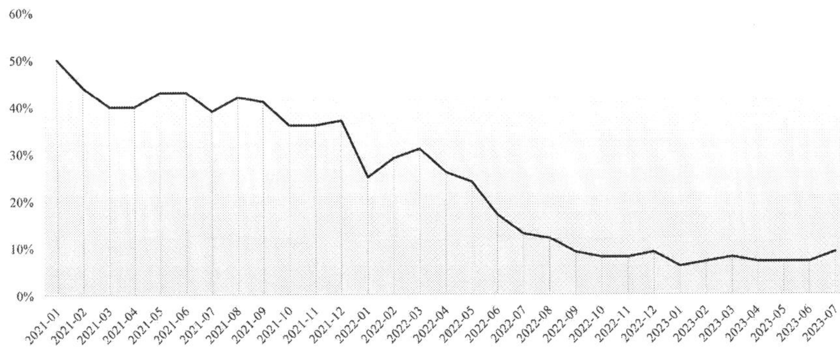

Figure 2.12 Share of Russian pipeline gas in total EU natural gas imports, 2019–2023

Source: Based on data from Eurostat.

energy purchases for all EU nations and select European allies (European Council, 2024). Through the implementation of novel measures, it is now feasible for EU nations and energy companies to purchase gas together on a global market. Aggregating the demand of EU members guarantees that they will be in a stronger position when it comes to buying gas on global markets, eliminating the risk of them outbidding each other in the process. The new rules also promote collaboration treaties between EU countries. Nations that haven't yet concluded a treaty with another EU member can request solidarity when the need arises. Additionally, the new regulation institutes a new price index, that will ensure uniform and foreseeable pricing for liquefied natural gas transactions, in addition to the Title Transfer Facility. The Energy Council officially adopted the measures on December 19, 2022.

Since then, the percentage of Russian gas has been decreasing rapidly while other suppliers have seen an increase in their market share. In particular, this process experienced a surge in 2022. Eurostat data shows that the EU's reliance on Russian gas decreased from 39% in the third quarter of 2021 to 8% in the third quarter of 2023.

Recent developments have led to updated energy supply agreements with international partners, in particular, the EU is receiving higher amounts of LNG from the United States and Canada, while Norway is supplying more gas. Collaboration with Azerbaijan has also been strengthened, and there are plans for new deliveries from Israel and Egypt.

In light of inconsistent gas deliveries, the Council swiftly implemented measures to secure gas supply during winter months and decrease demand within the EU. A new regulation on gas storage was enacted by the Council in June 2022 (European Council, 2024). To mitigate the risk of energy shortages, the EU ensured its gas storage facilities were filled up to 95% prior to the winter of 2022–2023. The EU also successfully met its goal of filling gas storage facilities to 90% by August 18, exceeding the deadline of November 1, 2023, by over two months. The new regulations also implemented solidarity measures among Member Nations to support those lacking storage capabilities within their borders (European Council,

2024). These nations must maintain reserves equivalent to 15% of their yearly domestic gas usage in storage facilities situated in a different Member Nation. To mitigate the risk of external interference, the regulation outlined the compulsory certification of all operators of underground gas storage sites.

After a long period of decline, coal consumption experienced a reversal in 2021 that carried over into 2022. It is worth mentioning that solid fossil fuels reached a historically low level in 2020, the lowest since data has been collected (i.e. since 1990), partly as a result of COVID-19 lockdown measures (Eurostat, 2023b). The significant rise seen in 2021 was predominantly driven by the post-lockdown recovery of the industrial sector, coupled with the increased consumption of coal for power and heat generation in specific EU Member States, as a substitute for the increasingly costly natural gas. Coal-based electricity and heat production continued to rise in 2022, partly influenced by gas supply interruptions and initiatives to lower gas consumption. Despite the rising numbers noted in 2022, solid fossil fuels remained at their third lowest level since 1990.

Compared to 2021, the EU witnessed a 5.8% increase in inland usage of lignite, a 0.7% uptick in other bituminous coal, and a 14.5% growth in oil shale and oil sands (Eurostat, 2023b). Conversely, there was a 1.2% decline in inland consumption of coking coal and a 7.5% decrease in coke oven coke (Eurostat, 2023b). The production of manufactured gases, primarily associated with coal usage in the iron and steel sector, saw a considerable decline, except for gas works gas. An analysis of coal consumption within the EU during the years 2017–2019 reveals a significant decline across all products, with no exceptions. During the years 2017–2019, the most significant decrease was seen in gas works gas (−82.7%), sub-bituminous coal (−59.7%), peat (−48.3%), and anthracite (−46.3%) (Eurostat, 2023b).The supply of hard coal remained relatively steady in relation to 2021(−0.1%) caused by a surge in imports (+25.0%), while the consumption of brown coal within the country saw a 5.7% increase, mainly driven by a rise in domestic production (+7.0%) (Eurostat, 2023b).

The EU market experienced a growth (+2.4%) in gross inland deliveries of all petroleum products in 2022, surpassing the figures from 2021 (Eurostat, 2023b). Although certain products experienced a decline in gross inland deliveries, the majority of them saw an increase, particularly kerosene-type jet fuel, indicating a near return to pre-pandemic air travel levels in 2022.

In a manner similar to natural gas, oil domestic production shows a downward trend, while rising demand is usually fulfilled by imports, which make up approximately 90%. In comparison to gas, the total supply has been slowly dwindling over time, with the exception of the aftermath of the COVID-19 pandemic.

The latest statistics also reveal that refineries are seeing a rise in demand for primary oil, particularly crude oil, after a notable decrease in 2020 (Eurostat, 2023b). In 2021, the refinery intake showed a 3.0% rise from the previous year, followed by a 4.0% increase in 2022 compared to 2021 (Eurostat, 2023b). The supply of refined petroleum products from refineries showed a similar trend (+3.2 % in 2021/2020 and +4.5% in 2022/2021) (Eurostat, 2023b). Yet, refinery intake and output both saw a 6.0% decline compared to the 2017–2019 period. In the EU, the most prominent oil products produced in 2022 were gas oil, diesel oil, and motor gasoline, making up a combined 58.5% of the total refinery output, showing a slight decrease from the previous year (Eurostat, 2023b).

Since March 2022, there has been a 90% decline in Russian oil imports into the EU, with no major effects on the EU economy. In accordance with EU legislation, Member States are responsible for storing emergency oil supplies. Despite the EU's sanctions and the G7's price limit on Russian oil, the EU's oil security was not compromised and Russian oil profits were effectively reduced. The EU's 11th set of sanctions includes measures to prevent the import of oil products produced in other countries using Russian oil or ones of unknown origin. The Oil Coordination Group, along with experts from Member States, is closely monitoring oil markets due to potential cuts from OPEC and Russia that could lead to increased market tightness.

Considering electricity (Figure 2.13), the EU experienced a 28% decline in overall supply compared to 2021, and a 33% drop compared to the pre-pandemic period of 2017–2019. Initial data suggests noteworthy yearly fluctuations among different fuel sources. Following a brief period of renewable energy surpassing fossil fuels for electricity generation in 2020, 2021 marked a shift back to fossil fuel dominance, which persisted and strengthened in 2022. The latest data for 2022 indicates a notable surge in electricity generated from solar photovoltaic energy (+29.3%) on the EU level, followed by wind (+8.9%) (Eurostat, 2023b). Conversely, the production of hydroelectricity experienced a significant decrease (−17.7%) as a result of unfavourable weather conditions, while electricity generation from natural gas

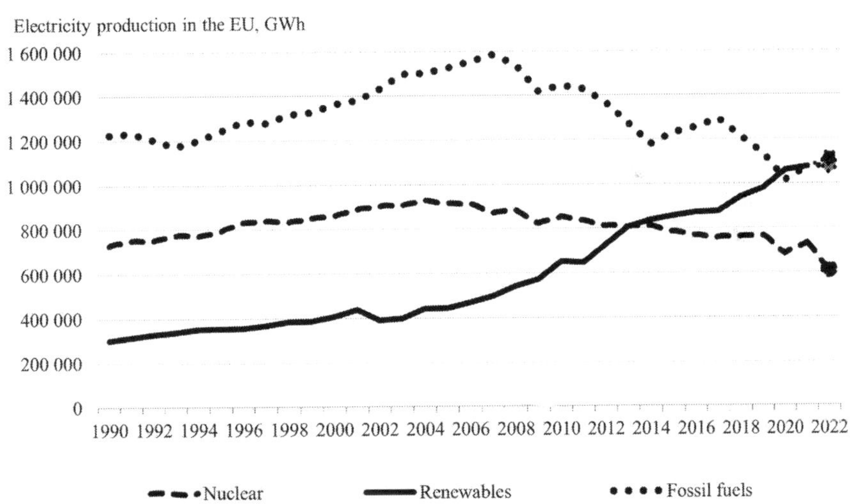

Figure 2.13 Electricity production in the EU, 1990–2022

Source: Own elaboration based on data from Eurostat (online data codes: nrg_ind_pehcf, nrg_ind_pehnf).

remained relatively stable (−1.3%) (Eurostat, 2023b). The year 2022 saw a rise in electricity generation from key solid fossil fuels, such as other bituminous coal (+10.0%) and lignite (+6.7%) (Eurostat, 2023b). As a result of both maintenance concerns and the permanent decommissioning of multiple reactors, the output of nuclear power plants dropped by 16.7% (−122.5 TWh) in contrast to 2021. The EU electricity generation system saw nuclear energy as the primary source of fuel, making up 21.8% of the total. This was closely followed by natural gas (19.5%), wind (15.0%), hydro (11.0%), lignite (8.6%), other bituminous coal (7.5%), and solar photovoltaic (7.3%) (Eurostat, 2023b).

The heat supply in the EU for 2022 dropped by 6.2%, a significant decrease from the previous year and a 5.2% decrease from the 2017 to 2019 period (Eurostat, 2023b). It should be noted that these numbers do not include self-consumed heat. The use of natural gas, which is the primary source of heat production in the EU, experienced a decline of 11.9% (Eurostat, 2023b). Meanwhile, solid biofuels, the second leading source, also saw a decrease of 8%, and heat generated from other bituminous coal decreased by 4.7% (Eurostat, 2023b). The amount of heat generated from waste remained relatively consistent compared to 2021. Other sources played a smaller role in overall heat production, and early data suggests varying patterns. The EU's heat supply is solely reliant on domestic heat production, as imports and exports of heat play a minimal role.

In response to the energy crisis, the EU took swift action to expand the use of renewable energy technologies, bolstering its energy supply, and ultimately reducing dependence on Russian fossil fuels. The installation of 57 GW of renewable energy capacity, primarily through solar PV and wind turbines, surpassed the previous year's installations by approximately 50% in 2022. Despite the dip in hydropower production in 2022 (12% of total power production), this helped to even things out, as 2023 saw a return to average levels due to increased rainfall and higher reservoir levels. In the renewable heating sector, "heat pump sales are breaking records, with more than 3 million heat pumps sold in 2022 – a year-on-year increase of +38.9%" with particularly strong relative growth in Belgium, the Czech Republic, and Slovakia, followed by Poland (EHPA, 2023). The use of renewable energies has markedly increased in 2022 and 2023, with the EU making a commitment to accelerate their deployment with a target of 42.5% in the EU energy mix by 2030, and the ambition to reach 45% European Commission (2023b).

2.5 Ukrainians on the EU Labour Market

As a result of Russia's invasion, the European Council unanimously approved an implementing decision on March 4, 2022, granting temporary protection for those seeking refuge from Ukraine. Temporary protection status and conditions of applications are defined by Council Directive 2001/55/EC of July 20, 2001, whereas Council Decision 2022/382 of March 4, 2022, establishing the existence of a mass influx of displaced persons from Ukraine within the meaning of Article 5 of Directive 2001/55/EC, is the first one to introduce temporary protection. It is a solution that offers immediate and temporary safety to individuals displaced from non-EU nations and those who cannot go back to their home country. It is applicable in cases where the standard asylum system may be overwhelmed by a large number of arrivals, posing a threat to the efficient processing of applications. Following discussions on September 28, 2023, the European Council reached a decision to extend the temporary protection programme for individuals fleeing from Russia's aggressive war against Ukraine, extending the end date to March 4, 2025.

As of November 30, 2023, the EU was providing temporary protection to approximately 4.3 million non-EU citizens (i.e. 4,274,630) who had fled Ukraine due to the Russian invasion in 2022. It was reported by Eurostat (2024) that around 60% of those who received temporary protection were identified by Germany (1,235,960 people; 28.9% of total EU), Poland (955,110; 22.3%), and Czech Republic (369,330; 8.6%) (Figure 2.14). The ratio of temporary protection beneficiaries to the overall EU population was 9.5 per thousand at the end of November 2023. Czech Republic (34.1), Bulgaria (26.3), Estonia (26.3), Lithuania (26.1), Poland (26.0), and Latvia (23.1) had the highest ratios among the EU Member States (Figure 2.15).

At the end of November 2023, adult women represented 46.3% of beneficiaries of temporary protection, 55% of them were women aged 35 to 64 years with higher-than-average educational levels (Figure 2.15). According to the results of OECD survey (2023a), the vast majority of them were employed before the war with a non-negligible share worked in the health and education sectors. Children represented 33.3%, while the proportion of adult men in the total number of beneficiaries of temporary protection was only 20.4%.

The integration of Ukrainian refugees into the labour force has progressed more quickly compared to other refugee groups. In certain European OECD countries, the percentage of Ukrainian refugees of working age currently employed is above 40% with the Netherlands, Lithuania, Estonia, and the United Kingdom leading the way (OECD, 2023a). The rates also seem comparable in Poland and the Czech Republic, when taking into account temporary and informal jobs. In other countries, the percentage is lower but increasing. The influx of early employment has been concentrated in low-skilled jobs, resulting in an abundance of skills discrepancies. Furthermore, the prevalence of part-time employment amongst Ukrainian refugees is likely due to childcare commitments.

Bearing in mind the formal qualification standards, the matters of skills transferability and foreign qualification assessments are especially relevant. Some states have advanced their procedures, including through enhanced promotion and intelligence. Governments have also facilitated entrance to regulated professions by simplifying acknowledgement procedures or eliminating particular occupational demands, particularly in the healthcare sector.

Table 2.4 shows an overview of the regulations concerning access to the labour market in different EU countries within the framework of this legislation and the extent of support Ukrainian citizens can receive at those countries' public employment services (hereafter: PES).

Moreover, to help people escaping from Russia's invasion of Ukraine, a new online job-search tool has been created to make it easier for them to find

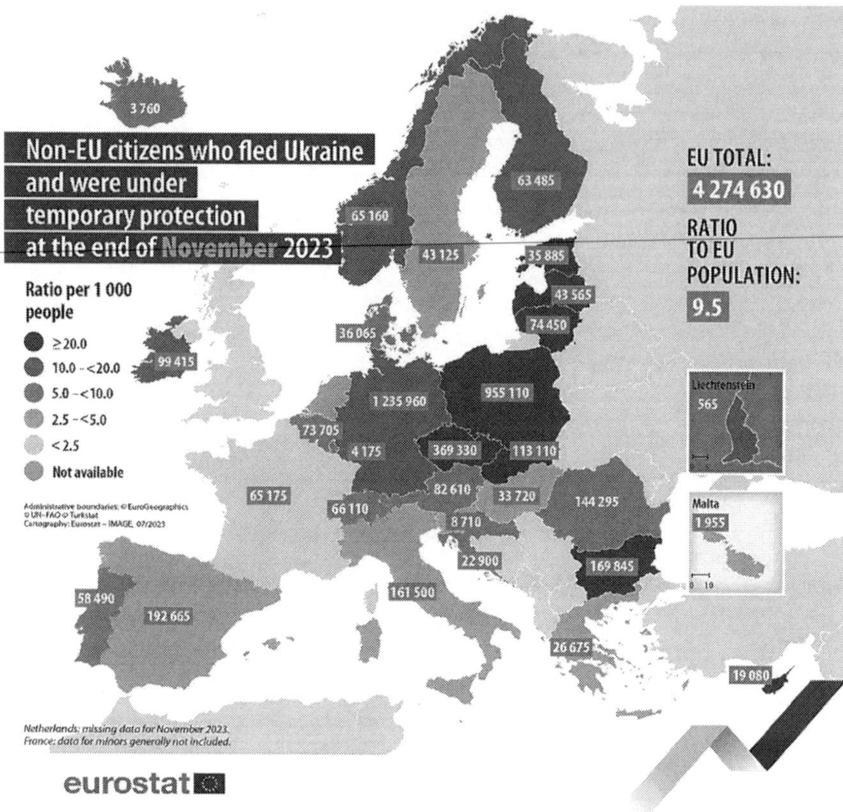

Figure 2.14 Temporary protection for persons fleeing Ukraine

Source: Eurostat (2024).

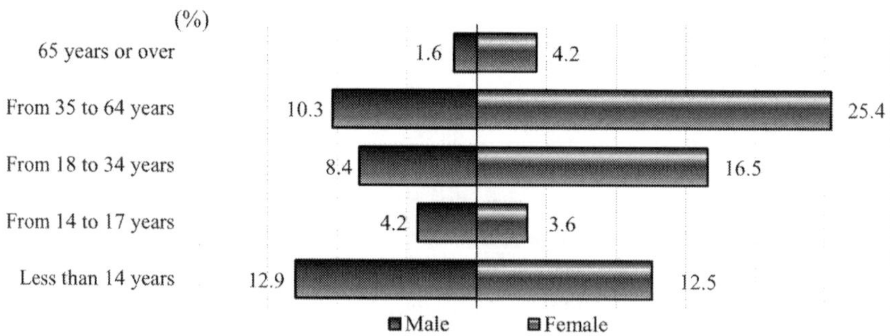

Figure 2.15 Structure by age and sex of beneficiaries of temporary protection in the EU, end of November 2023 (%)

Note: EU total calculated with data at the end of October 2023 for the Netherlands; EU total excluding: Hungary (data by age group not available); France (data for minors generally not included).

Source: Own elaboration based on data from Eurostat (migr_asytpsm).

Table 2.4 Access to the labour market of Ukrainian citizens in certain European countries

Country	*Access to the labour market / PES support*
Austria	Work permit required. PES provides assistance in the following fields: guidance, job placement, German language instruction, professional development/internship, special aid for women, childcare information.
Belgium–Brussels region	Gaining temporary protection through enrolment in the municipality, which grants access to the Brussels job market and the services they offer. Upon enrolment as a job seeker, a Ukrainian is able to access the common services of PES or can be directed to a team that affords more comprehensive guidance.
Belgium–Flanders region	Gaining temporary protection through enrolment at the municipality (obtaining the so-called 'A' card), which grants access to the labour market and services offered by PES in the Flanders region.
Croatia	Gaining temporary protection (issued by the Ministry of the Interior for a period of one year). It is possible to register at a nearby/regional employment office, upon presenting the temporary protection card and individual identification number (OIB).
Czech Republic	Granting free entry to the Czech labour market with residence permit (employment card, temporary protection, long-term visa for the purpose of toleration; employment cards for government-approved programmes). Electronic registration itself extends the temporary protection until September 30, 2024. However, it is necessary to complete the registration by booking a date to visit the Ministry of the Interior (with travel document and proof of accommodation) to have a new visa marked.
Denmark	Gaining residence permit under the Special Law on Temporary Residence Permits for Displaced Persons from Ukraine (issued by the Immigration Service). Access to the labour market and support of the labour office and municipality.
Estonia	Gaining temporary protection – full access to the labour market, PES, and unemployment benefits. In the case of residence on a visa or visa-free stay, the possibility of taking up only short-term work.
Finland	Gaining temporary protection – access to the labour market and PES.
France	Gaining temporary protection – access to the labour market and PES.
Germany	Possibility to apply for a residence permit, under the Directive, giving the right to work without a work permit. The residence permit is issued by the migration authorities with an expiration date of max. 4.03.2024.
Great Britain	Upon arrival in the UK, the passport stamp serves as evidence that an individual is authorised to work, rent a home, and utilise public services like medical care and education. Entry visa under the Homes for Ukraine, Family visa, or Extension visa scheme also allows to work straight away on arrival in the UK.
Greece	Within the 90-day period a one-year temporary protection by the Asylum Service of the Ministry of Migration and Asylum; this gives the right of access to the labour market and to medical care.

(*Continued*)

Table 2.4 (Continued)

Country	*Access to the labour market / PES support*
Hungary	The possibility of obtaining asylum, humanitarian, or temporary residence permits. The person eligible for employment must register as an applicant for service with the district employment office within five working days after receiving the first regular subsistence allowance.
Ireland	Ukrainians with a TPD (who are over one year on the Live Register and deemed Long-Term Unemployed) are available for employment support services with the Departments Intreo Partners National Employment Service.
Italy	Article 7 of Ordinance No. 872/2022 states that displaced persons coming from Ukraine can access employed and seasonal work, as well as self-employment on the basis of the sole application for a residence permit submitted to the competent Police Headquarters (Questure).
Portugal	Gaining temporary protection – access to the labour market and PES.
Slovakia	Two main projects providing assistance to the displaced persons from Ukraine were extended until December 2023. "We Are Helping Displaced Persons", for instance, aims to facilitate social inclusion and integration into the labour via education, mobility support, volunteering, and job orientation.
Spain	Gaining temporary protection – a residence permit is issued together with a work permit (within 24 hours). Access to the labour market and PES. The possibility of getting a so-called job seeker's card. Individual support path.
Sweden	Gaining temporary protection, obtaining a so-called coordination number. Registration in PES grants access to assistance including counselling (with a translator if necessary), job placement, and support in finding the right path.

Source: Own elaboration based on AMS; Safe.brussels (2023a, 2023b); Forem (2023a, 2023b); Hrvatska za Ukrajinu; Jobguide.Ukraine.dk. (2023); Eesti Tootukassa; Finnish Immigration Service; TE-palvelut; EU4UA (2022); job4ua.fr (2023); Bundesagentur fur Arbeit; The Germany4Ukraine; Instituto do Emprego (2023); Swedish Public Employment Service; Office of the Commissioner for Fundamental Rights of Hungary; ELA (2023); ACCACE (2024); ukrainianrefugeehelp.co.uk.

employment in the European Union. After signing up to the EU Talent Pool pilot initiative, those under temporary protection can upload their CVs, so that they can be seen by more than 4,000 employers, national employment centres, and private employment agencies. The EU Talent Pool pilot, which can be accessed in English, Ukrainian, and Russian, is available via EURES, a job-searching portal managed by the European Labour Authority. This portal unites national employment services, private employment agencies, and employers from all over the EU, and contains 3 million job vacancies.

Investigation[2] conducted by the European Union Agency for Asylum (EUAA) and the Organisation for Economic Co-operation and Development (OECD) across a few EU states between April 11, 2022, and August 15, 2022, has demonstrated that 71% of Ukrainian refugees indicate to have a tertiary-level qualification, with the majority being holders of a master's degree or higher. Only 8% of respondents attained no higher than a secondary level of education.

The data[3] of public employment services from 2022 is likely to show the most reliable representation of the situation but remain deficient. Thus, the share of highly educated refugees from Ukraine is:

- 78% – as to the Ifo online survey in Germany
- 79% – selected group from recently arrived refugees under Ukraine Humanitarian Schemes in the United Kingdom
- 68% – among those registered by public employment support events in Ireland
- 64% – among those registered with the Swiss PES
- 62% – among those registered in Spain
- 52% – among the slightly less than 6,000 Ukrainian refugees registered at the Belgium PES

According to the survey in the United Kingdom, Ukrainian refugees often demonstrate a high level of proficiency in English (ONS, 2022; 2023). The United Kingdom Humanitarian Response Insight Survey conducted in April 2022 revealed that approximately one-third of those who arrived in the country under the Ukraine Humanitarian Schemes are proficient or highly proficient in English. Meanwhile, only a small share of refugees speaks other languages. In Poland, for example, a significant share of Ukrainians (38%) stated their fluency in Polish, while a mere 4% in Germany stated they had proficiency in German. Not having the required language skills creates a barrier to integration into their host country, but also restricts them from realising their skill potential in the job market (OECD, 2021). A clear majority of respondents, approximately 60%, perceived language obstacles to be the most noteworthy difficulty they faced in adapting to their new environment (IOM, 2022). The same opinion has displaced persons in Poland, Belgium, the Slovak Republic, and Spain (UNHCR, 2022a; 2022b).

Data from surveys suggest that large number of refugees (i.e. 77% as to the OECD-EUAA survey) have a work or business background (UNHCR, 2022a; UNHCR, 2022b; INFO GmbH, 2022; Panchenko, 2022). Among them, the majority indicated to have worked in intellectual and scientific professions. Middle-skilled vocations, e.g., cashiers, secretaries, and machine operators, had lower involvement, around 30% in Ireland and Switzerland as well. Only 4% of refugees in both countries had jobs that require simple, routine tasks and physical effort. A considerable amount of refugees have been employed in education or healthcare. Findings indicate that the previous experience in education have 13% of respondents in the United Kingdom, 8% – in Lithuania, 7% – in Switzerland; meanwhile in the healthcare, about 8% respondents staying in the United Kingdom, Spain, and Lithuania (UNHCR, 2022a; ONS, 2022). It has been observed that the health and education sectors tend to have country-specific access requirements which may present challenges and delays when it comes to the integration of Ukrainian refugees into the labour market.

By studying the Ukrainian citizens living in Poland, it is noticeable that a considerable decline of almost twofold in the male population has occurred (from 57% in 2021 to 31% in 2023) (EWL Group, 2023). A significant rise of almost one-half can be seen in the share of Ukrainians aged 18–25 (23% vs. 16%), while the number of people over 45 years decreased (12% against 23%) (EWL Group, 2023). There is also a significant drop in those who are looking to stay in Poland for an extended period of time (40% vs. 60%). Taking into account professional qualifications, it is clear that there has been nearly a twofold decrease in the share of Ukrainians employed in Poland that are in line with their qualifications (35% vs. 68%) and almost a threefold reduction in the amount of Ukrainians considering launching their own business in Poland (15% vs. 42%) (EWL Group, 2023). In 2022, the majority of Ukrainian citizens worked in manufacturing (31%), followed by transport and storage (17%), administrative and support services (16%) and construction (12%). They were generally hired as personnel to performing simple tasks – 45%, industrial workers and craftsmen – 18%, operators and assemblers of machinery and equipment – 15%, office staff – 8%, service and sales workers – 6%, others – 8% (of which 2% were specialists) (EWL Group, 2023).

Nonetheless, Poland has achieved considerable success in providing employment opportunities to refugees from Ukraine, a great majority of whom have been able to find their initial job. In the opinion of 35% of the surveyed, the most beneficial element for Ukrainian integration in Poland is promotion of labour market access and healthcare (36%). Ukrainians in Poland mostly find jobs on their own (31%) or through family/friend's recommendations (31%). This brings to light not only the resourcefulness of labour migrants, but also that the citizens of Ukraine have become an essential element of the European labour market. The acceptance of Ukrainians by Poles and the cultural similarities between countries are of the utmost significance for economic migrants as well as war refugees.

For many years, a considerable migration of people from Ukraine to Poland for economic purposes has had a major influence on the Polish economy. The National Bank of Poland has reported that the contribution of Ukrainian immigration to Poland's GDP between 2014 and 2018 amounted to an impressive 11%. Strzelecki et al. (2022) found that influx of Ukrainian workers between 2013 and 2018 resulted in an annual increase of 0.8% in Poland's available labour force, and were responsible for about 13% of Poland's GDP growth.

Even before the war, the IMF's research suggests that Ukrainian migrants will play a significant role in boosting output in 2026 with estimates ranging from 2.2 to 2.3% in Estonia, Poland, and Czechia, and 0.6–0.65% in Germany (IMF, 2020). According to OECD projections, the combined workforce of EU member countries was expected to increase by 5% in 2022, that is twice as high as the previous migration surge from 2014 to 2017 (OECD, 2022). The Czech Republic (2.2%), Poland (2.1%), and Estonia (1.9%) are predicted to experience the most significant impact, while other countries, such as Hungary, Latvia, Slovakia, Lithuania, and Romania may see an increase of 1.0–1.5%. As a result, employment within the EU could potentially grow by 0.4%.

According to Bird and Amaglobeli (2022), the fiscal impact of Ukrainian migrants on EU economies is estimated to be approximately €30–37 billion, equivalent to 0.19–0.23% of the EU's GDP in the short term with the highest costs falling on bordering countries and Baltic nations. The European Investment Bank's (2022) calculations indicate that Latvia, Estonia, Hungary, Poland, and Czechia potentially spent from 4 to 9% of their GDP for migrant adaptation. While there may be some short-term challenges for public finances, the IMF predicts (Bird & Amaglobeli, 2022) that Europe will experience a positive net fiscal impact in the future due to the active integration of Ukrainians into the European labour market. Specifically, the integration of Ukrainian migrants into the labour market is demonstrated by their tax contributions in Poland. Calculations made by the Centre for Migration Research at the University of Warsaw show that between the beginning of the full-scale war and the end of 2022, Ukrainians residing in Poland have paid a total of 10 billion Polish zloty (equivalent to $2.4 billion) in taxes (Ukrainian World Congress, 2022).

Thus, due to its close proximity to Europe and strong cultural ties, as well as the presence of a Ukrainian diaspora and temporary protection status, Ukraine is expected to see a rise in labour force participation among displaced individuals in the European countries.

Key Takeaways

The European Union responded to Russia's invasion of Ukraine through 12 rounds of sanctions from 2014 to 2024, targeting various industries and individuals. The objectives included demonstrating solidarity, weakening Russia's military strength, and impacting its economy and ruling class. Despite successes, challenges in implementation and circumvention emerged, leading to legislative measures criminalising sanction violations.

Scientific studies indicate that wars have significant economic outcomes, both positive and negative. While military production can boost GDP, wars disrupt economic activity, imposing heavy fiscal costs and long-term consequences on education and income.

The war in Ukraine poses ongoing challenges for predicting its impact on the EU economy. Asymmetric consequences exist among Member States, influenced by trade links, energy dependence on Russia, and financial market vulnerability. The war triggered shocks to energy and food markets, causing supply reductions and historically unprecedented price increases, leading to inflationary pressure in the euro area. Key economic indicators of the EU show a rebound in consumption spending, investments, and other expenditure measures in 2021 and 2022 after a decrease in 2020. However, industrial production declined, impacting the private sector, and both consumer and business confidence witnessed negative trends.

Volatile energy prices since mid-2021, influenced by post-COVID economic recovery, lifted travel restrictions, and unexpected increases, posed challenges. Russia's decision to cut gas supplies in 2022 led to supply uncertainty, significant gas price hikes, and increased electricity costs in the EU. Emergency regulations were implemented to address these challenges, reduce electricity use, cap producer revenues, and secure contributions from fossil fuel businesses. Despite a reversal in coal consumption in 2021–2022, the EU experienced a decline in solid fossil fuels overall. The EU focused on renewable energy, constituting 42.5% of the energy mix by 2023, aiming for 42.5% renewable energy by 2030 to ensure energy security and transition towards sustainable sources.

The energy crisis affecting the EU has shown the importance of preparedness and resilience. At the same time, coordination at EU level and joint action between the EU and Member States have proven to be effective, resulting in increased unity among Member States and greater EU geopolitical influence and weight. Going forward, both resilience and alignment of Member State and EU action will remain crucial for ensuring energy security, enhancing the EU's energy independence and completing the clean energy transition. Recent developments have also highlighted that energy security is crucial for EU economic security as most economic sectors depend on a stable energy supply and supply chains.

Russia's invasion led to the EU granting temporary protection to refugees from Ukraine, covering approximately 4.3 million non-EU citizens by November 2023. Integration efforts focused on employment, with adult women comprising a significant proportion of recipients. Initiatives, including the EU Talent Pool and online job search platforms, were implemented to facilitate labour market access for Ukrainian refugees. The influx of Ukrainian refugees had a notable impact on the labour force and GDP growth in host countries. Economic studies projected positive fiscal impacts in the long term, estimating contributions to GDP and tax payments.

Notes

1 Annual inflation is the change of the price level of consumer goods and services between the current month and the same month of the previous year. Monthly inflation is the change of the price level between the current month and the previous month.

2 The EUAA-OECD Survey of Arriving Migrants from Ukraine includes an online study of 3,932 adult respondents between April 11th, 2022 and August 15, 2022 via mobile phones. The sample was predominantly female (82%), with an average age of 38 years (median age of 37). The majority (79%) of the sample fell within the 18 to 44 year bracket, with 18% of the sample in the 45 to 64 year group and a 2% aged 65 and above. The sample is largely composed of Ukrainian nationals (96%), with just 4% (161) being non-Ukrainian residents of Ukraine prior to February 24, 2022. Consequently, the results of the Survey may not be representative of the overall refugee population.

3 The period of investigation and the quantity of the sample differs in different countries.

References

Abadie, A., & Gardeazabal, J. (2003). The Economic Costs of Conflict: A Case Study of the Basque Country. *American Economic Review 93*(1): 113–132.

Accompagnement des ressortissants étrangers. (December 04, 2023a). *Forem*. https://www.leforem.be/particuliers/accompagnement-ressortissants-etrangers.html

Accompagnement des ressortissants ukrainiens. (December 04, 2023b). *Forem*. https://www.leforem.be/citoyens/ukraine.html

Acemoglu, D., Johnson, S., & Robinson, J. (2005). The Rise of Europe: Atlantic Trade, Institutional Change, and Economic Growth. *American Economic Review 95*(3): 546–579.

Alvarez-Cuadrado, F. (2008). Growth Outside the Stable Path: Lessons from the European Reconstruction. *European Economic Review 52*(3): 568–588.

Baczynska, G. (2023, May 08). EU Takes Aim at Chinese Firms in proposed New Russia Sanctions. Reuters. https://www.reuters.com/world/eu-takes-aim-chinese-firms-third-country-exports-tighten-russia-sanctions-2023-05-08/

Barro, R. J., & Lee, J.-W. (1994). Sources of Economic Growth. *Carnegie-Rochester Conference Series on Public Policy 40*(1):1–46.

Bird, N., & Amaglobeli, D. (2022, September 8), Policies to Address the Refugee Crisis in Europe Related to Russia's Invasion of Ukraine. *IMF Notes No* 2022/003.

Blattman, Ch., & Miguel, E. (2010). Civil War. *Journal of Economic Literature 48*(1): 3–57.

Broadberry, S., & Harrison, M. (2005). *The Economics of World War I.* Cambridge University Press.

Brück, T. (2001). Mozambique: The Economic Effects of the War. In F. Stewart, E. V. K. FitzGerald (Eds.), *War and Underdevelopment* (pp. 56–88). Oxford University Press.

Brussels helps Ukraine. (2023a, December 12). Safe.brussels. https://www.helpukraine.brussels/en

Cappelen, Å., Gleditsch, N. P., & Bjerkholt, O. (1984). Military Spending and Economic Growth in the OECD Countries. *Journal of Peace Research 21*(4): 361–373.

Caprile, A., & Delivorias A. (2023). EU Sanctions on Russia: Overview, Impact, Challenges. European Parliamentary Research Service. https://epthinktank.eu/2023/03/13/eu-sanctions-on-russia-overview-impact-challenges/

Cerra, V., & Saxena, S. Ch. (2008). Growth Dynamics: The Myth of Economic Recovery. *American Economic Review 98*(1): 439–457.

Chupilkin, M., & Kóczán, Z. (2022). The Economic Consequences of War: Estimates Using Synthetic Controls. The EBRD Working Paper No. 271. https://www.ebrd.com/publications/working-papers/the-economic-consequences-of-war

Collier, P. (1999). On the Economic Consequences of Civil War. *Oxford Economic Papers 51*(1):168–183.

Council Directive 2001/55/EC of 20 July 2001 on Minimum Standards for Giving Temporary Protection in the Event of a Mass Influx of Displaced Persons and on Measures Promoting a Balance of Efforts between Member States in Receiving Such Persons and Bearing the Consequences Thereof

Council Implementing Decision (EU) 2022/382 of 4 March 2022 Establishing the Existence of a Mass Influx of Displaced Persons from Ukraine within the Meaning of Article 5 of Directive 2001/55/EC, and Having the Effect of Introducing Temporary Protection ST/6846/2022/INIT. http://data.europa.eu/eli/dec_impl/2022/382/oj

Council of the EU. (2022). Press Release. Sanctions: Council Adds the Violation of Restrictive Measures to the List of EU Crimes (October 28, 2022). https://www.consilium.europa.eu/en/press/press-releases/2022/11/28/sanctions-council-adds-the-violation-of-restrictive-measures-to-the-list-of-eu-crimes/

Deane, Ph. (1975). *War and Economic Development: Essays in Memory of David Joslin.* CUP Archive.

Deleidi, M., & Mazzucato, M. (2021). Directed Innovation Policies and the Supermultiplier: An Empirical Assessment of Mission-Oriented Policies in the US Economy. *Research Policy 50*(2). https://doi.org/10.1016/j.respol.2020.104151

DTM Germany – Third Country Nationals Arriving from Ukraine in Germany. (2022, July 18). International Organization for Migration (IOM). https://dtm.iom.int/reports/germany-third-country-nationals-arriving-ukraine-germany-june-2022

ECB (2023, February 24), One Year Since Russia's Invasion of Ukraine – The Effects on Euro Area Inflation. [The ECB blog]. https://www.ecb.europa.eu/press/blog/date/2023/html/ecb.blog20230224~3b75362af3.en.html

Eesti Tootukassa. UpToDate. Retrieved December 10, 2023, from https://www.tootukassa.ee/en

ELA (2023). Overview of National Measures Regarding Employment and Social Security of Displaced Persons Coming from Ukraine. https://www.ela.europa.eu/sites/default/files/2023-03/IT-Country-Fiche_ELA_Ukraine-update_February-2023.pdf

Employment/Training. Looking for a Job. (December 13, 2023b). Safe.brussels. https://www.helpukraine.brussels/en/lookingfor/looking-job

Euro Area Composite PMI. (December 9, 2023a). Trading Economics. https://tradingeconomics.com/euro-area/composite-pmi

Euro Area Manufacturing PMI. (December 7, 2023b). Trading Economics. https://tradingeconomics.com/euro-area/manufacturing-pmi

Euro Area Services PMI. (December 04, 2023c). Trading Economics. https://tradingeconomics.com/euro-area/services-pmi

European Commission. (2022). European Business Cycle Indicators, Consumer Confidence in Turbulent Times – the Case of the Candidate Countries. Technical Paper 055. https://doi.org/10.2765/333981

European Commission. (2023a). European Economic Forecast. Spring 2023. Institutional Paper 200. Publications Office of the European Union. https://economy-finance.ec.europa.eu/system/files/2023-05/ip200_en_1.pdf

European Commission (2023b, March 30). European Green Deal: EU Agrees Stronger Legislation to Accelerate the Rollout of Renewable Energy. [Press Release]. https://ec.europa.eu/commission/presscorner/detail/en/ip_23_2061

European Commission. (2023c). Autumn 2023 Economic Forecast: A Modest Recovery Ahead after a Challenging Year. Economic Forecasts. https://economy-finance.ec.europa.eu/economic-forecast-and-surveys/economic-forecasts/autumn-2023-economic-forecast-modest-recovery-ahead-after-challenging-year_en

European Commission. (2023d, June 23). EU Adopts 11th Package of Sanctions against Russia for its Continued Illegal War Against Ukraine [Press Release]. https://ec.europa.eu/commission/presscorner/detail/en/ip_23_3429

European Council (2022, November 24). Council Agrees on Substance of New Measures on Joint Purchases of Gas and a Solidarity Mechanism. [Press Releases]. https://www.consilium.europa.eu/en/press/press-releases/2022/11/24/further-measures-to-tackle-the-energy-crisis-council-agrees-on-joint-purchases-of-gas-and-a-solidarity-mechanism/

European Council. (2023a). EU Response to Russia's Invasion of Ukraine. https://www.consilium.europa.eu/en/policies/eu-response-ukraine-invasion/#sanctions

European Council. (2023b). EU Response to Russia's Invasion of Ukraine. Impact of Russia's Invasion of Ukraine on the Markets: EU Response. https://www.consilium.europa.eu/en/policies/eu-response-ukraine-invasion/impact-of-russia-s-invasion-of-ukraine-on-the-markets-eu-response/

European Council. (2024). Energy Prices and Security of Supply. https://www.consilium.europa.eu/en/policies/energy-prices-and-security-of-supply/#EU

European Heat Pump Market and Statistic Report 2023. EHPA (2023). https://www.ehpa.org/news-and-resources/press-releases/market-report-2023/

European Investment Bank. (2022). How Bad is the Ukraine War for the European Recovery? Economics – Thematic Studies. EIB, Luxembourg. https://www.eib.org/attachments/publications/how_bad_is_the_ukraine_war_for_the_european_recovery_en.pdfEurostat. (2022, January). EU Trade with Russia – Latest Developments. https://ec.europa.eu/eurostat/statistics-explained/index.php?oldid=558089#Latest_developments

Eurostat. (2023). How is the EU Responding to the War's Market Impact? https://ec.europa.eu/eurostat/web/interactive-publications/energy-2023

Eurostat. (2023a, March 3). EU Trade with Russia Continues to Decline. https://ec.europa.eu/eurostat/web/products-eurostat-news/w/DDN-20230303-1

Eurostat. (2023b, December 5). Shedding Light on Energy – 2023 Edition. https://doi.org/10.2785/405482

Eurostat. (2023c, June). Energy Production and Imports. https://ec.europa.eu/eurostat/statistics-explained/index.php?title=Energy_production_and_imports

Eurostat. (2024). Temporary Protection for Persons fleeing Ukraine – Monthly Statistics. UpToDate. Retrieved December 11, 2023, from https://ec.europa.eu/eurostat/statistics-explained/index.php?title=Temporary_protection_for_persons_fleeing_Ukraine_-_monthly_statistics#Where_in_the_EU_did_people_fleeing_Ukraine_go.3F

Eurostat. Data Browser. UpToDate. Retrieved December 11, 2023, from https://ec.europa.eu/eurostat/databrowser/explore/all/all_themes?lang=en&display=list&sort=category

EWL Group. (2023). Report on Cross-border Mobility 'Citizens of Ukraine on the Polish Labour Market. New Challenges and Perspectives, 4th Edition. https://ewl.com.pl/wp-content/uploads/2023/05/REPORT_CROSSBORDER_2023_ENG.pdf (accessed: 09.06.2024).

Feigenbaum, J. J., Lee, J., & Mezzanotti, F. (2018). Capital Destruction and Economic Growth: The Effects of Sherman's March, 1850-1920. NBER Working Papers 25392. National Bureau of Economic Research, Inc.

Find a job in France! Employement for Ukrainians (October 28, 2022). EU4UA. https://www.eu4ua.org/jobs-articles/find-a-job-in-france-jobs-for-ukrainians

Finding Work As A Ukrainian Refugee. (November 15, 2023). UKrainian Refugee Help. https://ukrainianrefugeehelp.co.uk/finding-work/

Forced displacement from and within Ukraine: Profiles, experiences, and aspirations of affected populations. Joint EUAA, IOM and OECD Report (2022, October 28). EUAA https://euaa.europa.eu/sites/default/files/publications/2022-11/2022_11_09_Forced_Displacement_Ukraine_Joint_Report_EUAA_IOM_OECD_0.pdf

Geflüchtete aus der Ukraine. (2022, April 4). INFO GmbH.

Geflüchtete Personen aus der Ukraine einstellen (2023, December 9). AMS. https://www.ams.at/unternehmen/service-zur-personalsuche/gefluechtete-personen-aus-der-ukraine-einstellen

Gross, D. P., & Sampat, B. N. (2020). The World War II Crisis Innovation Model: What Was It, and Where Does it Apply? National Bureau of Economic Research Working Paper Series, No. 27909.

Guenctte, J. D., Kenworthy, Ph., & Wheeler, C. (2022). Implications of the War in Ukraine for the Global Economy, World Bank Group, EFI Policy Note 3.

Harrison, M. (1998). The Economics of World War II: An Overview. In M. Harrison (Ed.), *The Economics of World War II: Six Great Powers in International Comparison* (pp. 1–42). Cambridge University Press.

Hoeffler, A., & Reynal-Querol, M. (2003). *Measuring the Costs of Conflict*. World Bank.

How to Employ Refugees from Ukraine in the Czech Republic? (2024, January 9). ACCACE. News Flash. https://accace.com/wp-content/uploads/2024/01/CZ-2024-01-09_How-to-employ-refugees-from-Ukraine-in-CZ-EN.pdf

Hrvatska za Ukrajinu. UpToDate. Retrieved December 09, 2023, from https://hrvatska-zaukrajinu.gov.hr/

Ichino, A., & Winter-Ebmer, R. (2004). The Long-Run Educational Cost of World War II. *Journal of Labor Economics 22*(1): 57–87. https://doi.org/10.1086/380403

IMF (2020). The Macroeconomic Effects of Global Migration. In *World Economic Outlook: The Great Lockdown* (Chapter 4: 77–101). https://www.imf.org/-/media/Files/Publications/WEO/2020/April/English/ch4.ashx

Important Information for Persons Fleeing Ukraine. Office of the Commissioner for Fundamental Rights of Hungary. https://www.ajbh.hu/en/web/ajbh-en/important-information-for-persons-fleeing-ukraine

Jobguide.Ukraine.dk. UpToDate. Retrieved December 11, 2023, from https://jobguideukraine.dk/for-ukrainian-jobseekers/

Jobs for Ukrainians in France. UpToDate. Retrieved December 9, 2023, from https://www.job4ua.fr/

Koubi, V. (2005). War and Economic Performance. *Journal of Peace Research 42*(1): 67–82.

Kuznets, S. (1964). *Postwar Economic Growth: Four Lectures*. Harvard University Press.

Kuznets, S. (1971). *Economic Growth of Nations: Total Output and Production Structure*. Harvard University Press.

Lafond, F., Greenwald, D., & Farmer, J.D. (2022). Can Stimulating Demand Drive Costs Down? World War II as a Natural Experiment. *The Journal of Economic History 82*(3): 727–764. https://doi.org/10.1017/S0022050722000249

Main job opportunities in Portugal. (2023, December 5). Instituto do Emprego. https://www.iefp.pt/documents/10181/11349748/Job_Opportunities_2022_03_07.pdf/ddf11507-81a2-43d7-b312-a663d3d8014f

Moretti, E., Steinwender, C., & Van Reenen, J. (2019). The Intellectual Spoils of War? Defense R&D, Productivity and International Spillovers. National Bureau of Economic Research, Working Paper No 26483. https://doi.org/10.3386/w26483

OECD. (2021). *Language Training for Adult Migrants. Making Integration Work*. OECD Publishing. https://doi.org/10.1787/02199d7f-en.

OECD. (2022, July 27). The Potential Contribution of Ukrainian Refugees to the Labour Force in European Host Countries. https://www.oecd.org/ukraine-hub/policy-responses/the-potential-contribution-of-ukrainian-refugees-to-the-labour-force-in-european-host-countries-e88a6a55/

OECD (2023, January 6). Policy Responses: Ukraine Tackling the Policy Challenges. https://www.oecd.org/ukraine-hub/policy-responses/what-we-know-about-the-skills-and-early-labour-market-outcomes-of-refugees-from-ukraine-c7e694aa/

OECD. (2023a). OECD Economic Outlook, 2023(2). Preliminary Version. https://doi.org/10.1787/7a5f73ce-en

OECD. (2024a, January 14). Business Confidence Index (BCI). https://doi.org/10.1787/3092dc4f-en

OECD. (2024b, January 14), Consumer Confidence Index (CCI) (indicator). https://doi.org/10.1787/46434d78-en

Olson, M. (2008). *The Rise and Decline of Nations*. Yale University Press.

Organski, A. F. K., & Kugler, J. (1977). The Costs of Major Wars: The Phoenix Factor. *American Political Science Review 71*(4): 1347–1366.

Organski, A. F. K., & Kugler, J. (1980). *The War Ledger*. University of Chicago Press.

Panchenko, T. (2022). Prospects for Integration of Ukrainian Refugees into the German Labor Market: Results of the IFO Online Survey. *CESifo Forum 23*(4), 65–75.

Portugal for Ukraine. Instituto do Emprego. https://www.iefp.pt/portugal-for-ukraine

Rada Europejska. (2023). Rynkowe skutki rosyjskiej inwazji na Ukrainę: reakcja UE. https://www.consilium.europa.eu/pl/policies/eu-response-ukraine-invasion/impact-of-russia-s-invasion-of-ukraine-on-the-markets-eu-response/

Rasler, K., & Thompson, W. R. (1985). War and the Economic Growth of Major Powers. *American Journal of Political Science 29*(3): 513–538. https://doi.org/10.2307/2111141.

Recruter un ressortissant étranger. Forem. https://www.leforem.be/entreprises/recruter-ressortissant-etranger-infos.htmlRussia's attack on Ukraine. (2024, January 1). Finnish Immigration Service. https://migri.fi/en/faq-ukraine

Russia's attack on Ukraine. Local TE-service. (2024, January 2). TE-palvelut. https://toimistot.te-palvelut.fi/en/ukraine

Russia Sanctions Tracker – EU. (2024, January 5). Ashurst. https://www.ashurst.com/en/insights/eu-sanctions/

Ruttan, V. W. (2006). *Is War Necessary for Economic Growth? Military Procurement and Technology Development*. Oxford University Press.

S&P Global. (2023). HCOB Eurozone Composite PMI. News Release. Market Sensitive Information. https://www.pmi.spglobal.com/Public/Home/PressRelease/1429581789984ef5b8747ce4dfd8a66f

Sanctions against Russia – A Timeline (2024, January 4). S&P Global. https://www.spglobal.com/marketintelligence/en/news-insights/latest-news-headlines/sanctions-against-russia-8211-a-timeline-69602559

Strzelecki, P., Growiec, J., & Wyszyński, R. (2022). The Contribution of Immigration from Ukraine to Economic Growth in Poland. *Review of World Economics 158*: 365–399. https://doi.org/10.1007/s10290-021-00437-y

Surico, P., & Antolin-Diaz, J. (2022). The Long-run Effects of Government Spending. CEPR Discussion Papers 17433.

Swedish Public Employment Service. UpToDate. Retrieved December 11, 2023, from https://arbetsformedlingen.se/other-languages/ukrainska-ukrainska/vi-z-ukraini

Taran, S. (2023, May 16). 11th Package of EU Sanctions: Focusing on Circumvention, European Policy Centre. EPC Flash Analysis. https://www.epc.eu/en/publications/11th-package-of-EU-sanctions-Focusing-on-circumvention~50d944

The Investopedia Team (2023). Purchasing Managers' Index (PMI). Definition and How It Works. https://www.investopedia.com/terms/p/pmi.asp

The Germany4Ukraine Informational Guide. (2024, January 5). The Germany4Ukraine. https://www.germany4ukraine.de/hilfeportal-ua

The International Working Group on Russian Sanctions. (2023). Action Plan 2.0. Strengthening Sanctions against the Russian Federation. Working Group Paper No. 11. https://www.president.gov.ua/storage/j-files-storage/01/18/49/82e4b94da9b413ac4958b08bcea980b2_1682403883.pdf

Thorp, W. L. (1941). Postwar Depressions. *The American Economic Review 30*(5): 352–361.

Ukrainian World Congress (2022, November 09). Ukrainian Refugees Uphold Rather than Burden Polish Economy. [Press Release]. https://www.ukrainianworldcongress.org/ukrainian-refugees-uphold-rather-than-burden-polish-economy/

UNHCR. (2022a, September 23). Lives on Hold: Intentions and Perspectives of Refugees from Ukraine #2. https://data.unhcr.org/en/documents/details/95767#_ga=2.201651225.945945676.1664114023-984147863.1644414250

UNHCR. (2022b). The Un Refugee Agency, Lives On Hold: Profiles And Intentions of Refugees From Ukraine. Czech Republic, Hungary, Republic of Moldova, Poland, Romania & Slovakia, UNHCR Regional Bureau for Europe.

Unterstützung für Geflüchtete aus der Ukraine. (2024, January 5). Bundesagentur fur Arbeit. https://www.arbeitsagentur.de/ukraine

Van Raemdonck, D. C., & Diehi P. F. (1989). After the Shooting Stops: Insights on Postwar Economic Growth. *Journal of Peace Research 26*(3): 249–264.

Visa holders entering the UK under the Ukraine Humanitarian Schemes: 20 to 27 April 2022. (2022, May 16). ONS. http://community/populationandmigration/internationalmigration/datasets/visaholdersenteringtheukundertheukrainehumanitarianschemes (accessed: 15.01.2024).

Visa holders entering the UK under the Ukraine Humanitarian Schemes: 16 to 24 June 2022. (2023, July 7). ONS. https://www.ons.gov.uk/peoplepopulationandcommunity/populationandmigration/internationalmigration/datasets/visaholdersenteringtheukundertheukrainehumanitarianschemes (accessed: 15.01.2024).

Wheeler, H. (1980). Postwar Industrial Growth. In J. David Singer (Ed.), *The Correlates of War: II* (pp. 258–284). Free Press.

3 Ukraine's Relevance to European and Global Trade from 2013 to 2022

The Evolution of Ukraine's Trade Policy in the Context of the Annexation of Crimea and Russian Military Aggression in 2022

Maryana Prokop

Introduction

The Russian military invasion of Ukraine in February 2022 significantly contributed to substantial market changes in European and global trade because Ukraine and Russia were significant players in the global market for goods and services. Following the outbreak of the war, there are significant difficulties in continuing Ukrainian trade with European countries, as well as the rest of the world. Russian missile attacks contributed to the destruction not only of critical infrastructure but also of industrial infrastructure and stocks of raw materials. In addition, there was a marked migration of people, including abroad – all of which undoubtedly impacted Ukraine's trade exchange with Europe and the world. A whole range of sanctions and restrictions have been introduced against the Russian Federation as a tool of economic leverage and opposition to Russian hostilities. On the part of European countries and the US, there is a deliberate shift away from Russian economic cooperation including trade. In the case of Ukraine, the gradual shift away from the Russian market for the sale of goods after 2013 was due to economic instability, Russian actions in the east of Ukraine, the annexation of Crimea, and military aggression in 2022.

The aim of this chapter is to analyse trade between Ukraine and EU countries and selected countries of the world (the most important from the perspective of markets for Ukrainian goods), in order to establish the importance of Ukraine as a trade actor for the European and global market before and after the Russian military aggression in 2022. The chapter also aims at establishing the process of Ukraine's trade policy course in the context of the implemented foreign policy known as multi-vectorality. The analysis of trade with EU countries does not include the UK, due to GB's exit from EU structures in 2020. The time caesura covers the period 2013–2022. The year 2013 was considered as the starting caesura, due to the fact that until 2013, Ukraine's main trade partner was Russia, which accounted for 24% exports and 30% of imports in this period; however, the annexation of Crimea and Russian support for the activities of separatist movements in the Lugansk and Donetsk regions contributed to a redefinition of Ukraine's approach to economic policy and its most important trading

DOI: 10.4324/9781003435433-3

partners. The end caesura, on the other hand, is determined by the course of the Russian-Ukrainian war and the EU's actions vis-à-vis Ukraine through the introduction of a number of measures to facilitate trade under wartime conditions.

3.1 Methodological Assumptions

The analysis of the importance of Ukraine as a trade partner for the EU and the world required a breakdown of the share of Ukrainian exports and imports in the European and world market, and a comparison of these results up to the outbreak of war in 2013–2021 and 2022. Given the annexation of Crimea, the results for exports and imports do not include data from the annexed peninsula and in the temporarily occupied territories in the east of the country. Establishing the importance of Ukraine in trade with the EU required, on the one hand, an overall analysis of the share of Ukrainian import exports in the EU economy after 2013. Second, it was also very important to establish the importance of Ukrainian exports/imports for individual EU countries. Juxtaposing the overall results for the EU and for individual national economies will make it possible to verify whether Ukraine is an important trade partner for the EU as a whole or perhaps only for its individual members. The author attempted to answer the research question [Q]: what is the importance of Ukraine in trade with the EU and selected world countries between 2013 and 2022 and to what extent Russian military aggression implied on the dimension of Ukraine's trade with Europe and the world. The following specific questions were distinguished within the research question:

[Q1] What place does the EU hold in Ukrainian trade between 2013 and 2022?
[Q2] What is the place of Ukraine's trade with the EU between 2013 and 2022?
[Q3] What place does Russia hold in Ukraine's trade between 2013 and 2022?
[Q4] What is the importance of Ukraine in the trade of the world (excluding the EU and Russia) between 2013 and 2022?
[Q5] Whether and to what extent is there a change in the scope of trade between Ukraine and the EU after the Russian military aggression against Ukraine?
[Q6] Whether and to what extent is there a change in the scope of trade between Ukraine and countries of the world after the Russian military aggression against Ukraine?
[Q7] Whether and to what extent is the structure of exports/imports between Ukraine and the EU changing after the Russian-Ukrainian war?
[Q8] Whether and to what extent is the structure of exports between Ukraine and the countries of the world changing after the outbreak of the Russian-Ukrainian war?
[Q9] Whether and to what extent do the EU countries with the highest share of Ukrainian exports determine the overall share of Ukrainian exports in the EU economy?

The main hypothesis [H] was taken to be: Ukraine is an important partner for EU countries and the world, and since the annexation of Crimea in Ukraine there followed efforts to reduce trade with Russia and target of Western countries, and Russian military aggression contributed significantly to the consolidation and deepening of Ukraine's trade with the EU.

Specific hypotheses: [H1] The EU occupies an important place in Ukrainian trade and there is an increase in the EU's share of Ukrainian exports between 2013 and 2022.

[H2] Ukraine is an important player in EU trade between 2013 and 2022.
[H3] The importance of Russia's trade with Ukraine in the period 2013–2022 weakens as a result of events of a political nature (annexation of Crimea, Russia's support for separatist movements in eastern Ukraine, Russia's military aggression against Ukraine).
[H4] Ukraine's importance in world trade between 2013 and 2022 is mainly shaped by its agricultural export account.
[H5] After the Russian military aggression against Ukraine in 2022, there is a significant decline in trade between Ukraine and the EU, due to the operation of the Ukrainian state under martial law.
[H6] Trade between Ukraine and countries of the world after the Russian military aggression against Ukraine is significantly restricted by Russian actions blocking the flow of goods.
[H7] The export/import structure between Ukraine and the EU after the outbreak of the Russian-Ukrainian war has not changed significantly.
[H8] The structure of exports/imports between Ukraine and countries of the world after the outbreak of the Russian-Ukrainian war has not changed significantly.
[H9] The EU member states with the highest share of Ukrainian exports significantly determine the overall share of Ukrainian exports in the EU economy.

In order to establish the importance of Ukraine for the EU and world economies, the author further aggregated data on Ukrainian exports and imports from 2013 to 2022. The study analysed only exports and imports of goods; the score for exports and imports of services was not taken into account. This made it possible to analyse what the specifics of trade exchange between Ukraine and the EU, Ukraine and Russia, and Ukraine and key players looked like from the perspective of Ukrainian exports and imports (the world category was included through aggregation into regions, due to the very broad scope of the material). In addition, a commodity structure was established for exported and imported goods, which made it possible to determine the most significant elements of Ukraine's trade with the EU, Russia, and the world.

Determining the importance of Ukraine to the EU market was done using Vilfredo Pareto's Activity-Based Costing (ABC) analysis method by classifying EU countries in terms of the value of Ukrainian exports and imports to each country's economy, thus identifying the leaders in EU-Ukraine trade. In the classic approach, according to the ABC method, group A includes components that account for 20% of the total and at the same time represent 80% of the criterion value, group B includes approximately 30% of the components and at the same time represent 15% of the criterion value, while group C includes the remaining 50% and 5% of the value. The process of determining Ukraine's most significant trade partners among EU countries was based on the Pareto principle, according to which 20% of goods generate 80% of the flow of goods (Kavitha et al., 2016: 167–170). At the first stage of the ABC breakdown, the EU countries should be ranked according to the declining share of Ukrainian exports/imports in their economies. The next step will be to calculate the percentage share of Ukrainian exports/imports of EU countries in Ukraine's total exports/imports to the EU. After ranking the EU countries according to the three groups A, B, C, the most relevant in this comparison will be whether the significant result of Ukrainian exports and imports to the EU is shaped by the account of the entire EU market or by the group of countries with the highest ratio in trade.

3.2 Events Impinging on the Dimensions of Ukraine's Trade Policy from 2013 to 2022 (Selected Aspects)

Ukraine's trade exchange of the last decade took place during the ongoing Ukrainian-Russian conflict of 2014, also referred to as hybrid war, which culminated in the Russian military aggression against Ukraine on February 24, 2022. The genesis of the events is considered to be late 2013, when then Ukrainian President Viktor Yanukovych refused to sign the Association Agreement with the European Union. This became a significant premise for mass protests by Ukrainian citizens in Independence Square in Kiev, referred to in the public space as the "Revolution of Dignity" or "Euromaidan". At the same time, in the eastern and southern parts of the country, there were anti-European and pro-Russian protests called "Anti-Maidan" (Bryjka, 2016: 201–205; Tomala & Prokop, 2021: 40–48; Prokop, 2023a: 17). With the benefit of hindsight, we can say that these events developed into the biggest political crisis in the history of independent Ukraine. When we refer to the events of a decade ago, "Orange Revolution". Then the Revolution of Dignity in its background had a bloodier character in the form of clashes between protesters and the forces of the Berkut special units.

The next step in Russian efforts to disrupt Ukrainian Euro-integration was the annexation of Crimea. At the end of February 2014, local self-defence units and unmarked units of Russian soldiers "SpecNaz" appeared on the territory of the peninsula and took control of critical infrastructure. The local authorities proclaimed Crimea's independence, and already in March, following a referendum, it was annexed by Russia. The peaceful annexation of Crimea to the Russian Federation sparked demonstrations by the Russian-speaking population living in the eastern part of Ukraine, who also demanded the annexation of their inhabited territories to Russia. From as early as April, the demonstrations escalated into actions of occupying government administration buildings and replacing Ukrainian flags with Russian ones. The largest demonstrations took place in the Donetsk and Luhansk regions. There, the separatists announced the creation of the Donetsk People's Republic (DPR) and the Luhansk People's Republic (LPR) and announced their desire to be annexed to Russia, which has intensely supported the separatists' activities by sending soldiers and providing the rebels with weapons, thus destabilising eastern Ukraine and continuing the conflict until a Russian attack on Ukraine in 2022 (Головко et al., 2015: 5–28; Російсько-український конфлікт, 2014: 2–19; Plokhy, 2023: 136–145).

On February 24, 2022, Russia attacked Ukraine with missiles, thus turning a war with a hybrid dimension into a conventional war, although the fighting in the east of the country can also be considered the traditional course, when Russia supported separatist movements but did not officially engage in war. According to the Ukrainian State Special Service for Communications and Information Protection, more than 800 cyber attacks have been carried out on various facilities since the Russian aggression in February 2022, including government offices and institutional websites, defence, financial, energy, transport, and telecommunications infrastructure as well as mass media. It is also worth mentioning that the first such mass attacks were carried out by Russia even before the military aggression in January and February 2022 by blocking state official websites, halting information, telecommunication, and banking systems of Ukraine (Водотика & Магда, 2016; Державна служба, 2023; Магда, 2015; Harding, 2022; Prokop, 2023b). On the day of the Russian army invasion, February 24, 2022, martial law was imposed in Ukraine under the law "On the Legal Regime of Martial Law" of 2015. Martial law allows the military command and military administration to regulate, in a manner determined by the cabinet of ministers of Ukraine, the work of providers of electronic communications networks and/or services, print shops, publishing houses, television and radio organisations, television and radio centres and other enterprises, institutions, cultural organisations, and the media, as well as allows for the use of local radio stations, television centres, and print shops for military purposes (Закон України, 2015). Another legal act is the order of the commander-in-chief of the armed forces of Ukraine, Valeriy Zaluzhny, "On the organisation of interaction between the Armed Forces of Ukraine, other components of the defence forces and media representatives for the duration of the martial law regime" dated March 3, 2022, supplemented by provisions dated July 12, 2022 (Наказ, 2022).

It is also worth noting that the political situation in Ukraine implied on the emergence of an economic crisis in 2014–2015. In 2015, four consecutive quarters of GDP recession were recorded. The main reasons for the negative dynamics were the cyclical recession, geopolitical changes, conflict in the east of the country, falling production volumes in metallurgy, chemical industry, mechanical engineering, and agriculture (Бесчастна & Уварова, 2015: 9–13; Руденко, 2015).

When analysing Ukraine's trade with the EU and Russia, it is also worth noting that its dimension is also largely determined by Ukraine's geopolitical location, where Western and Eastern influences have clashed. This was of key importance for the formation of Ukrainian foreign and security policy. Analysing the concepts of Ukraine's foreign and security policy, taking into account the factor of the international environment, Yeropolk Tymkiv (2007) distinguishes three concepts which have been implemented at different stages of the state's functioning: neutrality (non-blockade), the concept of multi-vectorality, and the concept of directionality, which can be implemented in two dimensions – Euro-Atlantic, through integration with European and Euro-Atlantic institutions, and Eurasian through cooperation with Russia. By analysing the bilateral relations between Ukraine and Russia, Maryana Prokop concludes how the above-mentioned concepts impacted the relations between the states under the respective presidencies. From 1993 to 1997, during the presidencies of Leonid Kravchuk and Leonid Kuchma, the policy of the Ukrainian state oscillated according to the doctrine of neutrality; this stage can be described as the formation of relations with Russia. From 1998 to 2010, L. Kuchma (second term) served as head of state and from 2005 V. Yushchenko, and it was during this stage that the Ukrainian concept of multi-vectorality developed, which meant the absence of a clearly defined foreign policy dimension. With regard to relations with Russia, there is Russian interference in Ukraine's internal politics (the results of the 2004 presidential election) and the gas crisis. Under the presidency of the pro-Russian candidate Viktor Yanukovych (2010–2013), Ukraine broke with its multi-vector policy in favour of intensifying relations with Russia. Following the events of the "Revolution of Dignity", Ukraine's post-2014 foreign policy adopted a Euro-Atlantic dimension, which continued under both the presidencies of Petro Poroshenko and Volodymyr Zelensky. In relations with Russia, this translated into an escalation of conflicts through the annexation of Crimea, Russia's support for separatist movements in the Donbas and military aggression in 2022 (Prokop, 2023a: 7–11). The above rationale shows that it is very important for Ukraine to move away from Russian influence both politically and socially, as well as economically.

Similar steps as a reaction to Russian actions in Ukraine were taken by the EU and the US by employing a number of sanctions and economic instruments against Russia. The actions were aimed at imposing numerous sanctions of a political, economic, financial nature on Russia and citizens supporting the separatist side. The restrictions applied by the US concerned the introduction of trade barriers, including a ban on the export of goods and technology for Russian oil projects, and affected, among others, the following companies: Rosneft, Novatek, state-owned Vnesheconombank and Gazprombank, Almaz-Antey, Yuzhmash (Executive Order 13660; Executive Order 13661). In turn, EU sanctions targeted, among others, oil and energy companies – Rosneft, Transneft, GazpromNeft, and included as well a ban on investment, the provision of services, including in the field of tourism, and trade with Crimea and Sevastopol (Foreign Affairs Council, 23 June 2014; Special meeting of the European Council, July 16, 2014; Reinforced restrictive measures against Russia). By 2022, the EU and US successively introduced and extended the sanctions. Yet, after the outbreak of a full-scale war, the scope of sanctions was further extended, bans on imports and exports of goods with Russia were introduced, measures were taken to weaken the Russian currency and joint scientific and technological projects initiated were suspended (Hajduk & Stępniewski, 2015: 135–151; Tomala & Prokop, 2021: 45–46; Wasiuta & Wasiuta, 2017: 210–213).

An analysis by the National Institute for Strategic Studies (NISS) shows that the post-2014 political situation in Ukraine (including the "Revolution of Dignity" and the hybrid war with Russia) also implied on the functioning of Russia's economy. Sectoral sanctions against the Russian Federation and geopolitical tensions impacted the decline of investment activity in Russia, restrictions on investment projects caused the withdrawal of foreign capital from the Russian market. Restrictions imposed by the Russian Federation on imports from Ukraine, EU countries, and the United States also put strong inflationary pressure on the Russian economy. In the case of Ukraine, military operations in the Donbass led to a decrease in production in the region, a decrease in interest in external financing and an increase in budget expenditure to finance law enforcement and the reconstruction of damaged infrastructure, an increase in budget indebtedness due to the need to finance the deficit and debt Naftohaz created in previous years, and the depletion of international reserves, which complicates the use of National Bank intervention as a tool to curb the increase in demand for foreign currency created by panic and speculation. The worsening of the crisis in 2014 was the result of a reduction in the industrial potential of the Luhansk and Donetsk regions as a result of the hostilities and the loss of the Russian market. The country's dependence on imported energy resources created the need to seek new opportunities and ways of trading (NISS Report, 2014). As a result of these events, one of Ukraine's leading economic policy actions has been to try to move away from Russian markets for goods and services in favour of seeking new ones, which can undoubtedly be seen as a move towards consolidating Ukraine as a significant partner in the European market.

The legal basis for Ukraine's relations with the European Union is the Association Agreement between the European Union and Ukraine (full name: Association Agreement between the European Union and the European Atomic Energy Community and their member states, on the one hand, and Ukraine, on the other) whose non-signing by President Yanukovych led to the outbreak of the "Revolution of Dignity". The signing of the Association Agreement by President Poroshenko took place in November 2014; the agreement entered into force on September 1, 2017. The agreement gave rise to measures aimed at enabling political association and economic integration of Ukraine with the EU by promoting gradual rapprochement between the parties on the basis of shared values; deepening political dialogue and cooperation in the area of freedom, security, and justice; promoting peace and stability; creating conditions for enhanced economic and trade relations in pursuit of Ukraine's gradual integration into the EU internal market; and creating conditions for increasingly close cooperation in other areas of common interest (*Association Agreement between the European Union and Ukraine*, 2014). This agreement completely replaced the Partnership and Cooperation Agreement that was concluded between Ukraine and the EU in 1994 and entered into force on March 1, 1998; it provided the legal framework for relations between the EU and Ukraine (*Partnership and Cooperation Agreement between the European Union and the Ukraine*, 1994).

On trade and trade-related issues, the 2014 agreement provided for the creation of a Deep and Comprehensive Free Trade Area (DCFTA), developing trade and investment and stimulating competition. The DCFTA entails the gradual elimination of tariffs and tariff rate quotas, which, combined with a broader process of approximation of Ukraine's legislation with EU legislation, standards, and practices (the acquis communautaire), will contribute to further economic integration with the EU internal market. The provisions of the DCFTA entered into force on January 1, 2016, formed part of the Association Agreement between Ukraine and the European Union, abolished most import duties, facilitating Ukrainian companies and consumers to exchange goods and services with companies and consumers in the EU (EU-Ukraine DCFTA). On February 28, 2022, four days after the Russian aggression, Ukraine applied for EU membership. On June 17, the European Commission published its opinion on Ukraine's application, recommending that the Council grant Ukraine the prospect of EU membership and candidate status, provided that steps are taken in this direction. On June 23, the European Council adopted a decision to grant Ukraine candidate status for EU membership (European Commission Opinions on the EU Membership applications of Ukraine, 2022).

3.3 Ukrainian Trade from 2013 to 2022 (General Aspect)

The annexation of Crimea and the escalation of the conflict in eastern Ukraine have led to measures to significantly reduce Ukrainian trade with the Russian Federation and the challenge of replacing it with new markets for goods and services. The aforementioned volatility of Ukraine's foreign policy vectors was also reflected in the economic policy pursued and, therefore, also in foreign trade. After 2014, Ukraine finally moved away from a policy of multi-vectorality in foreign policy, i.e., balancing between the Euro-Atlantic and pro-Russian options of the implementation voyage, orienting itself towards the West.

The annexation of Crimea and the war in the Donbass caused a deep decline in GDP in 2014 by 6.6% and 2015 by 9.8%. The process of GDP stabilisation was on an upward trend until 2019, and in 2020, due to the coronavirus pandemic, a slowdown of the Ukrainian economy was observed; the GDP level in 2019 was US$153.0 billion and in 2020 US$155. 3 billion, compared to a figure of US$198.3 billion already in 2021 (Державна служба статистики України. Державні фінанси). Halyna Petryshyn, analysing Ukraine's economic situation before the outbreak of the Russian-Ukrainian war, points out that the host crisis in 2020 showed that the Ukrainian economy was better prepared than for the previous crisis in 2014–2015, through the stability of the national currency and the high foreign exchange reserves of the National Bank of Ukraine. The scale of the crisis was determined by the state of the global economy, as Ukrainian industry and agriculture were heavily reliant on manufacturing exports and efforts to unfreeze the economy after Covid restrictions. As a result, the Ukrainian economy experienced a decline of 4% in 2020, which were recovered in 2021 recording growth for GDP (Petryshyn, 2022: 65–66). Figure 3.1 presents a year-by-year summary of Ukraine's total imports and exports from 2013 to 2022. The given summary is relevant in the context of the decline in Ukrainian GDP and the resulting economic crisis, which implied on the indicator for Ukrainian exports and imports (World Bank. Ukraine's exports and imports 2013–2022; Державна служба статистики України. Зовнішньоекономічна діяльність).

The data in Table 3.1 presents that as a result of the 2014–2015 crisis, Ukraine's imports of goods fell by 28.22% in 2014 and by 30.93% in 2015, with an increase

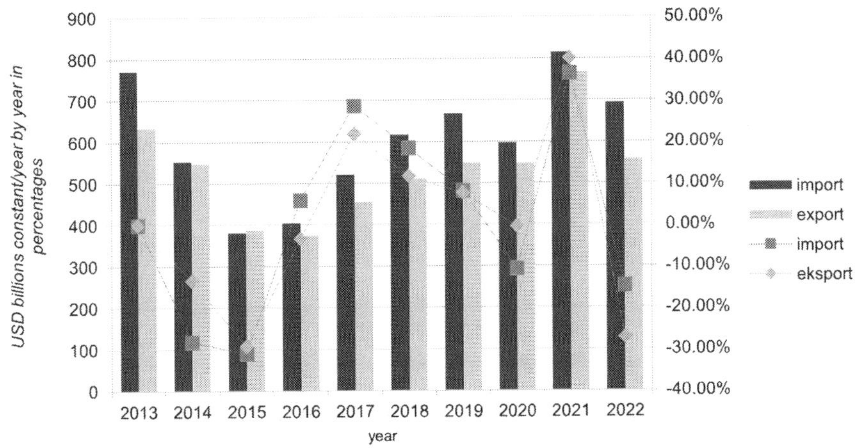

Figure 3.1 Global imports and exports of goods from Ukraine from 2013 to 2022 in USD billion constant 2013

Source: Own compilation based on World Bank's World Integrated Trade Solution. Exports and imports of Ukraine 2013–2022, and World Bank (CPI for years); Державна служба статистики України. Зовнішньоекономічна діяльність.

in subsequent years. The exception is 2020, which saw a 10.63% drop in imports due to the pandemic. In 2021, on the other hand, there was an increase in imports of 36.74%, albeit again a decrease of 14.75% due to the war. In the case of exports of Ukrainian goods, there was a significant decrease between 2014 (−13.48%) and 2015 (−29.20%) and 2016 (−3.435), with a significant increase of 21.98% in 2017. The pandemic in 2020 resulted in a renewed 0.43% decline in exports, which increased by 40.08% in 2021, eventually falling by 27.13% as a result of the first year of hostilities (World Bank. Ukraine's exports and imports 2013–2022). Figure 3.2 presents trade between Ukraine and the EU and Ukraine and Russia from 2013 to 2022. The juxtaposition of trade (exports and imports) for the EU and Russia allowed us to trace how the direction of Ukrainian trade policy changed after 2013 and after the military aggression in 2022. For the examined time caesura, results for exports and imports in constant prices 2013, which present the real value of goods taking into account price changes under the influence of various factors, e.g., inflation, were included (Table 3.2).

Current prices represent those at a given point in time. When included in exports and imports at high inflation the result could be distorted, representing an increase in exports and imports, which in fact could have been accounted for by price increases. Figure 3.2 shows that between 2013 and 2021 one can see an increase for Ukrainian exports to the EU. The exceptions are 2015 and 2016, as consequences after the economic crisis of 2014–2015 and the start of fighting in the east of the country, resulting in an increasing share of military spending.

Exports to the EU in 2014 accounted for $166.837107 billion, already falling to $128.68092 billion a year later, with an upward trend from 2016 when

Table 3.1 Ukraine's exports and imports statement 2013–2022

	2013	*2014*	*2015*	*2016*	*2017*	*2018*	*2019*	*2020*	*2021*	*2022*
import	769.860125	552.635968	381.6997517	404.3745516	520.2033391	616.425555	667.2427065	596.3160006	813.789672	693.758464
export	633.2046879	547.8789641	387.9150788	374.6144248	456.9575206	510.2253769	549.3191722	546.945407	766.1862791	558.3226309
import y-by-y	0.00%	−28.22%	−30.93%	5.94%	28.64%	18.50%	8.24%	−10.63%	36.47%	−14.75%
export y-by-y	0.00%	−13.48%	−29.20%	−3.43%	21.98%	11.66%	7.66%	−0.43%	40.08%	−27.13%

Source: Own compilation based on World Bank data; Ukraine's exports and imports 2013–2022; Державна служба статистики України. Зовнішньоекономічна діяльність.

Table 3.2 Consumer Price Index 2013–2022

Year	*2013*	*2014*	*2015*	*2016*	*2017*	*2018*	*2019*	*2020*	*2021*	*2022*
CPI USD 2010	106.83385	108.56693	108.69572	110.06701	112.41156	115.15730	117.24420	118.69050	124.26641	134.21121

Source: Own compilation based on World Bank data.

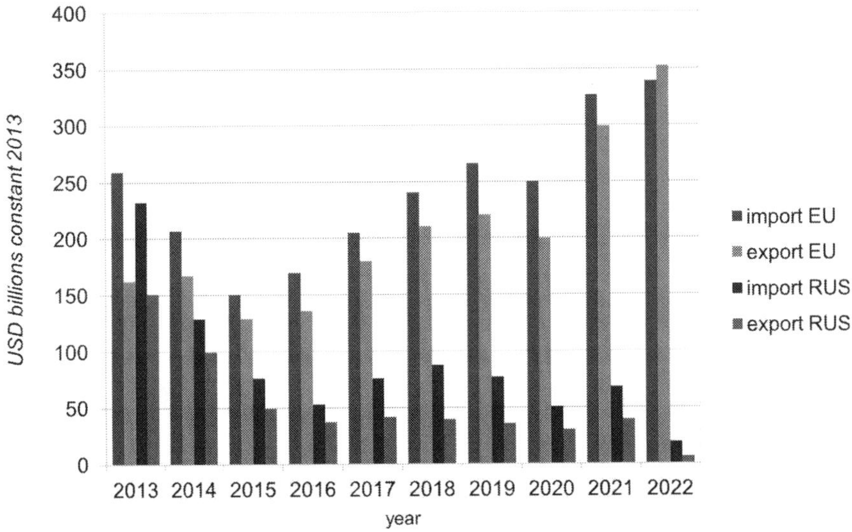

Figure 3.2 Imports and exports of goods from Ukraine to the European Union (excluding UK) and Russia

Source: Own compilation based on World Bank and World Bank Integrated Trade Solution data.; Державна служба статистики України. Зовнішньоекономічна діяльність.

2021 reached $299.049836 billion. In 2022, after the Russian attack on Ukraine, exports of goods to the EU reached US$352.114454 billion, mainly through a number of EU instruments simplifying the sale of Ukrainian goods. A similar trend was followed for Ukrainian imports from the EU, the result for imports in 2014 accounted for US$259.144075 billion, and just two years later a drop of over US$100 billion accounted for only US$150.173744 billion. Catching up with the 2013 result was only made possible in 2018. In contrast, the year before the war, imports of goods from the EU accounted for US$326.74713 billion, and in the year of the outbreak of the war they accounted for US$339.019043 billion (World Bank. Exports and imports of Ukraine 2013–2022). Detailed data on Ukrainian imports and exports to the EU, Russia, and the world's countries are presented in Table 3.1.

In the case of the Russian Federation, Ukrainian goods exports from 2013 onwards have a significant downward trend from US$150.772591 billion to US$38.9561058 billion in 2021, and already accounted for only US$6.19038082 billion in 2022 after a year of war. In 2013, the import of goods from Russia amounted to US 232.439943 billion, was very close to was very close to EU goods imports of US$259.144075 billion; however, after the annexation of Crimea it almost halved and in 2021 it accounted for US$68.0467892 billion. In the year of the war, on the other hand, Ukraine managed to reduce its imports of goods by more than three times, in relation to 2021, to US$19.3660921 billion (World Bank. Exports and imports of Ukraine 2013–2022; Table 3.3).

Table 3.3 Summary of exports and imports of Ukraine, EU, Russia, and the world in USD billion and %

	2013	*2014*	*2015*	*2016*	*2017*	*2018*	*2019*	*2020*	*2021*	*2022*
import EU	259.144075	206.983792	150.173744	169.286539	204.873093	240.635357	266.03579	250.468423	326.74713	339.019043
export EU	162.143899	166.837107	128.68092	135.81857	179.586779	211.00928	220.884755	199.471441	299.049836	352.114454
import RUS	232.439943	128.843597	76.2329904	53.0514944	75.7228875	87.2071588	76.6566308	50.5850171	68.0467892	19.3660921
export RUS	150.772591	99.5810759	49.1185412	37.015981	41.4909004	39.369902	35.5880963	30.0889361	38.9561058	6.19038082
import REST	278.276107	216.808579	155.293017	182.036518	239.607358	288.583039	324.550286	295.26256	418.995752	335.373329
export REST	320.288197	281.460782	210.115618	201.779873	235.879841	259.846195	292.846321	317.38503	428.180337	200.017796
EU i %	**33.66%**	**37.45%**	**39.34%**	**41.86%**	**39.38%**	**39.04%**	**39.87%**	**42.00%**	**40.15%**	**48.87%**
EU e %	**25.61%**	**30.45%**	**33.17%**	**36.26%**	**39.30%**	**41.36%**	**40.21%**	**36.47%**	**39.03%**	**63.07%**
Rus i %	**30.19%**	**16.74%**	**9.90%**	**6.89%**	**9.84%**	**11.33%**	**9.96%**	**6.57%**	**8.84%**	**2.52%**
Rus e %	**23.81%**	**15.73%**	**7.76%**	**5.85%**	**6.55%**	**6.22%**	**5.62%**	**4.75%**	**6.15%**	**0.98%**
rest i %	**36.15%**	**28.16%**	**20.17%**	**23.65%**	**31.12%**	**37.49%**	**42.16%**	**38.35%**	**54.42%**	**43.56%**
rest e %	**50.58%**	**44.45%**	**33.18%**	**31.87%**	**37.25%**	**41.04%**	**46.25%**	**50.12%**	**67.62%**	**31.59%**
import	769.860125	552.635968	381.699752	404.374552	520.203339	616.425555	667.242706	596.316001	813.789672	693.758464
export	633.204688	547.878964	387.915079	374.614425	456.957521	510.225377	549.319172	546.945407	766.186279	558.322631
import	0.00%	−28.22%	−30.93%	5.94%	28.64%	18.50%	8.24%	−10.63%	36.47%	−14.75%
export	0.00%	−13.48%	−29.20%	−3.43%	21.98%	11.66%	7.66%	−0.43%	40.08%	−27.13%

Bold values indicates percentages (%) used for export and import

Source: Own compilation based on World Bank and World Integrated Trade Solution data; Державна служба статистики України. Зовнішньоекономічна діяльність.

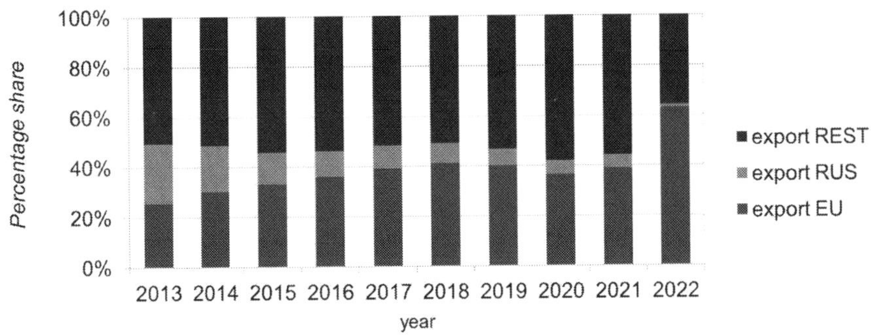

Figure 3.3 Ukrainian exports to the EU (without UK), Russia, and the rest of the world in 2013–2022 USD billion constant 2013.

Source: Own compilation based on World Bank and World Bank Integrated Trade Solution data; Державна служба статистики України. Зовнішньоекономічна діяльність.

In turn, Figure 3.3 presents a summary for Ukrainian exports in the period under review for the EU, Russia, and the rest of the world. The given graph shows a declining trend for Ukrainian exports to Russia which in 2013 accounted for 23.81% of Ukraine's total exports, a year later dropped to 15.73%, and from 2015 represents a single-digit figure of 7.76% and in 2021 dropped from to 6.15%. In contrast, after the Russian attack on Ukraine in 2022, Ukrainian exports to Russia accounted for less than 1% (0.98%). The shift away from the Russian market for goods has necessitated the search for new markets, which is undoubtedly the EU market. In 2013, Ukrainian exports to the EU accounted for 25.61%, so they were almost 5% less than exports to Russia; however, this increased to 30.45% in 2014 and accounted for 41.36% in 2018, then there is a slight decrease to 39.09% in 2021. The record rate of Ukrainian exports in the EU reached 63.07% in 2022 (World Bank. Exports and imports of Ukraine 2013–2022; Державна служба статистики України. Зовнішньоекономічна діяльність).

Considering Ukrainian imports from Russia, the situation is more difficult due to Ukrainian dependence on Russian raw materials. Although imports from Russia accounted for 30.19% in 2013, they almost halved to 16.74% after the events of the annexation of Crimea and the fighting in the Donbass in 2014, maintaining a downward trend until 2020, when they accounted for 6.57%, rising to 8.84% in the year before Russian aggression, and accounting for only 2.52% in 2022. Imports from the EU to Ukraine in 2013 accounted for 33.66%; a significant increase of 42.00% is recorded in 2020, and in 2022 it reached almost 50% of Ukraine's total imports (48.87%) (Figure 3.4).

The above charts show that since 2013 Ukraine has taken effective measures to become independent from Russia in terms of trade. Already in 2021, exports to Russia decreased to 6.15% of Ukraine's total exports and, in turn, imports accounted for only 8.4% of Ukraine's total imports, meaning that Ukraine was effectively implementing its plan to move away from trade with Russia. In the case of the EU, trade saw an increase in cooperation, and in 2022 the EU accounted

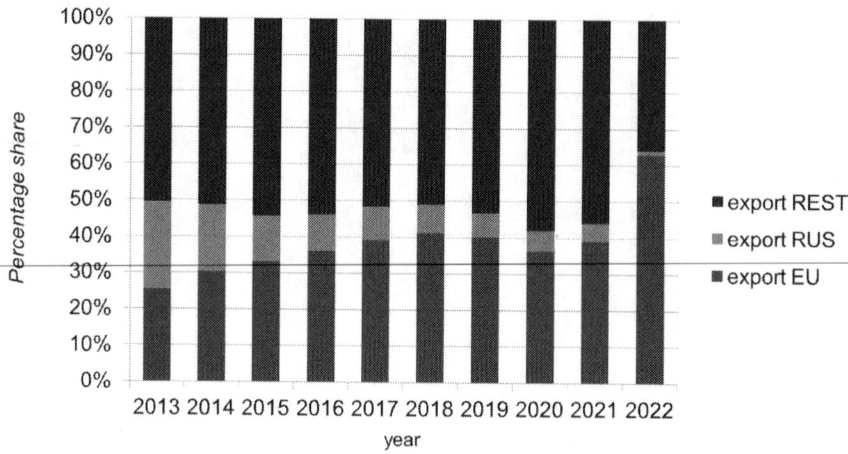

Figure 3.4 Ukrainian imports to the EU (without UK), Russia, and the rest of the world in 2013–2022 (USD billion) constant 2013.

Source: Own compilation based on World Bank and World Bank Integrated Trade Solution data; Державна служба статистики України. Зовнішньоекономічна діяльність.

for 63.07% of Ukrainian exports and 48.87% of imports. Thus, the EU has established itself as Ukraine's largest trading partner, accounting for 39.03% of exports and 40.15% of imports in 2021, and the Russian military aggression against Ukraine in 2022 further intensified cooperation between the EU and Ukraine. Total trade flows between the EU and Ukraine have almost doubled since the DCFTA came into force. The rest of the world countries filled 31.59% of Ukraine's exports and 43.56% of its imports, respectively; a detailed breakdown of the individual countries in this group is presented later in the chapter.

3.4 Commodity Structure of Ukrainian Exports to the EU and Russia

The importance of Ukraine on the world map in terms of its exports to other countries is determined by the fact that it is a world leader in the production of cereals including wheat, rye, barley, and maize. According to the State Statistical Service of Ukraine (Державна Служба Статистики України) and the Ministry of Economy of Ukraine (Міністерство економіки України), the decisive items in the commodity structure of agri-food exports are cereals and oil crops (sunflower and rapeseed), as well as meat products. Their combined share is more than 85% in agricultural exports.

Agriculture is one of the most important branches of the Ukrainian economy. In addition to agriculture, metallurgy, chemical, and transport industries were also important components of Ukrainian exports. Consequently, the position of Ukraine on the world and European market was determined by the sale of grain, meat products, metals, mineral products, fats and vegetable oils, crude oil, etc. The Russian aggression against Ukraine undoubtedly contributed to the redefinition of

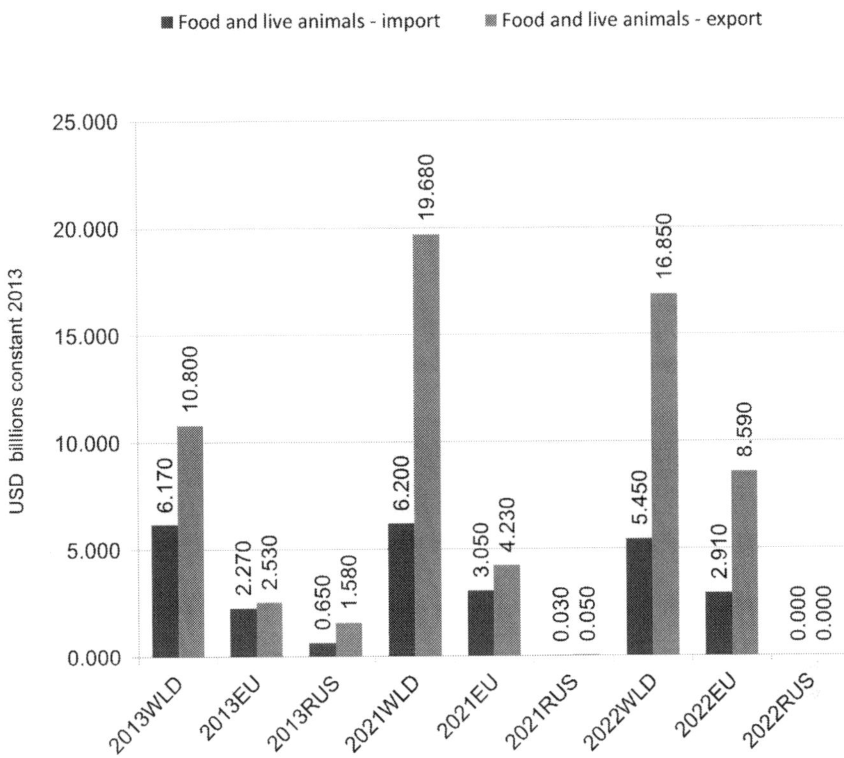

Figure 3.5 Value of Ukraine's exports and imports of the commodity group "Food and live animals": for the European Union (EU), Russia (RUS), and other countries (WLD)

Source: Own elaboration based on World Integrated Trade Solution World Bank and World Bank data; Державна служба статистики України. Зовнішньоекономічна діяльність.

Ukraine's trade policy and operation under difficult conditions. This part of the chapter focuses on the analysis of the commodity structure for Ukrainian exports from 2013 to 2022. The author's task was to determine, based on the overall results for Ukraine's exports and imports with the countries of the world, how Ukraine's trade evolved after taking measures to move away from the Russian market after the annexation of Crimea, and how the structure of trade with Russia changed after the Russian attack. This makes it possible to see whether all sectors of trade succeeded in replacing the Russian market with new outlets.

Important in the analysis of Ukraine's trade with the EU and Russia was the presentation of the commodity structure for Ukrainian imports and exports (Figures 3.5–3.14) based on data from the World Bank and the State Statistics Service of Ukraine (Державна Служба Статистики України) for Ukraine's trade with the EU, Russia, and the rest of the world. Taking into account the wide range of goods exported and imported by the Ukrainian state and the range of ten years, products were segregated in terms of types: food and live animals; beverages and tobacco, crude materials;

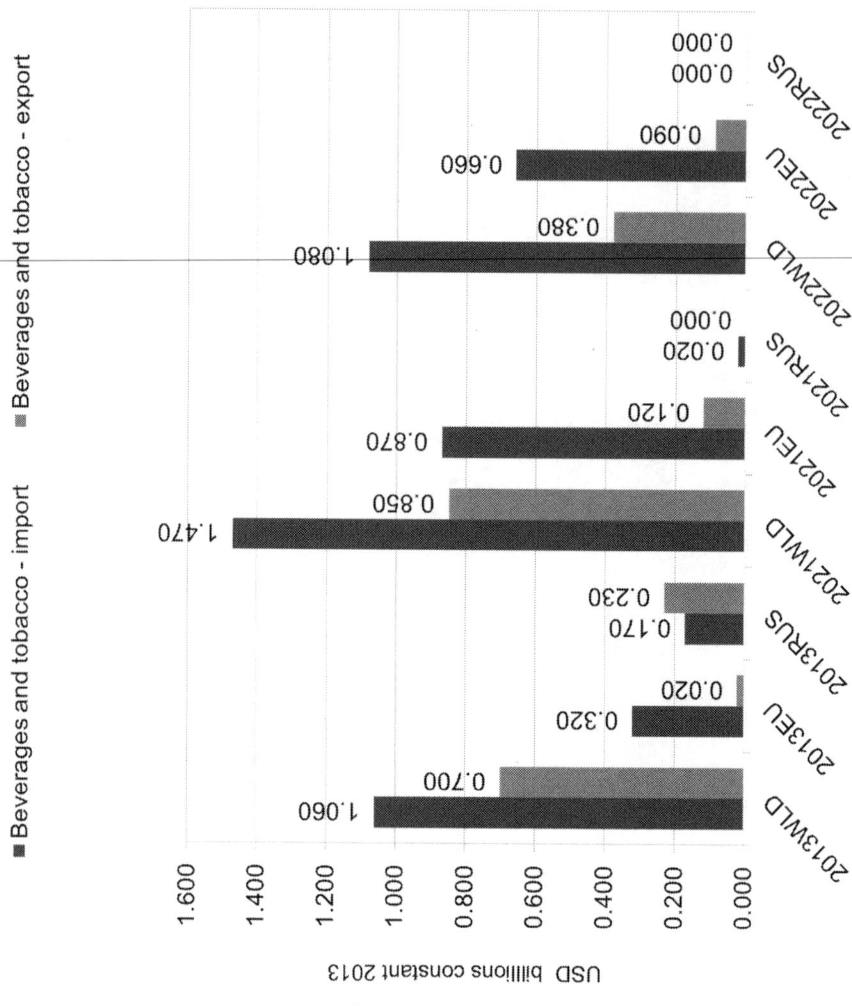

Figure 3.6 Value of Ukraine's exports and imports of the commodity group "Beverages and tobacco" for the European Union (EU), Russia (RUS), and other countries (WLD)

Source: Own elaboration based on World Bank and World Bank Integrated Trade Solution data; Державна служба статистики України. Зовнішньоекономічна діяльність.

inedible, except fuels, mineral fuels; lubricants and related materials; animal and vegetable oils; fats and waxes, chemicals and related products, not elsewhere specified (n.e.s.); manufactured goods classified chiefly by material; machinery and transport equipment; miscellaneous manufactured articles and commodities and transactions not classified elsewhere in the SITC. For the presentation of the commodity structure in Ukraine's trade with the EU and Russia, 2013 was chosen because of the starting caesura, 2021 because of the year before the war, and 2022 as the first year of the

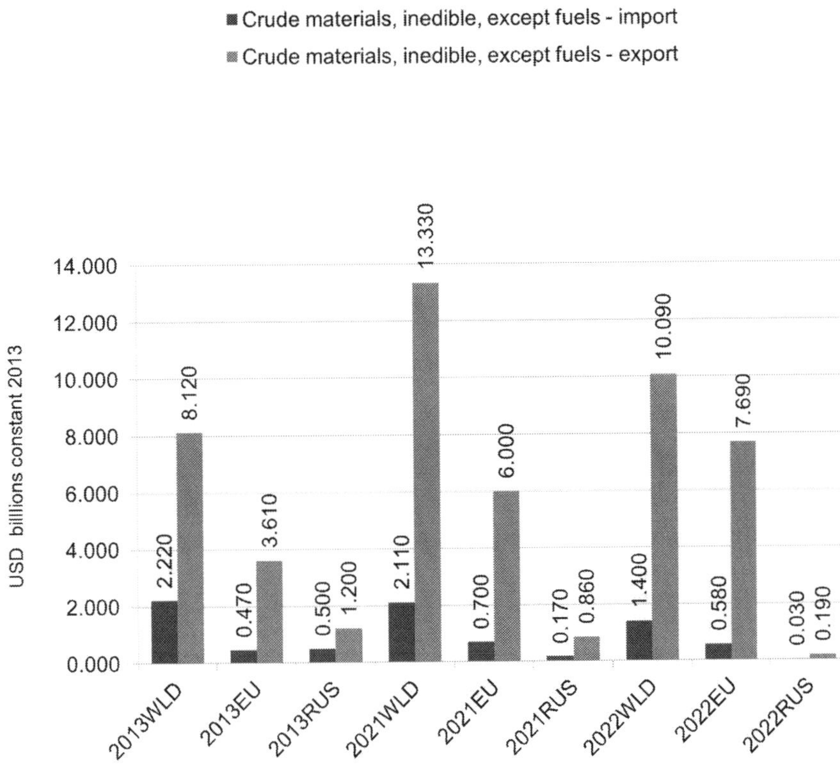

Figure 3.7 Value of Ukraine's exports and imports of the commodity group "Crude materials, inedible, except fuels" for the European Union (EU), Russia (RUS), and other countries (WLD)

Source: Own compilation based on data from World Integrated Trade Solution World Bank and World Bank; Державна служба статистики України. Зовнішньоекономічна діяльність.

course of the war. In this case, trade was tabulated in order to trace the change in the commodity structure for exports for the EU, Russia, and other countries in general (World Bank. Exports and imports of Ukraine 2013–2022; Державна служба статистики України. Зовнішньоекономічна діяльність).

Given the considerable number of charts presenting the commodity structure of the value of Ukrainian exports and imports, only a summary of their substance in the context of the Ukrainian concept of moving away from the Russian commodity market has been made. This juxtaposition in relation to total exports and imports made it possible to determine in which sectors of commodity exchange the goal was successfully realised, and in which changing the vector of trade policy was a much more difficult challenge. Detailed data on the value of Ukraine's exports and imports for each group of goods is presented in Table 3.4.

The given graph shows that in the product group "Food and live animals" until 2021, Ukraine has managed to significantly reduce exports (US$0.050 billion) and

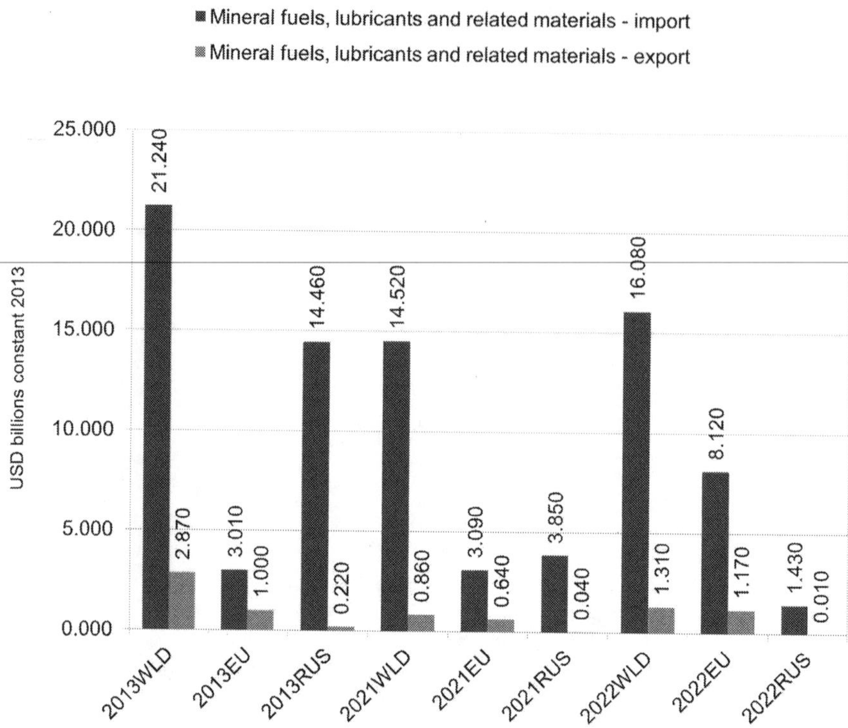

Figure 3.8 Value of Ukraine's exports and imports of the commodity group "Mineral fuels, lubricants and related materials" for the European Union (EU), Russia (RUS), and other countries (WLD)

Source: Own elaboration based on World Bank and World Bank Integrated Trade Solution data; Державна служба статистики України. Зовнішньоекономічна діяльність.

imports (US$0.030 billion) of goods compared to 2013 (US$1.580 billion and US$0.050 billion), and already in 2022 the trade result for represented US$0.000 billion. Considering the EU and the WLD, we see an increase in trade with Ukraine in 2021, with an expected decrease in 2022 as trade was conducted under war conditions. We can observe a similar trend in the "Beverages and tobacco" group of goods, where in 2013 exports and imports to Russia accounted for US$0.230 billion and US$0.170 billion, respectively, in 2021, imports accounted for US$0.020 billion and exports for US$0.000 billion, and in the year of war accounted for US$0.000 billion for both exports and imports. For the EU and WLD, the highest turnover was achieved in 2021 and the decline in 2022 was determined by the situation in Ukraine.

Exports and imports in the commodity group "Crude materials, inedible, except fuels" for Russia also marked a decline for 2013 and 2021; as in previous sectors in 2022, there was a significant reduction in trade in this sector to US$0.030 billion for exports and US$0.190 billion for imports. This positively impacted trade growth for the EU and WLD in 2021.

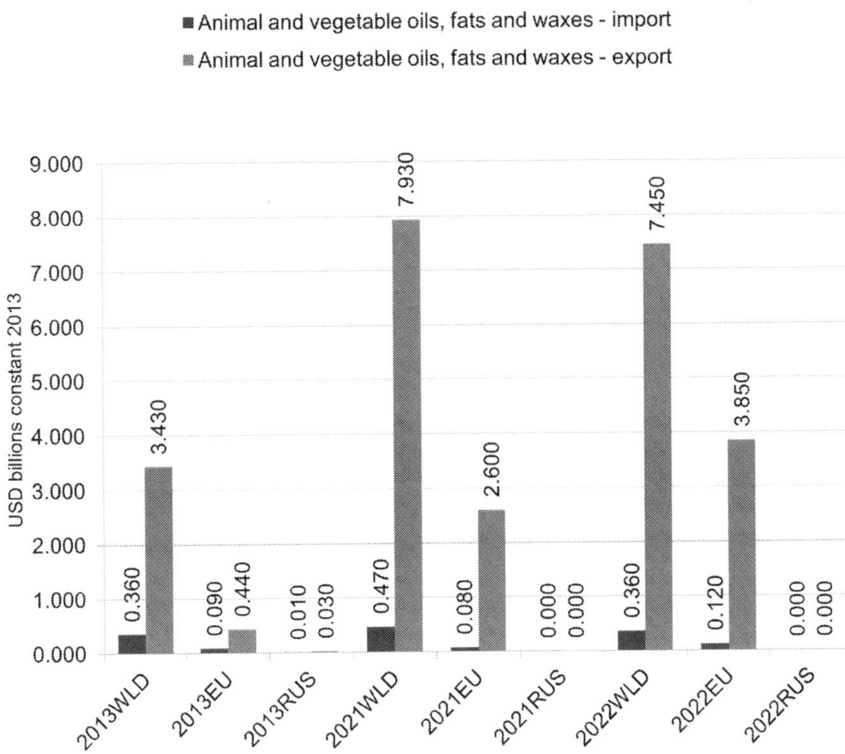

Figure 3.9 Value of Ukraine's exports and imports of the commodity group "Animal and vegetable oils, fats and waxes" for the European Union (EU), Russia (RUS), and other countries (WLD)

Source: Own elaboration based on data from World Integrated Trade Solution World Bank and World Bank; Державна служба статистики України. Зовнішньоекономічна діяльність.

In the case of "Mineral fuels, lubricants and related materials", in 2013, imports from Russia accounted for US$14.460 billion and exports for US$0.220 billion, although trade in goods in 2021 for exports already accounted for US$3.850 billion and for imports for US$0.040 billion, reaching US$1.430 billion in 2022, or around 10% for 2013 imports and US$0.010 billion, respectively, representing less than 5% of 2013 exports. The EU and the WLD achieve a decrease of about one-third for exports and imports in 2021, so that in 2022 both the EU and the WLD represent an increase for Ukrainian imports.

Considering "Animal and vegetable oils, fats and waxes", the 2021 and 2022 figures for Ukraine's exports and imports to and from Russia in this sector represent a trade score of US$0.000 billion against a turnover of US$0.030 billion for exports and US$0.010 billion for imports. In contrast, the low trade score for the EU in 2013 of US$0.440 billion exports and US$0.090 billion imports rose to US$3.850 billion for exports and US$0.120 billion for imports. An increase is also observed for the WLD score.

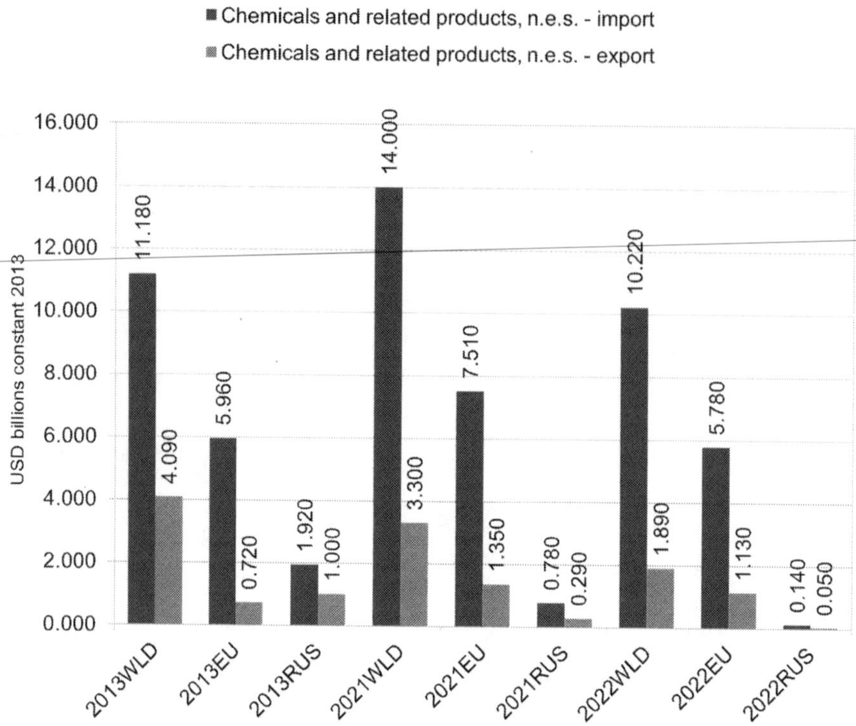

Figure 3.10 Value of Ukraine's exports and imports of the commodity group "Chemicals and related products, n.e.s." for the European Union (EU), Russia (RUS), and other countries (WLD)

Source: Own compilation based on data from World Integrated Trade Solution World Bank and World Bank; Державна служба статистики України. Зовнішньоекономічна діяльність.

Chemicals and related products, n.e.s. in Ukraine's exports and imports with Russia in the year of war accounted for US$0.050 billion and US$0.140 billion, respectively, against US$1.000 billion for exports and US$1.920 billion for imports in 2013. Declines for exports and imports also occur for the EU and WLD in both 2021 and 2022. Manufactured goods classified chiefly by material in 2022 score 0.230 billion for exports and US$0.210 billion for imports against 2013 results, US$1,000 billion and US$2,500 billion. Both the EU and WLD achieved declines in this sector in 2021 and 2022.

The structure of "Machinery and transport equipment" goods in the exchange with Russia in 2013 yielding US$5.310 billion in exports and US$2.650 billion in imports was reduced in exports to US$0.120 billion and in imports to US$0.110 billion in 2022. This means that Ukraine has effectively replaced Russia with European and world markets. The results for "Miscellaneous manufactured articles" also show a departure in Ukrainian exports and imports from trade with Russia in 2022 compared to 2013. In turn, in the case of the EU and WLD, we observe an

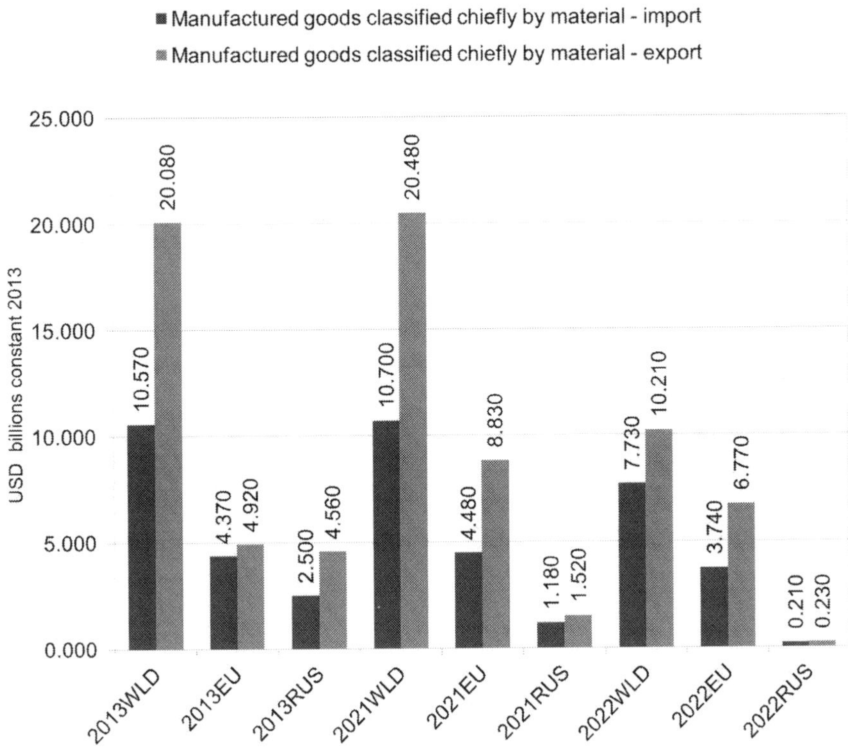

Figure 3.11 Value of Ukraine's exports and imports of the group of goods "Manufactured goods classified chiefly by material" for the European Union (EU), Russia (RUS), and other countries (WLD)

Source: Own elaboration based on World Integrated Trade Solution World Bank and World Bank data; Державна служба статистики України. Зовнішньоекономічна діяльність.

intensification of trade for the value of exports and imports in 2022 compared to 2013.

Commodities and transactions not classified elsewhere in the SITC for turnover with Russia in Ukraine's exports and imports in 2021 and 2022 account for US$0.000 billion against US$0.030 billion for exports and US$0.090 billion for imports. For the EU and WLD, it is interesting to note that the EU and WLD score a significant decrease in Ukraine's exports and a significant increase in imports.

The above comparisons of the value of Ukrainian exports and imports for the EU and Russia show that, similarly to the dimensions of overall exports and imports in individual trade sectors, we can observe a significant decrease in the value of trade with Russia. In as many as four groups of goods, the result for exports and imports in 2022 after the Russian military aggression against Ukraine was US$0.000 billion: food and live animals, beverages and tobacco, animal and vegetable oils, fats and waxes, and commodities and transactions not classified elsewhere. The remaining eight also saw significant declines in values

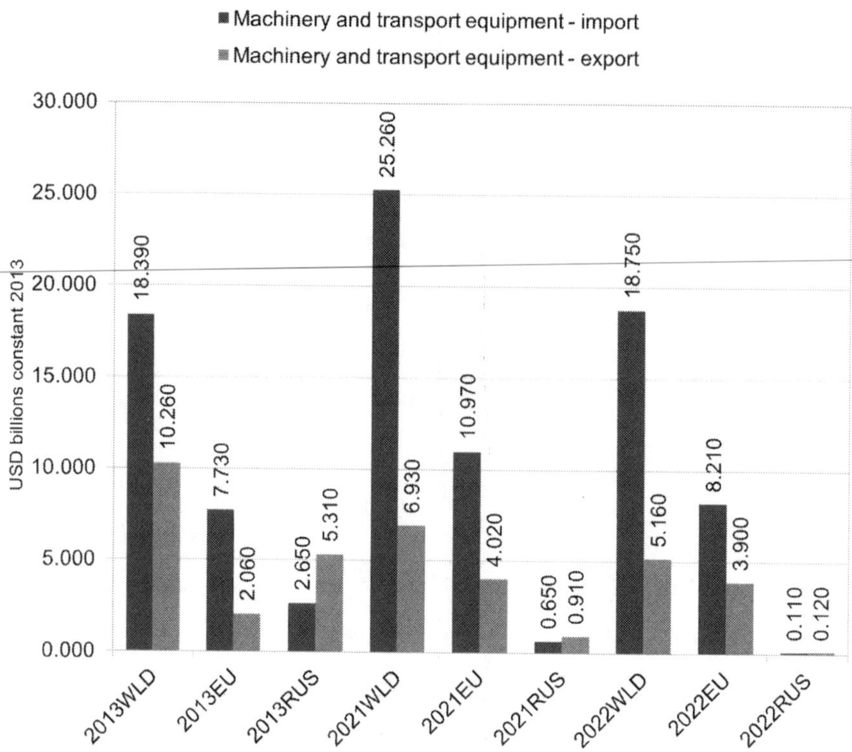

Figure 3.12 Value of Ukraine's exports and imports of the commodity group "Machinery and transport equipment" for the European Union (EU), Russia (RUS), and other countries (WLD)

Source: Own compilation based on data from World Integrated Trade Solution World Bank and World Bank; Державна служба статистики України. Зовнішньоекономічна діяльність.

for trade. In the case of values for Ukraine's exports and imports with the EU, we observe an upward trend, which is confirmed by the result for the overall dimension of Ukraine's exports and imports with the EU. The shift away from trade with Russia has been occurring successively since 2013 and the most noticeable changes in the year of Russian military aggression, resulting in Ukraine seeking European and global markets for goods.

3.5 Ukraine's Trade Exchange with Countries of the World

Relevant to the topic of this chapter is the analysis of Ukraine's importance to the global market. Therefore, an analysis of the value of Ukrainian exports was made in terms of the structure of global markets (Figure 3.15). This chart considers the values for Ukrainian exports in terms of regions: EAS – East Asia Pacific, ECS – Europe Central Asia, LCN – Lacin America Caribbean, MEA – Middle East North Africa, NAC – North America, OTR – other regions, SAS – South Asia,

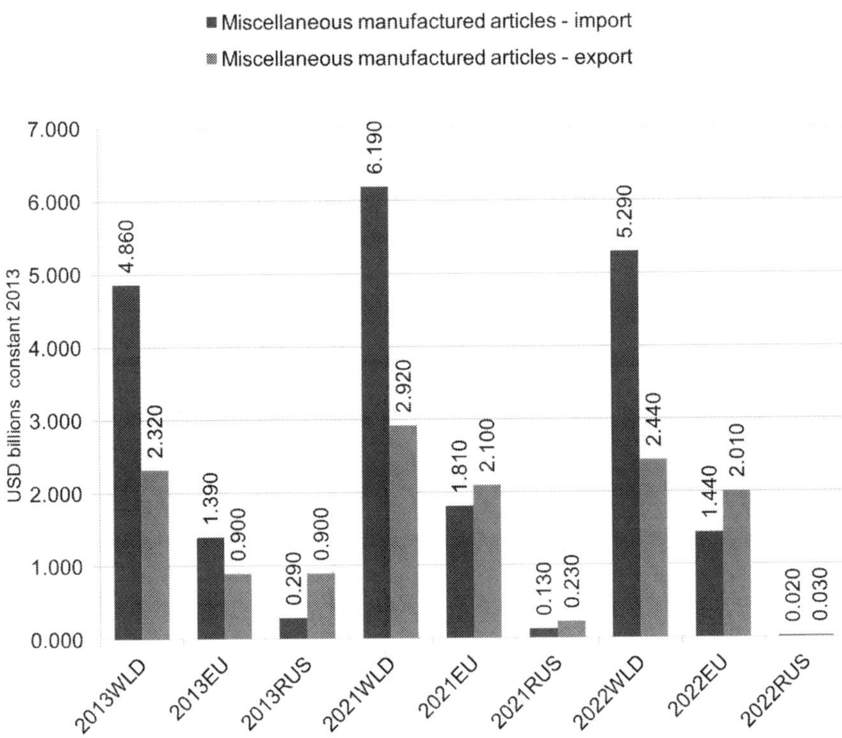

Figure 3.13 Value of Ukraine's exports and imports of the commodity group "Miscellaneous manufactured articles" for the European Union (EU), Russia (RUS), and other countries (WLD)

Source: Own compilation based on data from World Integrated Trade Solution World Bank and World Bank; Державна служба статистики України. Зовнішньоекономічна діяльність.

SSA – Sub-Saharan Africa, EU-UK – EU members excluding UK, RUS – Russia. WLD – worldwide.

The chart shows that Ukraine's most important global partner remains the EU, excluding the UK with US$241.34 billion representing 40.11% of Ukraine's total exports, the second place with over US$109.62 billion representing over one-sixth (18.11%) of Ukraine's total goods exports is with East Asia Pacific. In third place, trade with Europe Central Asia – US$97.96 billion (16.28%), Russia – US$86.81 billion (14.43%), trade with North America – US$29.85 billion (4.96%), South Asia – US$10.61 billion (1.76%), Latin America Caribbean accounted for US$9.71 billion (1.61%), Middle East North Africa – US$9.09 billion (1.51%), Sub-Saharan Africa – US$5.57 billion (0.93%), and other countries US$3.98 billion (0.66%) (World Bank. Ukraine's exports and imports 2013–2022).

Analysing the commodity structure for Ukrainian exports in the world (Table 3.5), it is worth mentioning that due to the wide time caesura of 2013–2022

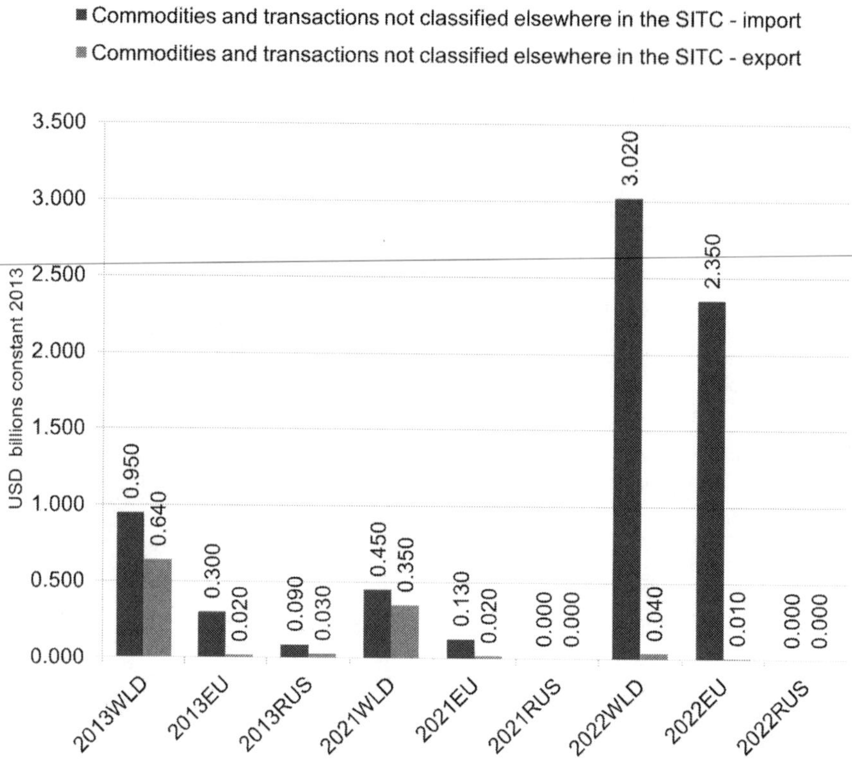

Figure 3.14 Value of Ukraine's exports and imports of the commodity group "Commodities and transactions not classified elsewhere in the SITC" for the European Union (EU), Russia (RUS), and other countries (WLD)

Source: Own compilation based on data from World Integrated Trade Solution World Bank and World Bank; Державна служба статистики України. Зовнішньоекономічна діяльність.

and the global scope for Ukraine's trade, it was decided to include the specifics of the commodity structure in 2013 as the initial stage for this work, 2021 as the year before the war and 2022 as the first year of the war. Thus, the author's intention was to present the overall value for the commodity structure of Ukrainian exports to the world for: food and live animals [0]; beverages and tobacco [1]; crude materials, inedible, except fuels [2]; mineral fuels, lubricants and related materials [3]; animal and vegetable oils, fats and waxes [4]; chemicals and related products, n.e.s. [5]; manufactured goods classified chiefly by material [6]; machinery and transport equipment [7]; miscellaneous manufactured articles [8]; commodities and transactions not classified elsewhere in the SITC [9].

Table 3.6 presents the commodity structure for Ukrainian exports to the world in percentages. For exports of the food and live animals commodity group, Middle East and North Africa is the leader with 28.58%, East Asia Pacific – 17.51%, and Europe and Central Asia with 15.20%. For Ukrainian exports of beverages

Table 3.4 Summary of Ukraine's export and import values for commodity groups 2013, 2021, and 2022 in billions.

Products import	*2013 WLD*	*2013 EU*	*2013 RUS*	*2021 WLD*	*2021 EU*	*2021 RUS*	*2022 WLD*	*2022 EU*	*2022 RUS*
Food and live animals – import	6.170	2.270	0.650	6.200	3.050	0.030	5.450	2.910	0.000
Beverages and tobacco – import	1.060	0.320	0.170	1.470	0.870	0.020	1.080	0.660	0.000
Crude materials, inedible except fuels – import	2.220	0.470	0.500	2.110	0.700	0.170	1.400	0.580	0.030
Mineral fuels, lubricants, and related materials – import	21.240	3.010	14.460	14.520	3.090	3.850	16.080	8.120	1.430
Animal and vegetable oils, fats and waxes – import	0.360	0.090	0.010	0.470	0.080	0.000	0.360	0.120	0.000
Chemicals and related products, n.e.s. – import	11.180	5.960	1.920	14.000	7.510	0.780	10.220	5.780	0.140
Manufactured goods classified chiefly by material – import	10.570	4.370	2.500	10.700	4.480	1.180	7.730	3.740	0.210
Machinery and transport equipment – import	18.390	7.730	2.650	25.260	10.970	0.650	18.750	8.210	0.110
Miscellaneous manufactured articles – import	4.860	1.390	0.290	6.190	1.810	0.130	5.290	1.440	0.020
Commodities and transactions not classified elsewhere in the SITC – import	0.950	0.300	0.090	0.450	0.130	0.000	3.020	2.350	0.000

Products export	*2013 WLD*	*2013 EU*	*2013 RUS*	*2021 WLD*	*2021 EU*	*2021 RUS*	*2022 WLD*	*2022 EU*	*2022 RUS*
Food and live animals – export	10.800	2.530	1.580	19.680	4.230	0.050	16.850	8.590	0.000
Beverages and tobacco – export	0.700	0.020	0.230	0.850	0.120	0.000	0.380	0.090	0.000
Crude materials, inedible except fuels – export	8.120	3.610	1.200	13.330	6.000	0.860	10.090	7.690	0.190
Mineral fuels, lubricants, and related materials – export	2.870	1.000	0.220	0.860	0.640	0.040	1.310	1.170	0.010
Animal and vegetable oils, fats and waxes – export	3.430	0.440	0.030	7.930	2.600	0.000	7.450	3.850	0.000
Chemicals and related products, n.e.s. – export	4.090	0.720	1.000	3.300	1.350	0.290	1.890	1.130	0.050
Manufactured goods classified chiefly by material – export	20.080	4.920	4.560	20.480	8.830	1.520	10.210	6.770	0.230
Machinery and transport equipment – export	10.260	2.060	5.310	6.930	4.020	0.910	5.160	3.900	0.120
Miscellaneous manufactured articles – export	2.320	0.900	0.900	2.920	2.100	0.230	2.440	2.010	0.030
Commodities and transactions not classified elsewhere in the SITC – export	0.640	0.020	0.030	0.350	0.020	0.000	0.040	0.010	0.000

Source: Own compilation based on data from World Bank's World Integrated Trade Solution and World Bank; Державна служба статистики України. Зовнішньоекономічна.

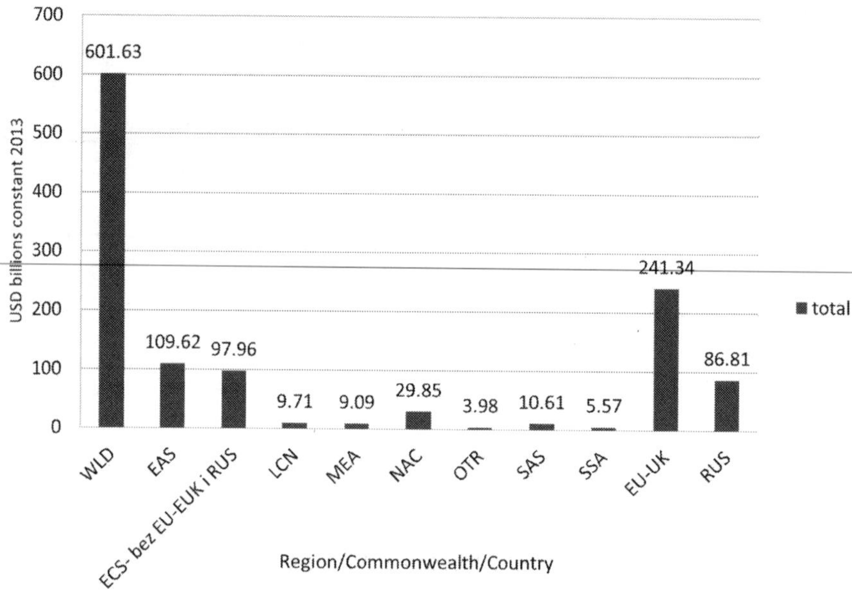

Figure 3.15 Value of Ukrainian exports by world region, total billion USD constant 2013

Source: Own compilation based on World Bank and World Integrated Trade Solution data.

Table 3.5 Value of Ukrainian exports for world regions, total USD billion constant 2013 and %

Value	*WLD*	*EAS*	*ECS-without EU & RUS*	*LCN*	*MEA*	*NAC*	*OTR*	*SAS*	*SSA*	*EU-UK*	*RUS*
Total bn USD	601.63	109.62	97.96	9.71	9.09	29.85	3.98	10.61	5.57	241.34	86.81

Source: Own compilation based on World Bank and World Bank World Integrated Trade Solution data; Державна служба статистики України. Зовнішньоекономічна діяльність.

and tobacco, the leaders are Europe and Central Asia – 47.02%, Middle East and North Africa – 14.44%, and East Asia Pacific – 10.63%. For crude materials, inedible, except fuels, the most important markets are East Asia Pacific – 20.97% and Europe and Central Asia – 13.57%. Exports from Ukraine mineral fuels, lubricants, and related materials achieved the highest score for Europe and Central Asia – 12.07%. Sales of animal and vegetable oils, fats and waxes had the highest result for Europe and Central Asia – 15.72%, and Middle East and North Africa – 15.95%. For chemicals and related products, n.e.s., the most important market is Europe and Central Asia – 26.70%. On the other hand, manufactured goods classified chiefly by material received the highest export value in Europe

Table 3.6 Commodity structure for Ukrainian exports to the world in % excluding EU and Russia

	EAS % MEAN	*ECS % MEAN*	*LCN % MEAN*	*MEA % MEAN*	*NAC % MEAN*	*OTR % MEAN*	*SAS % MEAN*	*SSA % MEAN*
0	17.51%	15.20%	0.39%	28.68%	0.46%	0.23%	3.86%	2.61%
1	10.63%	47.02%	0.78%	14.44%	1.00%	10.37%	0.05%	0.72%
2	20.97%	13.57%	0.22%	5.23%	0.37%	0.10%	1.40%	0.06%
3	0.57%	12.07%	2.78%	5.72%	0.46%	1.73%	1.54%	0.41%
4	15.72%	7.24%	0.32%	15.95%	0.54%	0.51%	30.51%	0.72%
5	3.27%	26.70%	2.85%	3.37%	2.99%	1.90%	5.40%	1.78%
6	3.60%	19.76%	1.99%	14.51%	4.94%	0.22%	1.05%	3.30%
7	4.71%	13.03%	0.94%	2.92%	1.63%	0.10%	2.84%	0.98%
8	1.67%	13.69%	0.23%	1.26%	1.27%	0.69%	0.94%	0.25%
9	21.22%	28.07%	0.19%	25.83%	2.74%	2.48%	7.47%	4.51%

Source: Own compilation based on World Integrated Trade Solution World Bank and World Bank data; Державна служба статистики України. Зовнішньоекономічна діяльність.

and Central Asia (excluding the EU and Russia) – 19.76%. Europe and Central Asia is the largest market for goods from Ukraine: machinery and transport equipment at 13.03%, miscellaneous manufactured articles – 13.69%, and commodities and transactions not classified elsewhere in the SITC – 28.07. Thus, based on the results of the commodity structure for Ukrainian exports, it should be concluded that Ukrainian goods go to different regions of the world. The undisputed leaders are Europe, Central Asia, East Asia Pacific, Middle East and North Africa (World Bank. Exports and imports of Ukraine 2013–2022; Державна служба статистики України. Зовнішньоекономічна діяльність).

When analysing Ukraine's trade after 2022, it is worth noting that the Russian aggression brought significant changes in the context of new difficult operating conditions for the Ukrainian economy. To a large extent, the destruction of production facilities and infrastructure, through Russian missile attacks on Ukrainian cities, the migration of the population including and abroad – in particular from the areas threatened by the attacks – contributed to this. The new realities of the functioning of the economy under wartime conditions required an adaptation of the economic policy of the state, not only of Ukraine but also of the partner countries. Thus, the existing conditions of the ongoing war have caused significant changes in the structure of trade in goods between Ukraine and the EU. This is mainly because agricultural products have become the priority products for European markets, while the production and sale of metal products have fallen significantly. Until the Russian invasion in 2022, metallurgy was Ukraine's largest export item, providing more than two-thirds of export revenues. According to the State Statistics Service, in 2021, Ukraine exported ferrous metals for a total of US$13.95 billion, 81.4% more than in 2020. Ukrainian cast iron was supplied to the United States, Italy, Turkey, the UAE, and Spain; ferroalloys to Turkey, Italy, China, and the Netherlands; and powder metals to EU countries (Державна служба статистики України. Зовнішньоекономічна діяльність). An undoubted reason for the stagnation of metal production in Ukraine is that a significant part of the production facilities is located in the occupied territories of the Donbass, where fighting has taken place or is still taking place, including the Illich Iron and Steel Plant in Mariupol, the Azovstal Iron and Steel Plant, the Makeevka Kirov Metallurgical Plant, the Alchevsk Metallurgical Plant, the Donetsk Metallurgical Plant, and the Yenakiieve Metallurgical Plant. In addition, there were a number of smaller, specialised metallurgical enterprises in the Donetsk region in Druzhkivka, Avdiivka, and Kramatorsk. However, not all metallurgical enterprises remained in the occupied territories. A significant number of them are located in Ukrainian-controlled territory. These include the ArcelorMittal, Kryvyi Rih, Zaporizhstal, Dniprostal, Dniprospecstal, and ferroalloy plants, as well as Zaporizhkoks (Гавриленко, 2022; Ляховська, 2023; Осіпова, 2022).

A very important measure for Ukrainian exports was the facilitation of access to the EU market through the removal of existing import duties, and safeguard measures for Ukrainian goods for one year, starting in June 2022. Another facilitation implying an increase in grain exports was the conclusion of the so-called grain agreement in July 2022, due to Russia blocking Ukrainian ports preventing the transport of Ukrainian grain to African and Middle Eastern countries. In 2021, almost 99% of Ukrainian grain exports were transported by sea; for oilseeds (including sunflower and rapeseed), the rate was over 90%. Russian military aggression led to the blockade of some Black Sea and Azov Sea seaports, which significantly hampered the delivery of Ukrainian goods. Before the war, around 15 (14.48) million tonnes of grain were shipped from the port of Chernomorsk, 12.30 million tonnes from the port of Nikolayev, around 10 (9.64) million tonnes from the port of Yuzhny. Also important for the realisation of exports from Ukraine were the ports of Olva, Berdyansk, Mariupol, and Kherson. “The Grain Agreement” was a covenant of sorts between Ukraine and Russia with the involvement of Turkey and the UN as signatories. The agreements provided for the partial unblocking of Ukrainian Black Sea ports (in Odessa, Chernomorsk, and Pivdenny) for the export of Ukrainian grain towards Istanbul along the humanitarian maritime corridor. On July 17, 2023, Russia declared its withdrawal from the grain agreement whose term was due to expire the following day. The Russian side said that the basis for the cancellation of the extension of the agreement was the failure to meet its arrangements with Russia to handle its food and fertiliser trade and to handle international bank payments and insurance transactions. The meeting between the Russian and Turkish leaders resulted in the Russian side ultimately refusing to extend the agreement for the resumption of Ukrainian grain shipments, on the basis that Russia’s expectations had not been met (Гавриленко, 2022; Ляховська, 2023; Осіпова, 2022; Державна служба статистики України. Зовнішньоекономічна діяльність) (Figure 3.16).

The undisputed leader in grain imports from Ukraine is the ECS (Europe-Central Asia) region, with Ukrainian grain imports accounting for 46.57% in 2013, falling to 27.90% in 2021, and already rising to 64.98% in 2022, due to a number of EU measures facilitating grain transport from Ukraine. The second place is occupied by countries from the EAS (East Asia Pacific) region,

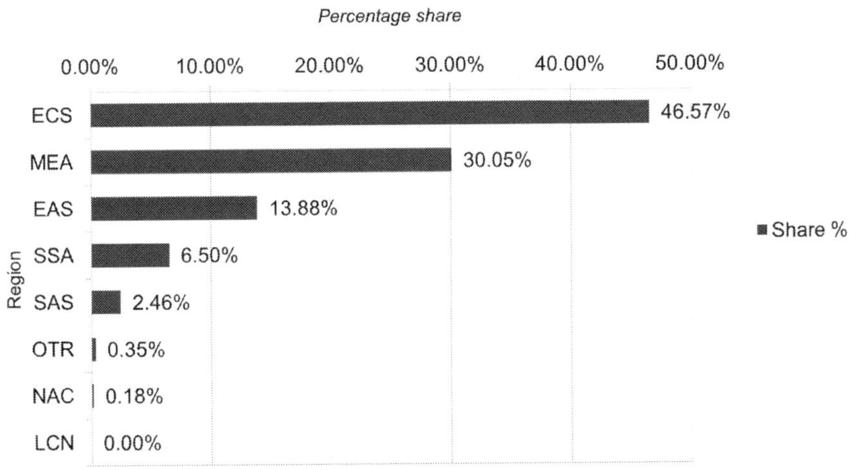

Figure 3.16 Ukrainian grain exports in % to countries of the world (SITC Revision 4 04) by region 2013

Source: Own compilation based on World Integrated Trade Solution World Bank and World Bank data; Державна служба статистики України. Зовнішньоекономічна діяльність.

in 2013 grain imports there amounted to only 13.88%, and already in 2021, this region became the leader accounting for as much as 38.12%, for 2022 it was 23.35%. The MEA (Middle East North Africa) region is also an important importer of grain, where imports in 2013 from Ukraine amounted to 30.05%, giving it second place in the ranking, and in 2021 – 19.82% and in 2022 – 11.11%. Countries from the SSA (Sub-Saharan Africa) and SAS (South Asia) region are also important players for Ukrainian grain imports, in 2013 they accounted for 6.50% and 2.46%, respectively, in 2021 their score for grain imports increased to 9.19% and 4.14%. However, after the outbreak of war, this score dropped to 0.16% for SSA and 0.32% for SAS. Considering individual countries, the most important importers of Ukrainian grain are China, Spain, Turkey, the Netherlands, Egypt, Bangladesh, Israel, and Portugal (Figure 3.17).

The main markets for Ukrainian products in 2021 were four areas – countries of the European Union, Africa, Asia, and the Commonwealth of Independent States. Together, they accounted for more than 97% of the value of Ukrainian agricultural exports. It is the most important region for Ukrainian agricultural exports. EU and African countries are also important, with a significant decrease observed in trade with the CIS (Figure 3.18; Table 3.7).

The above statements present that the undisputed leaders in grain imports from Ukraine are the ECS (Europe and Central Asia), EAS (East Asia Pacific), and MEA (Middle East and North Africa) regions. The situation related to Russian actions against the suspension of the supply of Ukrainian raw materials by blocking seaports made it necessary to support Ukraine through a number of instruments facilitating the realisation of grain supplies under crisis conditions.

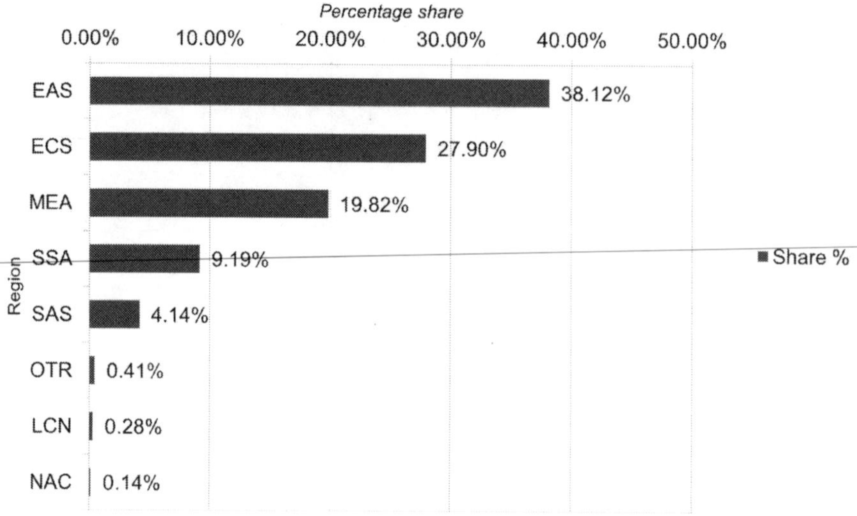

Figure 3.17 Ukrainian grain exports to world countries in % (SITC Revision 4 04) by region 2021

Source: Own compilation based on World Bank and World Bank World Integrated Trade Solution data; Державна служба статистики України. Зовнішньоекономічна діяльність.

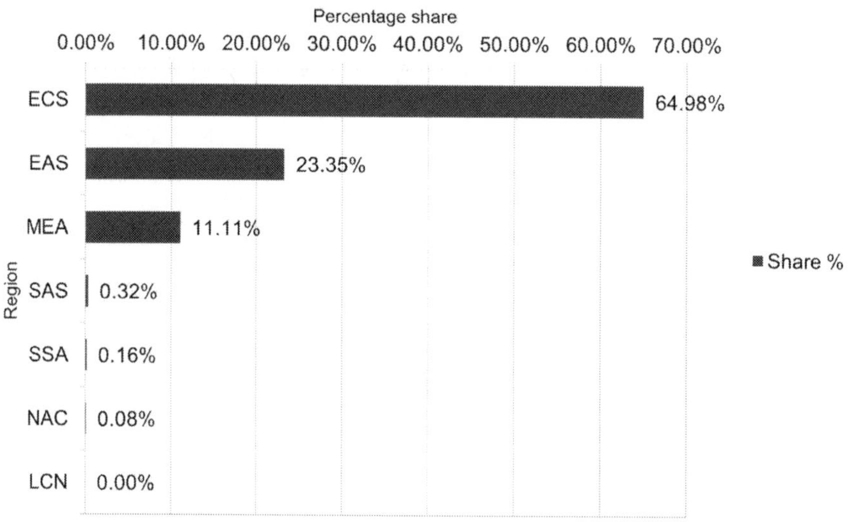

Figure 3.18 Ukrainian grain exports to world countries in % (SITC Revision 4 04) by region 2022

Source: Own compilation based on World Bank and World Bank World Integrated Trade Solution data; Державна служба статистики України. Зовнішньоекономічна діяльність.

Table 3.7 Ukrainian grain exports to world regions 2013, 2021, 2022 in billions and %

Region	*Year*	*Trade Value in US$1000*	*CPI Year*	*mld USD constant 2013*	*Udział %*
ECS	2013	2647192.373	106.83	2.65	46.57%
MEA	2013	1708535.767	106.83	1.71	30.05%
EAS	2013	794058.997	106.83	0.79	13.88%
SSA	2013	367919.631	106.83	0.37	6.50%
SAS	2013	141375.917	106.83	0.14	2.46%
OTR	2013	17866.046	106.83	0.02	0.35%
NAC	2013	12223.494	106.83	0.01	0.18%
LCN	2013	321.703	106.83	0	0.00%
EAS	2021	4741566.47	124.27	5.52	38.12%
ECS	2021	3470892.126	124.27	4.04	27.90%
MEA	2021	2470858.389	124.27	2.87	19.82%
SSA	2021	1143294.285	124.27	1.33	9.19%
SAS	2021	518679.806	124.27	0.6	4.14%
OTR	2021	51755.164	124.27	0.06	0.41%
LCN	2021	35319.893	124.27	0.04	0.28%
NAC	2021	18388.215	124.27	0.02	0.14%
ECS	2022	6425595.299	134.21	8.07	64.98%
EAS	2022	2309753.648	134.21	2.9	23.35%
MEA	2022	1097743.218	134.21	1.38	11.11%
SAS	2022	35492.176	134.21	0.04	0.32%
SSA	2022	18308.659	134.21	0.02	0.16%
NAC	2022	8960.194	134.21	0.01	0.08%
LCN	2022	437.437	134.21	0	0.00%

Source: Own compilation based on World Bank and World Bank World Integrated Trade Solution data; Державна служба статистики України. Зовнішньоекономічна діяльність.

3.6 Importance of Ukraine for the EU Market

The analysis made earlier indicates that the EU is undoubtedly an important market for Ukrainian goods. Analysing the analysis in more detail in terms of individual EU Member States, the author undertook the task of determining whether the significant share of the EU in Ukraine's exports (more than 40%) is behind the account of all Member States, whether it is the trade of selected EU countries with Ukraine that implies a significant result for the EU as a whole, to what extent the EU countries with the highest share of Ukrainian exports determine the overall share of Ukrainian exports in the EU economy, thus by juxtaposing the value result for imports from Ukraine to the EU in individual countries. Figure 3.19 is a breakdown of the value of imports from Ukraine to EU Member States in percentages in relation to total imports from Ukraine to the EU.

The advantage of the given summary is that it makes it possible to determine whether a given result for the EU of sales of Ukrainian goods in the EU is evenly distributed among all Member States, or whether it is shaped by the account of individual countries, which are the most important importers of Ukrainian goods; ABC data analysis was used to resolve the issue in question. By compiling the result for Ukrainian imports to the EU for individual countries, it was possible to

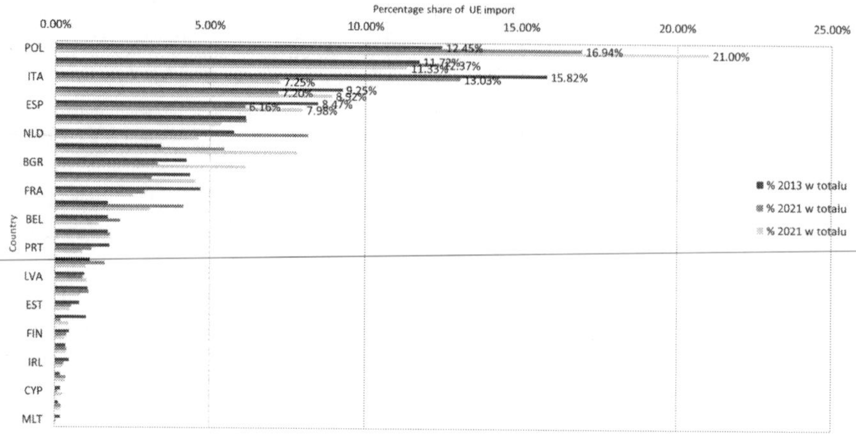

Figure 3.19 Value of imports from Ukraine for EU countries in 2013, 2021, and 2022 in %

Source: Own compilation based on World Integrated Trade Solution World Bank and World Bank data.

calculate the percentage share of Ukrainian exports in EU countries in the total Ukrainian exports to the EU. This was further categorised according to groups A (countries forming 80%), B (countries forming 15%), and C (countries forming 5%) (Kavitha et al., 2016: 167–170).

Detailed information on the value of imports from Ukraine in individual EU countries in 2013, 2021, and 2022 will be presented in Table 3.8. The largest market for goods from Ukraine within the EU is given by Poland and accounted for 12.45% in 2013, 16.94% in 2021, and 21.00% in 2022 of total EU imports from Ukraine. Germany is second with 11.72% in 2013, 12.37% in 2021, and 11.33% in 2022. In 2013, imports of goods to Italy from Ukraine accounted for 15.82% of total EU imports and this was the highest rate among Member States; in 2021, it was 13.03% and in 2022 it dropped to 7.25%. In contrast, Ukraine's imports to Hungary accounted for 9.25% of EU imports in 2013, in 2021 – 7.20%, and in 2022 – 8.92%. Spain in 2013 scored 8.47% of imports, in 2021 – 6.16% and in 2022 – 7.98%. On the other hand, for the Czech Republic, Netherlands, France, Austria, Belgium, Portugal, Greece, Denmark, and Estonia, we observe a decrease in the result of imports from Ukraine against 2013 and 2021 in 2022. In contrast, the result for Romania and Bulgaria in 2022 represented an increase of imports from Ukraine against previous years. For the rest of the countries, the summary showed no significant change for the percentage of imports from Ukraine.

By sorting according to the Pareto principle in 2013, Group A was formed, which included nine EU countries (33.33%) (Italy, Poland, Germany, Hungary, Spain, the Czech Republic, the Netherlands, France, and Slovakia) with a 78.74% share of Ukrainian exports to the EU; group B – seven EU countries (25.93%) (Bulgaria, Romania, Portugal, Austria, Belgium, Lithuania, and Greece) with a share of 15.59%; and group C is 11 EU countries (40.74%) (Denmark, Croatia, Latvia, Estonia, Finland, Ireland, Sweden, Slovenia, Cyprus, Malta, and Luxembourg) with a share of 5.66%. In 2021, nine countries re-enter Group A: Poland, Italy, Germany,

Table 3.8 Value of imports from Ukraine for EU member states in 2013, 2021, 2022 segregation ABC analysis

	Country 2013	*Bln USD 2013*	*% 2013*	*Country 2021*	*Bln USD 2021*	*% 2021*	*Posit 2022*	*Country 2022*	*Bln USD 2022*	*% 2022*
1	ITA	2.82	15.82%	POL	5.86	16.94%	1	POL	7.82	21.00%
2	POL	2.22	12.45%	ITA	4.51	13.03%	2	DEU	4.22	11.33%
3	DEU	2.09	11.72%	DEU	4.28	12.37%	3	HUN	3.32	8.92%
4	HUN	1.65	9.25%	NLD	2.82	8.15%	4	ESP	2.97	7.98%
5	ESP	1.51	8.47%	HUN	2.49	7.20%	5	ROM	2.9	7.79%
6	CZE	1.1	6.17%	CZE	2.14	6.18%	6	ITA	2.7	7.25%
7	NLD	1.03	5.78%	ESP	2.13	6.16%	7	BGR	2.3	6.18%
8	FRA	0.84	4.71%	ROM	1.89	5.46%	8	CZE	2	5.37%
9	SVK	0.78	4.37%	AUT	1.44	4.16%	9	NLD	1.73	4.65%
10	BGR	0.76	4.26%	BGR	1.15	3.32%	10	SVK	1.69	4.54%
11	ROM	0.61	3.42%	SVK	1.08	3.12%	11	AUT	1.15	3.09%
12	PRT	0.31	1.74%	FRA	1	2.89%	12	FRA	0.93	2.50%
13	AUT	0.3	1.68%	BEL	0.72	2.08%	13	LTU	0.65	1.75%
14	BEL	0.3	1.68%	LTU	0.61	1.76%	14	BEL	0.52	1.40%
15	LTU	0.3	1.68%	GRC	0.55	1.59%	15	LVA	0.38	1.02%
16	GRC	0.2	1.12%	PRT	0.41	1.18%	16	GRC	0.37	0.99%
17	DNK	0.19	1.07%	DNK	0.38	1.10%	17	PRT	0.33	0.89%
18	HRV	0.18	1.01%	LVA	0.31	0.90%	18	DNK	0.3	0.81%
19	LVA	0.17	0.95%	EST	0.18	0.52%	19	EST	0.17	0.46%
20	EST	0.14	0.79%	FIN	0.13	0.38%	20	HRV	0.16	0.43%
21	FIN	0.08	0.45%	SWE	0.13	0.38%	21	SWE	0.13	0.35%
22	IRL	0.08	0.45%	SVN	0.12	0.35%	22	SVN	0.12	0.32%
23	SWE	0.06	0.34%	IRL	0.1	0.29%	23	FIN	0.11	0.30%
24	SVN	0.03	0.17%	LUX	0.07	0.20%	24	IRL	0.09	0.24%
25	CYP	0.03	0.17%	HRV	0.06	0.17%	25	CYP	0.09	0.24%
26	MLT	0.03	0.17%	CYP	0.03	0.09%	26	LUX	0.07	0.19%
27	LUX	0.02	0.11%	MLT	0.01	0.03%	27	MLT	0.01	0.03%

Note: The Group A countries are marked with dark gray color in the table, Group B countries are marked with white color, and Group C countries are marked with light gray color

Source: Own compilation based on World Bank and World Bank's World Integrated Trade Solution data, using ABC method.

the Netherlands, Hungary, the Czech Republic, Spain, and two new countries Romania and Austria forming 79.65% for EU imports from Ukraine. Group B comprises six EU countries (22.22%) (Bulgaria, Slovakia, France, Belgium, Lithuania, Greece, and Portugal, with 14.76%; Group C comprises 12 countries (44.44%): Denmark, Latvia, Estonia, Finland, Sweden, Slovenia, Ireland, Luxembourg, Croatia, Cyprus, and Malta with a rate of 5.59%. In 2022, nine countries enter the group with a share of 80.47% of EU imports from Ukraine, where, in a different order, are the eight countries in Group A in 2021 (except Austria), which has been replaced by Bulgaria. Group B is seven EU countries (25.93%): Slovakia, Austria, France, Lithuania, Belgium, Latvia, and France giving 14.76% share of Ukrainian imports to the EU. Group C is 11 countries (40.74%): Portugal, Denmark, Estonia, Croatia, Sweden, Slovenia, Finland, Ireland, Cyprus, Luxembourg, and Malta accounting for 4.26% of Ukrainian exports to the EU (Table 3.9).

Table 3.9 Value of Ukrainian imports to the EU, 2013, 2021, 2022, summary for ABC groups

Year	*Group of countries*	*Number of countries*	*Percentage share of the group*	*Import share*
2013	A	9	33.33%	78.74%
2013	B	7	25.93%	15.59%
2013	C	11	40.74%	5.66%
2021	A	9	33.33%	79.65%
2021	B	6	22.22%	14.76%
2021	C	12	44.44%	5.59%
2022	A	9	33.33%	80.47%
2022	B	7	24.93%	15.29%
2022	C	11	40.74%	4.26%

Source: Own elaboration.

Table 3.10 Summary for Ukraine's exports and imports from the EU in % 2013, 2021, 2022

Year	*Percentage of import in global EU imports*	*Position*	*Percentage of export in global EU exports*	*Position*
2013	0.36%	46	0.59%	36
2021	0.47%	45	0.52%	37
2022	0.41%	44	0.46%	43

Source: Own elaboration.

The summary data presents that in all analysed years, one-third of the EU countries (9 – 33.33%) accounted for about 80% of Ukrainian exports to the EU. On this basis, it can be concluded that the trade rate between the EU and Ukraine is mainly driven by a few countries that dominate trade with Ukraine, as for two-thirds of the EU countries account for only one-fifth of Ukrainian exports to the EU (around 20%). Considering how important Ukraine is for the EU economy, the summary in Table 3.10 shows that in 2013 Ukraine accounted for 0.36% of EU global imports and 0.59% of EU global exports. In 2021, the ratios for imports and exports were 0.47% and 0.52%, respectively, while in 2022, the result was 0.41% and 0.46%.

The above analysis gives grounds to claim that overall Ukrainian exports for the EU economy are not significant, a much more important role Ukrainian exports play from the perspective of individual countries. The analysis, with the help of the ABC method, has established that one-thirds of the EU countries account for as much as 80% of total Ukrainian goods exports from the EU. Thus, it is these countries that shape the demand for Ukrainian goods within the European structures.

Conclusion

The Russian attack on Ukraine in February 2022 implied a redefinition of trade policy not only for Ukraine but also for European countries and the world. The main rationale for this is that both Ukraine and Russia were significant players in the global market. In solidarity with Ukraine, EU countries and the United States have imposed a series of sanctions on Russia in order to exert pressure due to military action. Russia, in turn, hinders Ukraine's trade with the world by destroying industrial infrastructure and Ukrainian raw material stocks, blocking the transport of Ukrainian grain by sea. The aim of this chapter was to analyse trade between Ukraine and EU countries and selected countries of the world, in order to establish the importance of Ukrainian trade for European and world markets. The assumptions of the chapter were also based on a juxtaposition in the perception of Ukraine as a trade actor before and after the Russian military aggression in 2022.

The author undertook the task of solving the main research problem [P]: what is the importance of Ukraine for trade with the EU and selected world countries between 2013 and 2022, and to what extent did Russian military aggression imply on the dimension of Ukraine's trade with Europe and the world. It was also important to find answers to specific questions:

[Q1] what place does the EU occupy in Ukrainian trade between 2013 and 2022?
[Q2] what is the place of Ukraine's trade with the EU between 2013 and 2022?
[Q3] what place does Russia hold in Ukraine's trade between 2013 and 2022?
[Q4] what is the importance of Ukraine in the trade of the world (excluding the EU and Russia) between 2013 and 2022?
[Q5] whether and to what extent is there a change in the scope of trade between Ukraine and the EU after the Russian military aggression against Ukraine?
[Q6] whether and to what extent is there a change in the scope of trade between Ukraine and countries of the world after the Russian military aggression against Ukraine?
[Q7] whether and to what extent is the structure of exports/imports between Ukraine and the EU changing after the Russian-Ukrainian war?
[Q8] whether and to what extent is the structure of exports between Ukraine and the countries of the world changing after the outbreak of the Russian-Ukrainian war?
[Q9] whether and to what extent do the EU countries with the highest share of Ukrainian exports determine the overall share of Ukrainian exports in the EU economy?

The resolution of the research problems posed was made possible by the verification of the hypotheses. The main hypothesis [H] was accepted: that Ukraine is an important partner for the EU countries and the world, and as the annexation of Crimea in Ukraine was followed by measures to reduce trade with Russia and the targeting of Western countries, and Russian military aggression contributed significantly to the consolidation and deepening of Ukraine's trade with the EU, was verified on the basis of specific hypotheses.

In the case of hypothesis [H1], the EU occupies an important place in Ukrainian trade and there is an increase in the share of the EU in Ukrainian exports between 2013 and 2022, it was fully confirmed. The Deep and Comprehensive Free Trade Area had a positive impact on the dynamics of Ukraine's bilateral trade in goods with the EU and facilitated the restoration of Ukraine's general trade after the 2014–2015 crisis. With the entry into force of the DCFTA, Ukraine's trade in goods with the EU began to improve significantly. The EU applied zero tariffs to goods from Ukraine for around 89% of tariff lines. In 2020, economic regression and reduced demand, due to the global COVID-19 pandemic, also occurred in goods trade between the EU and Ukraine. Instead, in 2021, we see a significant increase in demand for goods, which translates into trade between actors. In turn, the outbreak of the Russian-Ukrainian war in 2022 resulted in an even greater intensification of trade between the EU and Ukraine, a number of measures and instruments facilitating Ukraine's sales were reflected in the consolidation of the EU vector of Ukrainian trade policy, by moving away from trade with Russia. Since 2013, the EU's share of Ukraine's exports has been increasing from 25.61% to 30.45% (2014), 41.36% (2018), up to a record high in 2022 – 63.07%. On the other hand, the case study of imports of goods from the EU to Ukraine is the result in 2013 represented 33.66%, a significant increase is recorded in 2020 – 42.00%, and in 2022 it reached almost 50% of Ukraine's total imports (48.87%).

On the other hand, [H2] Ukraine is an important player in EU trade between 2013 and 2022 has not been fully confirmed, given that 80% of Ukrainian exports to the EU are consumed by only one-thirds of EU countries (nine) that actually shape demand for Ukrainian goods. In hypothesis [H3], the importance of Russia's trade with Ukraine between 2013 and 2022 is weakened as a result of events of a political nature (annexation of Crimea, Russia's support for separatist movements in eastern Ukraine, and Russia's military aggression against Ukraine) is fully confirmed. Confirmation for the given claim is provided by the fact that Ukrainian imports from Russia in 2013 accounted for 30.19%, and after the events related to the annexation of Crimea and the fighting in the Donbass in 2014, they almost halved to 16.74%, maintaining a downward trend until 2020 – 6.57%, and accounted for just 2.52% in 2022. In the case of Ukraine's exports to Russia, the result in 2013 was 23.81% of Ukraine's total exports, and since 2015 it has accounted for a single-digit figure of 7.76%, falling from Ukrainian export to Russia 6.15% in 2021. In contrast, after the Russian attack on Ukraine in 2022, Ukrainian exports to Russia accounted for less than 1% (0.98%).

In hypothesis [H4], the importance of Ukraine in the trade exchange of world states in 2013–2022 is mainly shaped by the account of agricultural production exports. This hypothesis was not confirmed, mainly because trade between Ukraine and the world countries took place in all ten sectors of food and live animals; beverages and tobacco; rude materials, inedible, except fuels; mineral fuels, lubricants and related materials, animal and vegetable oils, fats and waxes, chemicals and related products, n.e.s., manufactured goods classified chiefly by material, machinery and transport equipment, miscellaneous manufactured articles, commodities, and transactions not classified elsewhere in the SITC. Both in Ukraine's exports and imports with the rest of the world, important sectors, apart from agricultural production, were chemicals and related products, n.e.s.: machinery and transport equipment, miscellaneous manufactured articles, and manufactured goods classified chiefly by material.

The importance of Ukraine to European and global trade is evidenced by the fact that in 2021 it was the third largest exporter of raw materials in the world (after

Russia and Brazil), representing 23% of global exports. In addition, Ukraine provided 9% of global exports of semi-finished iron or non-alloy steel, the third largest exporter. In addition, Ukraine plays an important role in world exports of maize and wheat. In 2021, it was the third largest exporter of maize after the United States and Argentina, accounting for 11.4% of world exports. In addition, the country exported 8.5% of the world's wheat, making it the fifth largest exporter of wheat. The country also occupies a large share of global exports among oil exporters, while in sunflower oil it was the world leader, providing 37% of global exports in 2021.

In the case of [H5], following the Russian military aggression against Ukraine in 2022, there is a significant decline in trade between Ukraine and the EU, due to the operation of the Ukrainian state under martial law, the hypothesis is partially confirmed. However, it is worth adding that, considering the juxtaposition for Ukrainian exports at the end of 2021 and the beginning of 2022, the result of a significant increase (by 40.08%) of exports in 2021 against the previous year in trade between the EU and Ukraine determines the fact of a decrease in performance due to the COVID-19 pandemic. In the first year of the war, Ukrainian exports to the EU fell by 27.13%. However, comparing the given result for exports during the economic crisis in Ukraine 2014–2015, there was also a significant decrease in 2014(−13.48%) and 2015 (−29.20%). Thus, the value of the decrease in the state's exports during the war is similar to the result of the decrease during the economic crisis. In the case of imports of goods from the EU in 2021, there was an increase in imports of 36.74% (against a decrease of 10.63% in 2020), and a decrease of 14.75% in 2022 as a result of the war. In contrast, as a result of the 2014–2015 crisis, Ukraine's imports of goods fell by 28.22% in 2014 and by 30.93% in 2015. Thus, the decrease result for imports during the war is much lower.

[H6] The trade exchange between Ukraine and the countries of the world after the Russian military aggression against Ukraine is significantly limited by Russian actions blocking the flow of goods. This hypothesis is partially confirmed, as undoubtedly Russia's actions are limiting trade opportunities with world states. The decrease in the result for exports with world countries occurs, because the value of Ukraine's total exports and imports in 2022 against 2021 has decreased (see H5). Another issue is also that the share of Ukraine's exports and imports with world countries in 2022 decreased, with imports at 43.56% (54.42% in 2021) and imports at 31.59% (67.62% in 2021). However, it is also worth noting in this respect the increase in the share of exports and imports for countries from the EU (see H1).

In hypotheses [H7], the structure of exports/imports between Ukraine and the EU after the outbreak of the Russian-Ukrainian war did not change significantly and [H8] the structure of exports/imports between Ukraine and the countries of the world after the outbreak of the Russian-Ukrainian war did not change significantly, were not confirmed. Considering the structure of Ukraine's exports to the EU, there was a twofold increase in the food and live animals sector at US$8.590 billion in 2022 (from US$4.230 billion in 2021), an index increase for exports in the crude materials, inedible, except fuels sector at US$7.960 billion (from US$6.000 billion in 2021), a near doubling for the mineral fuels, lubricants, and related materials result of US$1.170 billion (US$0.640 billion in 2021), and an increase in the export of animal and vegetable oils, fats and waxes of US$3.850 billion (from US$2.600 billion in 2021). In contrast, six other sectors were pegged to decline in exports (beverages and tobacco, chemicals and related products, n.e.s., manufactured goods classified chiefly by material, machinery and transport equipment, miscellaneous manufactured articles, commodities and transactions not classified elsewhere in the SITC). In the case of imports of Ukrainian goods to the EU, growth occurred in three sectors: mineral fuels, lubricants, and related materials worth US$8.120 billion (from US$3.090 billion in 2021), animal and vegetable oils, fats and waxes of US$0.120 billion (from US$0.080 billion in 2021), and a very significant increase in commodities and transactions not classified elsewhere in the SITC worth US$2.350 billion (from US$0.130 billion in 2021), while the remaining seven sectors saw a decrease. In exports to the rest of the world, there was an increase in 2022 only in the commodities sector of mineral fuels, lubricants, and related materials worth US$1.310 billion (from US$0.860 billion in 2021), the remaining nine sectors saw a decrease for the export result. For Ukrainian imports from the rest of the world, an increase was recorded in the mineral fuels, lubricants, and related materials sector of US$16.080 billion (from US$14.520 billion in 2021) and a very significant increase (similar to the EU countries) for commodities and transactions not classified elsewhere in the SITC of US$3.020 billion (from US$0.450 billion in 2021), with the remaining eight sectors showing a decrease for merchandise imports. To sum up the given theme, it should be pointed out that the trade structure for Ukrainian exports and imports in 2022 war changed, mainly because many sectors saw a significant decrease in value and only a few saw an increase.

In hypothesis [H9], EU member states with the highest share of Ukrainian exports significantly determine the overall share of Ukrainian exports in the EU economy was confirmed. Analysing with the help of the ABC method, it was possible to determine that one-thirds of the EU countries account for as much as 80% of all Ukrainian exports to the EU. Thus, it is these countries that shape the demand for Ukrainian goods within the European structures.

Referring to the above specific hypotheses, it was possible to resolve the main research problem [P] by verifying the main hypothesis [H] that Ukraine is an important trade partner for both the EU and the rest of the world. In the case of the EU, Ukraine's move away from trade after 2013 has led to an increase and deepening of trade with the EU. The latter uses a number of instruments to facilitate bilateral trade cooperation, due to Ukraine's operation under wartime conditions. Regarding Ukraine's trade with the world, it takes on a less dynamic character. Although Ukrainian goods go to various regions of the world, the undisputed leaders in this plan are Europe, Central Asia, East Asia Pacific, and Middle East and North Africa.

References

Association Agreement between the European Union and its Member States, of the one part, and Ukraine, of the other part. (2014). 02014A0529(01).

Bryjka, F. (2016). Rosyjska Wojna zastępcza w Donbasie. *Ante Portas – Studia nad Bezpieczeństwem 1*(6): 201–217.

EU-Ukraine DCFTA. Retreived from, https://trade.ec.europa.eu/access-to-markets/en/content/eu-ukraine-deep-and-comprehensive-free-trade-area

European Commission Opinions on the EU Membership applications of Ukraine. (2022). Retreived from https://www.eeas.europa.eu/ukraine/european-union-and-ukraine_en?s=232

Executive Order 13660. Blocking Property of Certain Persons Contributing to the Situation in Ukraine. Retrieved from https://obamawhitehouse.archives.gov/the-press-office/2014/03/06/executive-order-blocking-property-certain-persons-contributing-situation

Executive Order 13661 Blocking Property of Additional Persons Contributing to the Situation in Ukraine. Retrieved from https://obamawhitehouse.archives.gov/the-press-office/2014/03/17/executive-order-blocking-property-additional-persons-contributing-situat

Foreign Affairs Council, 23 June 2014. Retrieved from https://www.consilium.europa.eu/en/meetings/fac/2014/06/23/

Hajduk, J., & Stępniewski, T. (2015). Wojna hybrydowa Rosji z Ukrainą: Uwarunkowania i instrumenty. *Studia Europejskie 4*: 135–151.

Harding, L. (2022). *Russian's Bloody War and Ukraine's Fight for Survival*. Guardian Faber.

Kavitha, S., Kandeepan, A., & Narmadha, N. (2016). ABC Analysis, an Inventory Management Technique at a Manufacturing Company. *International Journal of Operations Management and Services 19*(3): 167–170.

Partnership and Cooperation Agreement between the European Union and the Ukraine. (1994). https://edit.wti.org/document/show/ffc14f8f-aeee-4700-ae09-9c114328a99c?textBlockId=f3414f15-7619-4086-a95e-3be949fd93a5&page=1

Petryshyn, H. (2022). Sytuacja gospodarcza w Ukrainie przed wybuchem wojny rosyjsko-ukraińskiej. *Społeczestwo i Polityka 3*(72): 61–80.

Plokhy, S. (2023). *The Russo-Ukrainian War. The World's Foremost Historian of Ukraine Financial Times*. Penguin Random Hause.

Prokop, M. (2023a). Russia-Ukraine: Difficult Neighbourly Relatios. In A. Kasińska-Matryka & K. Pałka-Suchojad (Eds.), *The Russia-Ukraine War of 2022. Faces of Modern Coflict* (pp. 6–21). Routledge.

Prokop, M. (2023b). War in Ukraine. Media and Emotions. In A. Turska-Kawa, A. Kasinska-Metryka, K. Pałka-Suchojad (Eds.), *A Redefinition of the Essence of Social Media in Ukraine in the Era of Russian Aggression of 2022* (pp. 95–110). Palgrave Macmillan. https://link.springer.com/chapter/10.1007/978-3-031-37608-5_6

Reinforced restrictive measures against Russia, BACKGROUND ST 12944/14 PRESSE 460 Brussels, 11 September 2014. Retrieved from https://www.consilium.europa.eu/media/21992/144868.pdf

Report NISS. (2014). Щодо тенденцій розвитку економіки України у 2014–2015 pp. Аналітична записка, Retreived from https://niss.gov.ua/doslidzhennya/ekonomika/schodo-tendenciy-rozvitku-ekonomiki-ukraini-u-2014-2015-rr-analitichna

Special meeting of the European Council, 16.07.2014. Retrieved from https://www.consilium.europa.eu/en/meetings/european-council/2014/07/16/

Tomala, M., & Prokop, M. (2021). Zagrożenia militarne i wojenne a bezpieczeństwo gospodarcze państwa. Case study: Konflikt zbrojny między Ukrainą a Rosją w 2014 roku. Annales Universitatis Pedagogicae Cracoviensis. *Studia de Securitate 11*(2): 40–59.

Tymkiv, Y. (2007). Koncepcje polityki zagranicznej i bezpieczeństwa Ukrainy. In T. Pietraś & Kapuśniak (Eds.), *Ukraina w stosunkach międzynarodowych* (pp. 109–126). Wydawnictwo Uniwersytetu Marii Curie-Skłodowskiej.

Wasiuta, O., & Wasiuta, S. (2017). *Wojna hybrydowa Rosji przeciwko Ukrainie*. Wydawnictwo Arcana.

World Bank's World Integrated Trade Solution Ukraine World Bank. Ukraine's Exports and Imports 2013–2022. Retrieved from https://wits.worldbank.org/

World Bank. Ukraine's Exports and Imports 2013–2022. Retrieved from https://data.worldbank.org/indicator/FP.CPI.TOTL?end=2022&locations=US&start=2010

Бесчастна, Д., & Уварова, К. (2015). Аналіз економічної кризи 2014–2015 років в Україні крізь призму югославського конфлікту. *Науковий вісник Міжнародного гуманітарного університету 14*: 9–13.

Водотика, Т., & Магда, Є. (2016). *Ігри Відображень. У пошиках власного образу. Якою бачить Україну світ*. Харків, Віват.

Гавриленко, Н. (2022), вплив війни на зовнішню торгівлю України (за підсумками першого півріччя 2022 р.), Центр зовнішньополітичних досліджень. Retrieved from https://niss.gov.ua/sites/default/files/2022-08/_us-gavrilenko-tablici_merged_0.pdf

Головко, В., Палій, О., Черевко, О., & Янішевський, С. (2015) Революція Гідності 2013–2014 рр. та агресія Росії проти України. In. П. Полянський (ed.) Науково-методичні матеріали. Київ: Київський університет імені Бориса Грінченка.

Російсько-український конфлікт (2014) стан, наслідки, перспективи розвитку подій. Національна безпека і оборона *5–6*: 3–38.

Державна служба статистики України. Зовнішньоекономічна діяльність. Retrieved from: https://www.ukrstat.gov.ua/ (accessed: 21.12.2023).

Державна служба статистики України. Державні фінанси, податки та публічний сектор. Retrieved from: https://www.ukrstat.gov.ua/ (accessed: 21.12.2023).

Державна служба. (2023). Спеціального зв'язку та захисту інформації України. Retrived fromhttps://cip.gov.ua/ua/statics/finansovo-ekonomichna-diyalnist

Закон України. (2015) Про правовий режим воєнного стану. Відомості Верховної Ради (ВВР), 2015, № 28, ст.250. Retrieved from https://zakon.rada.gov.ua/laws/show/389-19#Text

Ляховська, О. (2023) Особливості функціонування найбільших підприємств металургійної промисловості України під час війни, Економіка та суспільство, 47. Retrieved from https://economyandsociety.in.ua/index.php/journal/article/view/2180

Магда, Є. (2015). *Гібридна Війна. Вижити і перемогти*. Харків, Віват.

Міністерство економіки України, Reireived from https://www.me.gov.ua/Tags/DocumentsByTag?lang=uk-UA&id=565ab860-7fe2-4f51-8e27-0b70ff06c732&tag=ZovnishnoekonomichnaDiialnist

Наказ. (2022). Головнокомандувач Збройних Сил України Від 3 березня 2022 року N 73 Про організацію взаємодії між Збройними Силами України, іншими складовими сил оборони та представниками засобів масової інформації на час дії правового режиму воєнного стану Із змінами і доповненнями, внесеними наказом Головнокомандувача Збройних Сил України від 12 липня 2022 року N 196. Retrieved from https://ips.ligazakon.net/document/view/MUS36785?an=2&ed=2022_03_03

Осіпова, Л. (2022). Динаміка експорту України в умовах повномасштабної війни: проблеми та можливі шляхи їх усунення в контексті євроінтеграції. Вісник Хмельницького національного університету, 6/2, 50–54. Retrieved from http://journals.khnu.km.ua/vestnik/wp-content/uploads/2023/01/2022-312-62-09.pdf

Руденко, М. (2015). Фінансова криза в Україні 2014–2015 років: причини та інструменти регулювання. Науковий вісник НЛТУ України. *Серія еконімічна 25*(7): 2014–2020.

4 The War in Ukraine Impacting European Financial Market and Banking Sector

Oleksandra Struk

Introduction

The European financial market plays a crucial role in the accumulation of capital and fostering growth, making a significant impact on the development of countries in the region. The European financial landscape has achieved interconnectedness through a strong emphasis on market integration and connections to global financial markets, bringing both benefits and potential risks. Ongoing geopolitical shifts, including the Russian invasion of Ukraine, have brought about a variety of challenges that are influencing the security of energy, the availability of food, and the movement of individuals and goods. In response to the situation, investors moved their funds to secure assets, resulting in fluctuations in the values of stocks, commodities, and financial instruments. Thus, the financial markets saw an uptick in activity, with investment portfolios undergoing dynamic changes due to the impact of geopolitical tensions, political choices, and their potential ramifications on the global economy.

This chapter aims to analyse the effects of the war in Ukraine on the financial market and banking sector of Europe, with a specific focus on the EU.

In order to make a comprehensive analysis of the research problem, the following research questions were formulated:

- What is the nature of European financial market?
- What is the impact of World Uncertainty Index (WUI) and economic policy uncertainty (EPU) on stock market performance, particularly in the context of war-related uncertainties?
- How do investors' expectations and market sentiments change in response to geopolitical events, and what role do economic policy measures play in shaping these expectations?
- How did European stock market respond to the initiation of the war, and what trends were observed in their performance and volatility?
- In what ways did the military conflict in Ukraine affect various sectors in the European stock market, and what were the immediate and long-term consequences for different industries?

DOI: 10.4324/9781003435433-4

- How does the ongoing war in Ukraine impact different channels of the banking sector in Europe?

A combination of both quantitative and qualitative research techniques was employed in the study, including data analysis, synthesis, and interpretation, along with the comparative analysis. The chapter provides an in-depth examination of various scientific studies, statistical data, and international reports.

4.1 A Brief Overview of the European Financial Market

As a pivotal point for gathering and increasing capital, the financial market plays a vital role for both entities in need of funds for investments and for investors looking for optimal returns on their investments. The origin of the European financial market can be traced back to 1958, and it has since undergone significant changes, particularly with the adoption of the euro currency. These modifications have not only heightened the level of integration in financial markets, but have also impacted domestic economic structures by facilitating access to capital for entrepreneurs and promoting the development and transformation of nations. Transparency, reliability, efficiency, liquidity, and integrity are key functions of the European financial market. These functions are essential for establishing its credibility and promoting entrepreneurship, driving the transformation of nations, and fostering the growth of European economies (Juza & Dąbrowski, 2021). Internally, there has been a strong emphasis on promoting financial market integration, resulting in increased interconnectedness among the national markets of European states and the establishment of a common market. Externally, on the other hand, the European market has become an integral part of global financial markets, resulting in increased interdependence and risk, commonly known as the 'domino effect.' The implementation of the euro currency was accompanied by the establishment of a unified monetary policy and the formation of a unified European market.

The banking sector, with the exception of the UK, holds a key position in the financial landscape of Europe, largely due to historical and legal circumstances. Meanwhile, the financial system of economies has been impacted by the emergence of capital markets and the increasing cross-border capital flows in recent years (Łasak, 2016). Furthermore, it is worth mentioning the ongoing process of financialisation whereby financial markets, financial institutions, and financial elites gain greater influence over economic policy and economic outcomes. Financialisation transforms the functioning of economic systems at both the macro and micro levels.

Thus, considering the unique nature of the European financial market, it is crucial to consider its character, such as the prevalence of the banking sector in Germany, France, and Poland, versus the dominance of the capital market in the United Kingdom. Moreover, the financial systems of EU countries differ primarily due to discrepancies in their legal systems (Bilski et al., 2016). Therefore, regulations for the financial market's operations should be tailored to the varying characteristics of member countries and their financial systems.

The European financial market is comprised of two main categories of actors: issuers, who are authorised to issue securities, and investors, including individuals, companies, financial institutions, insurance companies, and foreign investors (see: Juza & Dąbrowski, 2021). Investment carries different implications depending on the entity For individuals, it involves utilising available resources to achieve material, monetary or educational benefits, while for companies, it aims at increasing productive capacity. Households, who hold the majority of assets in the financial market, typically employ the services of financial brokers. Non-financial corporations commonly allocate funds in short-term securities, and their involvement in the market is frequently driven by the acquisition efforts of competing firms. In order to finance budget deficits, public authorities turn to the financial market, utilising financial institutions as intermediaries to create investment portfolios that aim to achieve maximum returns. Foreign investors also participate in investing capital outside their own countries.

The European financial market offers a diverse range of dematerialised financial instruments for facilitating efficient transactions. Some examples of these are stocks, which represent ownership in a company's capital; bonds, which signify the issuer's responsibility to repay a sum with interest; and certificates of deposit, which grant rights to specific deposits; mutual funds, which allocate funds into a range of assets; ETFs, also known as exchange traded funds; currencies, representing different monetary units; investment certificates, evidencing participation in an investment fund; and commercial paper – short-term securities issued by companies as a form of short-term financing.

The European economies were confronted with multifaceted obstacles regarding energy security, food supply, and the movement of people and goods as a consequence of the Russian invasion in Ukraine. These events have greatly disrupted investors, leading to fluctuations in the values of stocks, commodities, and financial instruments. Due to concerns about the conflict, investors directed their funds towards safe assets, including gold, government bonds, and currencies like the US dollar and Swiss franc. Meanwhile, industries tied to energy, raw materials, and infrastructure saw changes in their value based on their vulnerability to supply interruptions caused by the war. Investors closely observed the actions taken by financial institutions and governments in response to the crisis, assessing the potential consequences on markets. Consequently, the financial markets in Europe experienced a surge in investment activity, characterised by frequent changes in investment portfolios. The decision-making process for investments has included forecasts regarding Ukraine's developments, political choices, and their impact on the global economy. Ultimately, the geopolitical landscape has played a crucial role in shaping investment choices and the establishment of financial markets in Europe (see: European Council, 2023; Mallia et al., 2022).

4.2 World Uncertainty and Economic Policy Uncertainty versus Financial Stability in Recent Studies

Apart from the COVID-19 pandemic, most of the top concerns for investors in the 21st century revolve around geopolitical factors. Namely, the emergence of

China as a major player in the world economy has greatly influenced the narrative of globalisation. Similarly, the origins of the subprime crisis can be traced back to the United States. Quantitative easing and a low-risk interest rate were both initiated by the US in the second decade of the century. The ongoing China–US trade war, which began in 2017, is undeniably influenced by the geographical, economic, and political factors of both nations. Finally, the ongoing military clashes between Russia and Ukraine highlight the prevalence of geopolitical risks, as well as the Israel-Hamas war or War in Yemen swirling key geopolitical relationships and growing concerns that the conflict may spread across the Middle East (Bossman & Gubareva, 2023; Bossman et al., 2023a, 2023b; Shen & Hong, 2023; Yousaf et al., 2022b). Each of the above-mentioned occurrences has had a unique impact on the stock market performances across the globe, with variations observed among different countries and regions. The EU's economic climate and financial markets are noticeably susceptible to the rise of geopolitical risk, making it imperative to thoroughly examine and address the connection between the two in regards to EU stocks (Bedowska-Sojka et al., 2022; Boungou & Yatié, 2022; Yousaf et al., 2022b).

Considering contemporary scientific publications, Chowdhury and Khan (2023) assessed the immediate impact of Russia–Ukraine war on the global stock markets for the first four months since Russia's first invasion attempt on February 24, 2022. Exponential Generalised Autoregressive Conditional Heteroskedasticity indicates the presence of significant volatility and leverage effect in all the markets. Regression estimates show significantly positive impact of the CBOE Volatility Index and negative impact of oil on the abnormal returns of the global stock markets.

Meanwhile, using daily data on stock returns for a sample of 94 countries over the period from January 22, 2022, to March 24, 2022, Boungou and Yatié (2022) show significant negative effects of the Ukraine–Russia war on global stock indices. Several scientific studies have shown that a succession of sanctions aimed at Russia and its allies for their unlawful military actions in Ukraine have greatly impacted the Russian economy, heightening cross-market and cross-asset interconnectedness (Bossman et al., 2023a, 2023b). However, Sverdlov et al. (2023), based on correlation analysis, proved the inefficiency of the sanctions on the Russian financial market. They also found that some stock and industry indices of the countries that initiated the sanctions became less attractive to investors.

The aforementioned studies demonstrate a complex relationship between economics, geopolitics, market sentiment, and stock market performance (see also: Albaity et al., 2023; Klement, 2021; Shen & Hong, 2023). A multitude of studies present that several financial markets have sensibly reacted to Russia's invasion of Ukraine by financial fluctuations of assets (see: Bedowska-Sojka et al., 2022; Boungou & Yatié, 2022; Bossman et al., 2023a, 2023b; Sun et al., 2022; Yousaf et al., 2022b). These works demonstrate that the effect of geopolitical risk on financial markets can be attributed to the prevalence of significant uncertainty and turmoil, which in turn causes the propagation of risk transmission and spillover effects (Bossman et al., 2023a, 2023b; Mensi et al., 2023a, 2023b).

To focus on these issues more closely, Figure 4.1 shows the WUI in the period 1990–2023 for 143 countries, while Figure 4.2 includes data of certain European

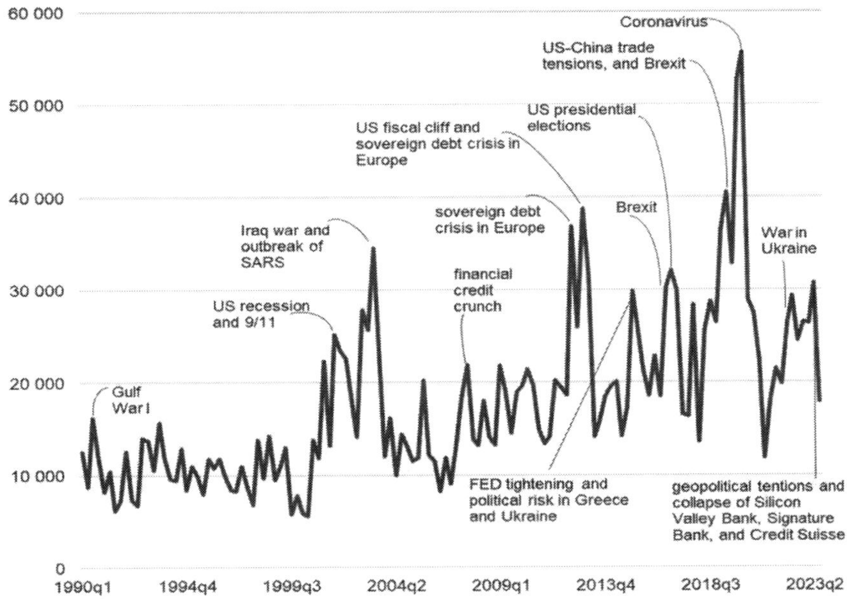

Figure 4.1 World Uncertainty Index, 1990Q1–2023Q3

Source: Own elaboration based on WUI (2024).

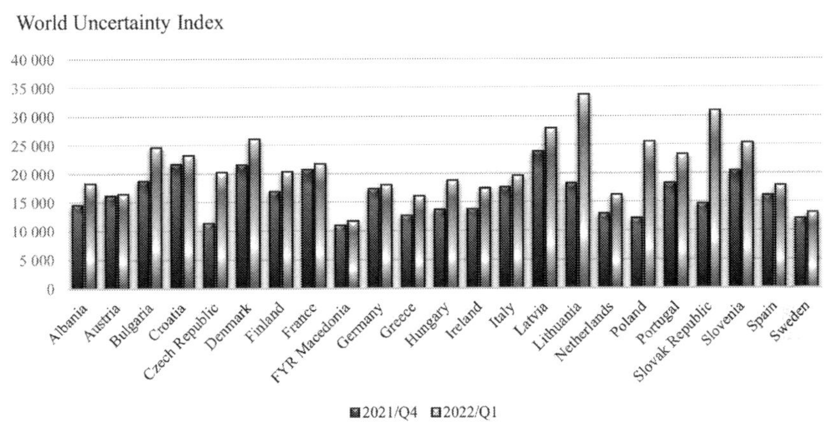

Figure 4.2 World Uncertainty Index, EU, 2021Q4 and 2022Q1

Source: Own elaboration based on WUI (2024).

states in the last quarter of 2021 and the first quarter of 2022. WUI is a metric designed to gauge worldwide uncertainty through the systematic examination of country reports published by the Economist Intelligence Unit. Thus, it is evident that there has been a rise in uncertainty across all countries, with a notable emphasis on Lithuania, Poland, and the Slovak Republic.

Considering EPU, there is a widespread recognition that it can have a range of effects on value of assets and liabilities. Initially, any lack of clarity regarding economic policies may prompt businesses and other economic participants to alter or delay significant decisions such as consumption, saving, investment, and employment (Gulen & Ion, 2016). Policy uncertainty also may have an impact on inflation, interest rates, and estimated risk premiums (Gubareva, 2021; Rebucci et al., 2022). Moreover, it could lead to a rise in production expenses, potentially resulting in a decrease in investment and overall economic performance (Julio & Yook, 2012). Finally, the uncertainty of policy may increase financial market risks by decreasing the value of market safeguards provided by the government (Pástor & Veronesi, 2012).

Following the global financial crisis, there has been a growing focus on analysing the effects of EPU. Figure 4.3 represents the EPU statistics from 2000 to 2023, indicating a considerable surge in recent times. Both investors and regulators have expressed concerns about how economic policies may impact stock market performance (Arouri et al., 2016). The emergence of the COVID-19 pandemic in 2020 has also provided an opportunity to evaluate the impact of EPU on stock market performance (Yousaf et al., 2023). Additionally, the ongoing military conflict between Russia and Ukraine poses a significant obstacle for geopolitics, as it has greatly escalated potential risks on a global scale (Bossman & Gubareva, 2023; Bossman et al., 2023a, 2023b). The current situation has emphasised the necessity of implementing economic policies to address externalities and endure financial volatility across various capital markets.

Kundu and Paul (2022) used the two-regime Markov-switching VAR model to analyse G7 countries during the period of 1998–2018. Their research uncovered that a rise in EPU leads to a decline of stock returns and an escalation of volatility in the immediate future. The findings also demonstrate that a rise in EPU results in a subsequent growth in stock returns, as investors seek heightened uncertainty premiums, resulting in a subsequent decline in volatility. The data indicates that the impact of EPU holds significance during the bear market, yet lacks significance during the bull market.

The investigation carried out by Albrecht et al. (2022) explores the interplay between EPU and equity markets. The researchers study time-variant comovement between the EPU index and several stock market indices, including S&P500, UK100, Nikkei225, and DAX30, across various investment time periods. The study reveals that during periods of financial instability worldwide, the EPU index shows a delayed reaction compared to the examined stock markets, particularly in the United States, Germany, and Japan. The time lag between fluctuations in the EPU index and the chosen equity market indices is between two and six months for investment horizons longer than 32 months. Furthermore, the researchers demonstrate the presence of the short-term impact of EPU on stock markets.

Javaheri et al. (2022) study EPU and the US stock market. According to their findings, a decrease in economic and political uncertainty indicators leads to an increase in stock market indices. Furthermore, their findings suggest non-linear

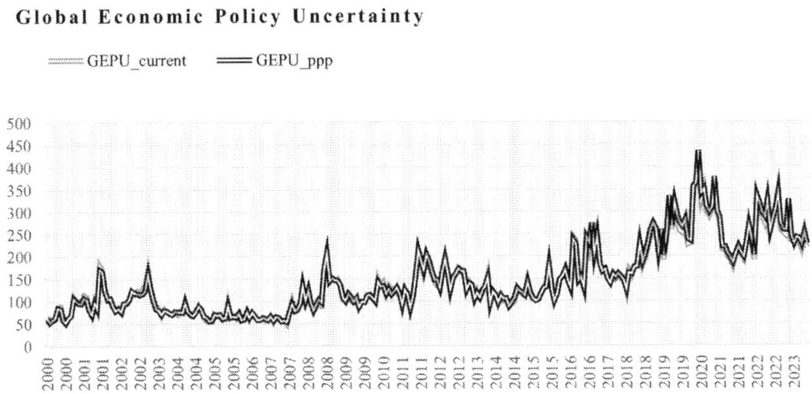

Figure 4.3 Global Economic Policy Uncertainty, 2000–2023

Source: Own elaboration based on EPU (2023).

patterns in the impact of inflation and GDP variables, i.e., an asymmetric impact of inflation and GDP on stock market activities.

Shen and Hong (2023) conducted a compelling analysis of the relationship between Germany's EPU and geopolitical risk in light of the Russia–Ukraine conflict. The authors prove that the ongoing military hostilities between Russia and Ukraine have elevated geopolitical risks and generated greater uncertainty in global economic policies, leading to an increasingly strained international landscape. By using Germany as a model, the study investigates the potential for geopolitical risks to impact time-varying risks in EPU.

The bond markets, faith-based assets, as well as commodities and digital currency markets, have experienced significant shifts in dynamics due to the COVID-19 pandemic (Akhtaruzzaman et al., 2022; Gubareva, 2021; Gubareva & Umar, 2020; Gubareva et al., 2023a, 2023b; Gupta et al., 2021; Hanif et al., 2023; Narayan et al., 2020; Umar et al., 2021, 2022a, 2022b; Wang & Park, 2021; Yousaf et al., 2022a). Besides, studies have revealed that turbulent periods of the pandemic have had a significant impact on cross-asset and cross-market connectedness, as well as comovement patterns. The introduction of unforeseen economic policies, specifically focused on reducing the spread of the pandemic and mitigating its consequences on the global economy, is seen as the driving force behind the significant changes in financial markets. The increased levels of policy uncertainty and market sentiment instability are prompting investors to seek out safe-haven and hedge assets, ultimately changing market interconnectedness (Agyei et al., 2022; Gubareva et al., 2023b; Hung & Vo, 2021; Mensi et al., 2023a, 2023b).

The event study analysis revealed that Russia's invasion of Ukraine had a noticeable impact on multiple financial markets (Sun et al., 2022; Yousaf et al., 2022b). Moreover, geopolitical risk has had a direct impact on the prices and returns of various assets (Bedowska-Sojka et al., 2022; Bossman et al., 2023a, 2023b; Boungou & Yatié, 2022). These works highlight the impact of geopolitical risk on financial markets, as the presence of geopolitical risk often creates a state of unpredictability and disturbance that can result in risk transmission and spillover (Bossman et al., 2023a, 2023b; Mensi et al., 2023a, 2023b).

Therefore, current studies suggest that global aspects, including policy uncertainty and geopolitical risk, have significant impact on investor sentiment and play a crucial role in financial markets (Bossman et al., 2023a; Mensi et al., 2023a, 2023b; Naeem et al., 2021; Xiao et al., 2018). Additionally, the fluctuation of prices in financial markets is impacted by shifts in investor sentiment and geopolitical uncertainty. These factors are also influenced by fiscal and monetary policies, as well as government interventions that shape the economic landscape (Agyei et al., 2022; Bossman et al., 2023b).

4.3 Investors' Market Expectations versus War in Ukraine

The Sentix indices, published by the Sentix research group, provide valuable insight into the relationship between the Ukrainian war and investor sentiment (Sentix, 2022; 2023a; 2023b; 2023c). The surveys are conducted weekly among investors of 12 different markets (i.e. German stock market, German technology company stock market, Eurozone stock market, US stock market, US technology company stock market, Japanese stock market, Eurozone long-term bond market, US long-term bond market, EUR/USD, USD/YEN, gold market, and oil market). Data is collected separately for institutional and individual investors.

According to the Sentix (2022), expectations have taken a sharp decline of 34.75 points, causing the overall index to reach its lowest level since November 2020. This was an unprecedented event in the 20-year history of the index. Even the Covid pandemic or the banking crisis had not led to such a sharp drop in the future outlook. This can be observed in Figure 4.4 presenting ten strongest slumps in the expectations in Euro area from 2008.

The Sentix economic indices in early October 2022 suggested a continued challenging economic climate, both in Europe and globally. The Eurozone indices, both representing current situation and expectations, plunged to the lowest point since May 2020, registering a drop of about −40 points in 2022, because of the financial concerns, the instability in gas and energy supply, as well as increasing possibility of an escalation of the military conflict in Ukraine (Sentix, 2023b). Considering overconfidence, the markets have also experienced a historical range of fluctuations (Sentix, 2023c). Meanwhile, with regards to the Sentix Report, it is evident that the overall index for the Eurozone displays an increase to −18.6 points in November and −16.8 in December 2023 (Sentix, 2023a, 2023b). In the meantime, the appraisal of the current state saw only a minor rise of +0.3 points, suggesting that the problem of recession is still present. According to the Sentix survey, professional and private investors are showing a decrease in their medium-term scepticism, which is a positive trend, thus economic expectations have recovered by 6.8 points to a value of −10 points in November and −9.8 points in December 2023 (Sentix, 2023a, 2023b). The current level is the highest since February 2023 and the second consecutive increase. The initial sign of improvement is reflected in the decrease

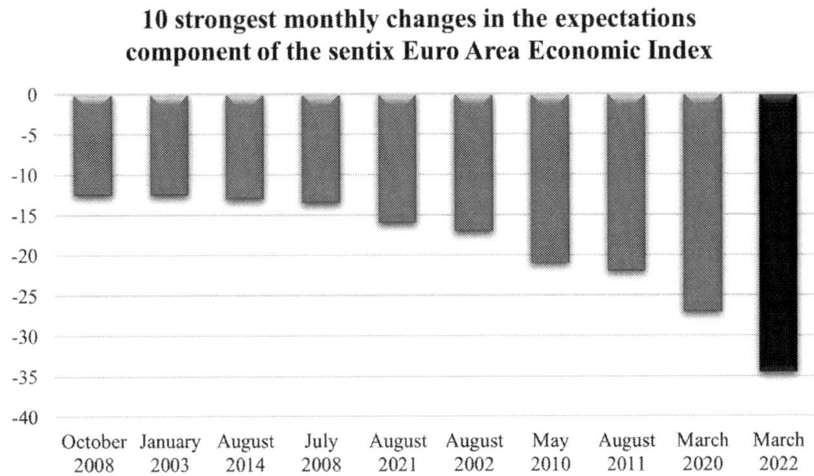

Figure 4.4 Ten strongest monthly changes in the expectations component of the Sentix Euro Area Economic Index, 2008–2022

Source: Sentix (2022).

of negative momentum. Nevertheless, the expectation values must shift to positive for complete confirmation. Without any alterations, the negative outlook suggests that the economy will still be seen as weaker in six months, despite its already weak position. Thus, the only prevailing influence is one of decline.

The reasoning behind this 'improvement' is based on the interest rate dynamics. The Sentix barometers provide evidence that the current economic stagnation and positive inflation projections are generating optimism for a potential conclusion to the central banks' trend of increasing interest rates. The implementation of this measure would greatly decrease the possible threat to certain economic sectors. However, this response of the central bank providing support to a struggling economy is still a distant prospect. Despite this, it appears that inflation is becoming less important as a negative influencing factor. After remaining in negative trend since the beginning of 2020, the Sentix 'inflation' index is now back in the positive trend with a +6.5 point rise (Sentix, 2023a). December saw a fifth consecutive improvement in the corresponding inflation barometer, reaching 16.25 points (Sentix, 2023b). With this favourable outlook on inflation, investors not only anticipate an end to the prolonged period of interest rate increases by central banks but also anticipate positive reinforcement from monetary policy. The theme barometer experiences a rise to 14.25 points, marking its highest level since April 2021.

4.4 European Stock Market versus War in Ukraine

The warfare unearthed worldwide stock markets at the bullish market driven by the escalation of tech firms' stock prices, hastening the alteration of trajectory and pivoting investor focus towards alternative sectors. The military conflict in Ukraine

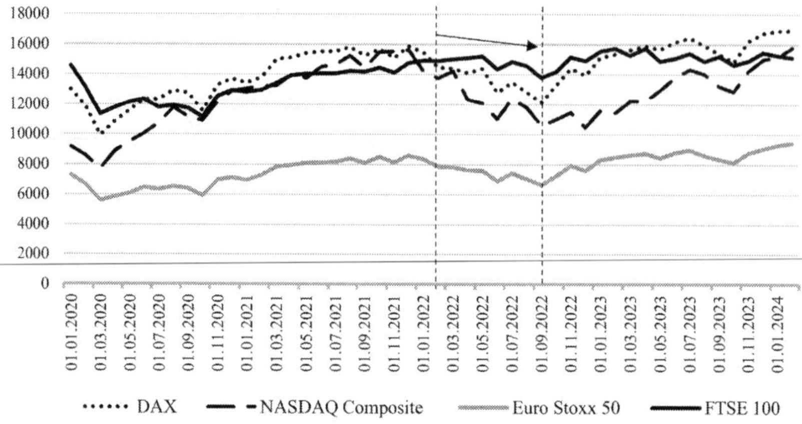

Figure 4.5 Dynamics of certain indices, 2019–2023

Source: Based on data from Google Finance.

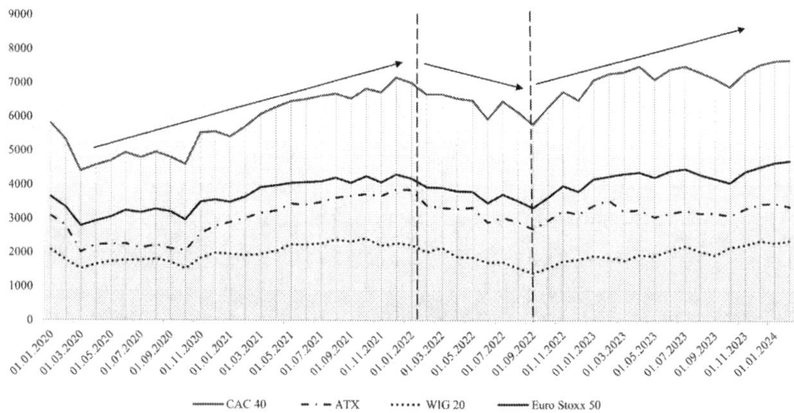

Figure 4.6 Dynamics of certain indices, 2019–2024

Source: Based on data from Google Finance.

caused significant disruptions in financial markets, in common with challenges investors are facing due to high inflation and potential interest rate increases. On that day, the STOXX® Global 1,800 Index dropped by as much as 3% due to the initiation of a war in Europe, leading to increased political and military tensions in the region similar to those observed during the Cold War. The same decline could be clearly observed among main indices like AEX, S&P 500, NASDAQ, Dow Jones, Euro Stoxx, FTSE 250, CAC40, and MSCI World (Figures 4.5 and 4.6). Due to its proximity to the conflict zone and significant trade connections with Russia, Europe experienced the greatest impact from the selling of developed-market stocks. The global benchmark recovered some of its losses as the day went on, but investors have still felt the impact of a 10% decline in the index for the year.

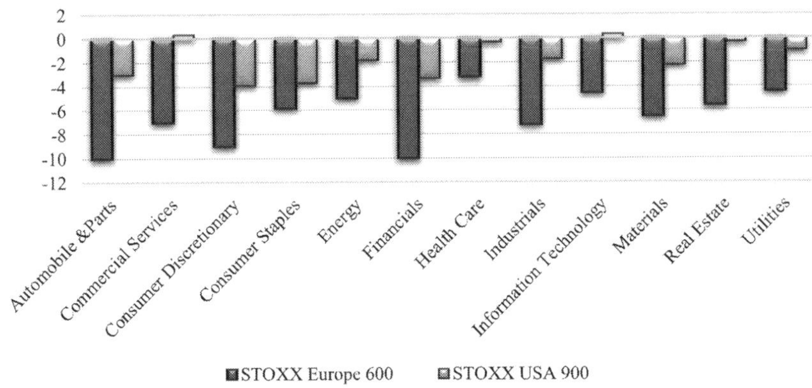

Figure 4.7 Total return – Industries – STOXX Europe 600 & STOXX USA 900, February 18–24, 2022 (%)

Source: Own elaboration based on data from Qontigo (2023c).

As of February 23, the STOXX Europe 600 Index had outperformed the STOXX USA 900 Index by 534 basis points in 2022. A day later, it had shrunk to just 82 basis points (−9.8% for the European index vs. −10.7% for the USA benchmark) (Qontigo, 2022). Meanwhile, the week ending February 24 saw below average performance across all 11 industries in Europe (Figure 4.7).

However, at the end of 2023, the EURO STOXX 50, comprised 50 foremost and most liquid stocks of top-performing Eurozone blue-chip companies, has achieved its 23-year peak of 4,542 points (Figure 4.8). The EU50, the primary stock market index in the Euro Area, has risen by 577 points or 15.22% since the beginning of 2023. According to Trading Economics global macro models and expert forecasts, it will reach a trading value of 3,929.27 within the next 12 months. Meanwhile, according to the macroNEXT service's indices (2023), the Eurozone is currently experiencing a challenging economic environment due to factors such as financial concerns, energy supply instability, and the potential for military conflict escalation.

In light of market's predictions of volatility, it is crucial to monitor the VSTOXX indices (Figure 4.9), which are derived from real-time options prices of EURO STOXX 50 and are designed to reflect the market's predictions of volatility in the near- to long-term period by calculating the implied variance among all options with a specific expiration date. A higher level of volatility implies that investors are shelling out more money for options premiums in order to hedge against potential drops in stock prices. Thus, the outbreak of war has resulted in a noticeable negative change in predictions concerning the financial markets, as shown by the increase in the index of volatility to 45 points (Figure 4.9).

Another noteworthy index is the STOXX Europe 600, which represents publicly traded firms with large, medium and small capital from the major European countries. It provides a thorough examination of Europe's developed economies, with a wide range of country and industry allocations, encompassing nearly 90% of the

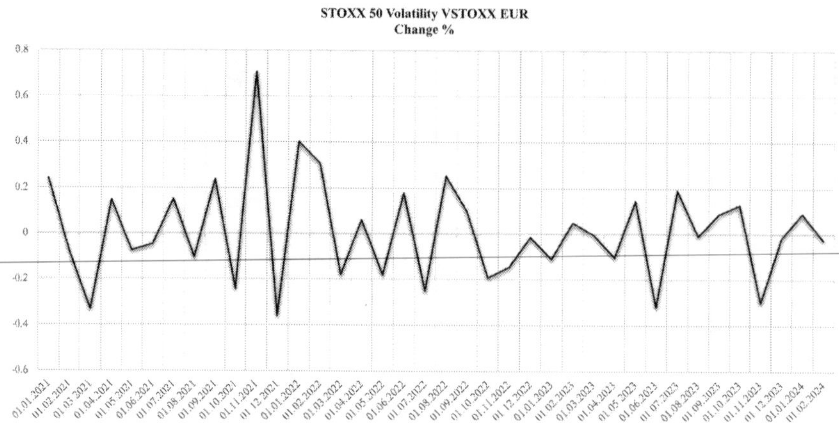

Figure 4.8 Euro Area Stock Market Index (EU50), 2014–2024

Source: Based on data from Trading Economics (2023a).

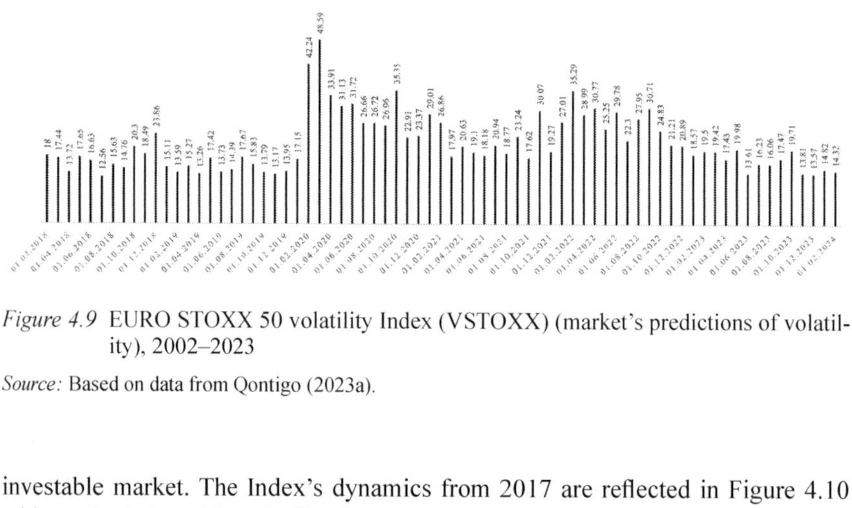

Figure 4.9 EURO STOXX 50 volatility Index (VSTOXX) (market's predictions of volatility), 2002–2023

Source: Based on data from Qontigo (2023a).

investable market. The Index's dynamics from 2017 are reflected in Figure 4.10 with particularly evident decline in 2022. Nonetheless, it is also important to consider the Sentix Economic Index, which reflects the level of investors' participation in the stock market. Data indicates a highly pessimistic sentiment among investors in the Euro area, along with a decline in value of equities in Europe following the onset of war (Sentix, 2023c).

Shaker et al. (2022) employed firms belonging to the STOXX Europe 600 index as a sample for investigating the influence of war on European financial market. Through the implementation of the event study approach, they observed a notable and adverse average abnormal returns within the event windows, specifically a decline of 0.41% on the event day, representing the largest decrease in stock values during the event period. The European stock market showed a significant

Figure 4.10 The STOXX Europe 600 Index (EU 600), 2015–2023

Source: Based on data from Trading Economics (2023b).

decrease in cumulative abnormal returns during the event days, pre-event days, and post-event days, indicating the adverse effects of the Russia–Ukraine crisis. They also noted a significant fluctuation in both average and cumulative abnormal returns during the event period taking into account the varying reactions of stock prices at the industry level. Additionally, it was noted that Dutch firms showed the most negative average abnormal returns, while businesses in the United Kingdom saw a significant positive average abnormal returns on the day of the event. During the event and the pre-event periods, it was noted that firms located in both Denmark and Switzerland experienced considerable drops in cumulative abnormal returns, highlighting a distinct disparity in the stock price reactions to the crisis at a country-wide level. Finally, the study revealed that small and medium-sized businesses suffered more from the crisis than large corporations.

The next STOXX Eastern Europe 300 Index is based on the STOXX Eastern Europe Total Market Index (TMI). across 18 countries in Eastern Europe, the STOXX Eastern Europe 300 Index comprises 300 components and includes companies of various sizes in terms of market capitalisation: Bulgaria, Croatia, Cyprus, Czech Republic, Estonia, Greece, Hungary, Latvia, Lithuania, Macedonia, Poland, Romania, Russia, Serbia, Slovak Republic, Slovenia, Turkey, and Ukraine. Thus, Figure 4.11 shows a sharp decline of the Index to 44,484 in March 2022.

The impact of the war on particular sectors can be assessed by analysing the STOXX Sector indices accessible for both global and regional markets, including Europe, the Eurozone, and Eastern Europe (Qontigo, 2023c). Companies are classified based on their primary source of income using the Industry Classification Benchmark (ICB) nomenclature. The classification system consists of four levels, which range from general to specific: ten industries are divided into 19 supersectors, 41 sectors, and 114 subsectors. There are 11 industries, 20 supersectors, 45 sectors, 173 subsectors. Table 4.1 shows that almost all of 20 ICB industries in the

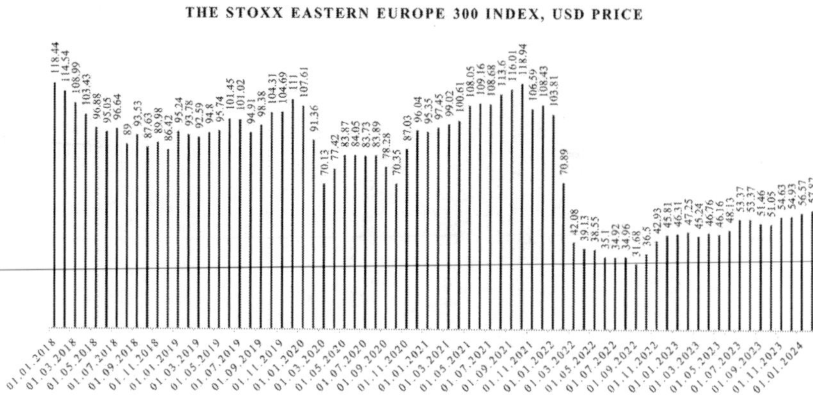

Figure 4.11 The STOXX Eastern Europe 300 Index, 2006–2023

Source: Based on data from Qontigo (2023b).

Table 4.1 The STOXX Sector indices for Europe 600, Eastern Europe 300, and global market in 2022–2023 (gross return in % and volatility in %)

The STOXX Sector indices	*2023 gross return in %*	*2023 volatility in %*	*2023 gross return in %*	*2023 volatility in %*	*2022 gross return in %*
	STOXX Europe 600		*Eastern Europe 300*		*Global 1800*
Health Care	21,09	13,99	**−16,58**	17,93	**−10,72**
Technology	4,91	24,43	5,49	21,24	**−18,25**
Energy	5,22	0,23	**−25,83**	54,6	15,87
Basic Resources	23,39	28,22	**−22,42**	42,65	6,11
Utilities	17,48	15,85	2,39	22,31	**−7,88**
Food & Beverage	23,59	12,7	**−22,42**	25,19	**−0,36**
Telecommunications	14,15	14,04	**−4,26**	17,34	**−4,72**
Insurance	13,8	16,88	4,98	26,59	**1,03**
Industrial Goods & Services	8,77	18,63	**−24,33**	28,99	**−11,14**
Retail	**−3,14**	19,85	**−33,38**	31,9	**−15,55**
Automobile & Parts	13,63	0,2	5,66	41,4	**−15,55**
Construction & Materials	33,38	0,17	**−15,51**	29,78	**−13,34**
Banks	29,87	0,2	**−14,92**	37,75	N/D
Consumer Products and Services	10,52	0,2	**−30,66**	27,27	**−14,99**

Note: The bold values represent particularly evident decline in the STOXX Sector indices (gross return in %)

Source: Own elaboration based on Qontigo (2023c).

STOXX Global 1800 have had a negative return in 2022. Besides, the gross return for Eastern Europe 300 in 2023 is considerably worse than that of STOXX Europe 600, along with a significantly higher degree of volatility. The price of Brent oil has jumped more than 30% to above \$100 a barrel, the highest since 2014, while the CRB Commodity Index has climbed 22% in 2022.

Considering expectations within the Euro Area, the ZEW Economic Sentiment Index is a tool used by analysts to measure their opinion regarding economic developments in the next six months. The index is derived from the contrast between the percentage of analysts with a positive outlook and the percentage of analysts with a negative outlook on the economy's development. Thus, the ZEW indicator assesses the level of confidence on a range of −100 (indicating a consensus among analysts for economic downturn) to 100 (indicating a consensus for economic growth). A score of 0 signifies a neutral outlook.

The results of the survey in December 2023 showed that 37.6% of analysts expected an improvement in economic conditions, 47.8% predicted stability, and 14.6% anticipated a deterioration. In November, the ZEW Indicator jumped to 13.8 from 2.3 in previous month, while in December 2023, it saw a significant increase of 9.2 points, reaching a ten-month high of 23 and surpassing market predictions of 11.2. At the same time, the current economic situation indicator dropped by 0.9 points to −62.7 and inflation expectations surged by 14.5 points to −58.2. Forecast suggests that such positive trend will also continue in 2024 (Figures 4.12 and 4.13).

According to Qontigo's Brown, "studies have shown that most conflicts have not had a lasting impact on equity markets – share prices tend to rise after a period and even become less volatile" and that's exactly what we have observed in 2023. In the meantime, the future remains uncertain, and as a result, we can consider two potential scenarios. The first one – increasing tensions in Eastern Europe and its negative implications on financial markets. And the second one – stable situation or even frozen conflict without negative effects.

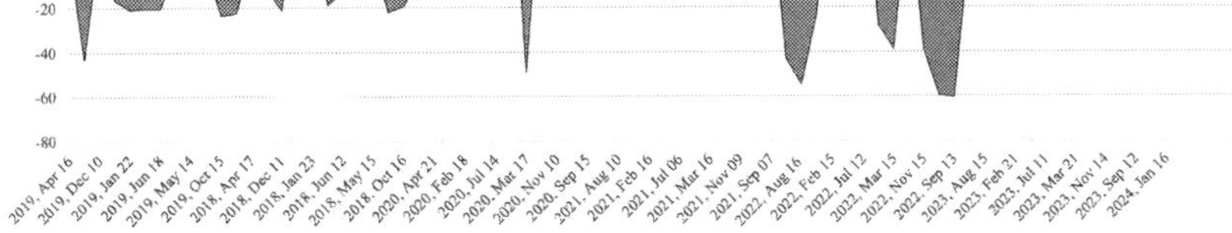

Figure 4.12 Euro Area ZEW Economic Sentiment Index, 2000–2022

Source: Based on data from Trading Economics (2023c).

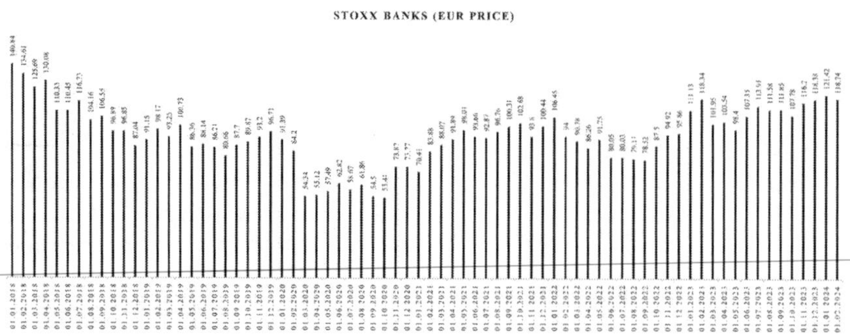

Figure 4.13 Euro Area ZEW Economic Sentiment Index, 2020–2024

Source: Based on data from Trading Economics (2023c).

4.5 Banking Sector versus War in Ukraine

According to existing research, banks and firms of countries near a war zone are likely to face a more severe penalty. Among industries, the European banking sector was particularly vulnerable to the effects of military conflicts. According to forecasts, the European economy may experience stagflation, leading to a potential decline in financial conditions for firms and households, a delay in investments, increased uncertainty among investors, and a weakening of business confidence. As a result, banking activity declines while non-performing loans increase, resulting in reduced future cash flows and financial market value for banks. The expected decrease in the stock market price of European banks can be linked to the change in investor sentiment due to war risk, affecting their optimal investment portfolio. A common practice among investors is to rebalance their portfolio by transitioning out of 'war-sensitive' industries, including the banking sector, and into industries deemed to be less risky.

Using an event study, for the 100 largest European listed banks, Martins et al. (2023) observed a negative and statistically significant stock price reaction at the beginning of the military conflict. As to the authors, the magnitude of the stock market reaction to the military conflict is reinforced or mitigated by bank-specific determinants, such as size, profitability, risk aversion, operational efficiency level, institutional ownership, and exposure to Russia.

According to the EBA (2023a; 2023b), the direct impact of Russia and Ukraine on financial stability is not significant, but the uncertainty surrounding the outcome of the war and its potential impact on the global and EU economy is a major concern. Thus, macroeconomic and geopolitical uncertainty remains high. Banks' direct asset exposures to Russia and Ukraine are mainly concentrated in a few countries and a limited number of financial institutions. Banks from Austria, France, and Italy reported the most significant level of exposure to Russian counterparts, while banks from Austria, France, and Hungary had notable exposure to Ukraine. Only Austrian and Hungarian banks reported more than 2% of their total exposures towards both. A vast majority of the overall financial risk pertains to loans and advancements, primarily directed towards non-financial businesses, specifically in the manufacturing (valued at EUR 16 billion) and mining and quarrying (valued at EUR 9 billion) industries (EBA, 2023b). A cumulative amount of EUR 82 billion has been accumulated through deposits made by counterparties from Russia and Ukraine.

While banks' profitability and capital ratios rose, loan growth was hindered by macroeconomic uncertainty. In 2023, the euro area institutions experienced a steady increase in their four-quarter trailing return on equity (ROE), reaching 8.9% in the second quarter, a level not seen in 15 years (ECB, 2023). ROE has experienced significant growth in recent years, largely due to the increase in net interest income (NII). The increase in lending activities was the primary catalyst for NII growth during the first quarter, while an expansion in margins played a significant role in the improved NII levels in the second quarter. Based on third quarter earnings reports from listed banks, it appears that the profitability of euro area banks remained relatively stable in the end of 2023 (ECB, 2023). Meanwhile, it is predicted to decrease gradually in the upcoming quarters due to the anticipated stabilisation or small rise in interest rates, as well as a gradual increase in operating expenses.

Decreased economic growth has a negative effect on loan growth. The Eurozone's private sector is already feeling the impact of stricter financing conditions, resulting in a slowdown in lending. Outstanding loans for both households and non-financial corporates showed no change over the second quarter of 2023. Credit risk is steadily rising, particularly for exposures that are susceptible to increases in interest rates. The rising trend of corporate bankruptcies in the EU suggests a decrease in asset quality at banks in the coming years. On average, asset quality remains strong, though there has been an uptick in non-performing loan (NPL) volumes in a few countries. Additionally, data suggests that for certain portfolios, asset quality may decline at a faster rate in the future.

Following the February 24 invasion, the STOXX index for European banks experienced a sharp decline of 60%, dropping to 71.546 on February 28, making it one of the weakest performing sectors in the region (Figure 4.14). In a like manner, the WIG index for Polish banks has experienced a substantial decrease, falling from around 9,300 in February to 4,600 in October of the same year (Figure 4.15).

The eventual economic expenses resulting from the ongoing war and its influence on different areas of the economy are heavily influenced by the progression of the political-military situation and the duration of military campaigns. However, it is already evident that these ongoing endeavours play a significant role in European economy and, consequently, in the functioning of the financial sector.

The Office of the Polish Financial Supervision Authority reported that the Polish banking sector held PLN 2,572.5 billion in total assets at the close of December 2021, making up 72.2% of the overall assets in the financial sector (NBP, 2022). Loans and other liabilities were the primary components of the asset structure in the Polish banking sector, comprising 55.6% of total assets by the end of 2021. In 2022, the net financial result of the banking sector amounted to 12.4 billion PLN, in comparison with 6,1 billion PLN in 2021 (NBP, 2023). The balance sheet total increased by 6.5% y/y and amounted to 2,723.5 billion PLN. The value of loans for

Figure 4.14 STOXX Banks (EUR), 2019–2023

Source: Based on data from Google Finance.

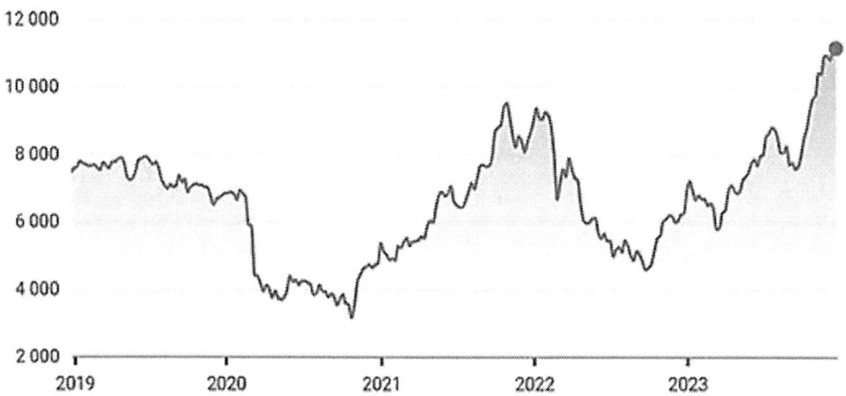

Figure 4.15 WIG Banks Index, 2019–2023

Source: Based on data from Google Finance.

the non-financial sector decreased by 1.4% y/y to 1,169.4 billion PLN, while the value of deposits of this sector increased by 6.5% y/y to 1,637.0 billion PLN (Statistics Poland, 2023). In contrast, EU countries have the highest percentage of total assets in the form of loans and advances (62%) in 2023, with cash balances and debt securities making up 13% and 12%, respectively. Derivatives make up 6% of total assets, while equity holdings account for only 1%. The average compound annual growth rate (CAGR) of loans during the period of 2015–2021 was 4.5%, while the average annual growth rate of total assets – 8.3%, suggesting a systematic decline in the share of loans in the banking sector's assets from 69% in 2015 (a decline of 13.4% points) (Statista, 2023).

By the end of 2021, the Polish banking sector had an average short-term liquidity coverage ratio (LCR) of 176%, surpassing the minimum requirement of 100% (NBP, 2022). Since January 1, 2015, banks have been required to keep a minimum of 60% in high-quality liquid assets (HQLA) in order to survive potential 30-day liquidity challenges. This minimum requirement was to increase annually by 10% until it reaches 100% as of 2019. By March 2023, all European nations had successfully fulfilled this minimum requirement. The highest liquidity coverage ratio among European countries was recorded in Lithuania (419.7%), followed by Cyprus (331.8%) and Slovenia (272.9%) (Statista, 2023).

The average NSFR levels of EU banks remain high, consistently above 120%. This suggests that despite unfavourable external and internal conditions, resulting, among other things, from the introduced epidemic emergency in 2020, the stability of the banking sector was not shaken. A strong influence in this context was exerted by the actions of public institutions directed not only to the entities of the financial sector (delays to the enactment dates for specific banking regulations, modifications, and exemptions regarding oversight of capital and liquidity standards, revisions to the level of macroprudential buffers, launch of a government bond buying scheme), but also to households and businesses (credit moratoria, direct subsidies, preferential credit terms). These actions prevented the loan portfolio from declining in quality, halted the suspension of lending to businesses and households, maintained stable liquidity and capital ratios, and safeguarded the overall stability of the financial sector.

The banking sector reports revealed a promising forecast for its growth in the upcoming months. Nevertheless, the dramatic events of Russia's invasion of Ukraine on February 24, 2022, led to a significant change and a surge of uncertainty surrounding European economic prospects and the stability of its financial sector. The ongoing conflict makes it nearly impossible to estimate the ultimate expenses of the war and its repercussions on the economy.

According to Jakubowski (2016), conflicts have multifaceted and long-lasting consequences that hinder a country's development opportunities for years. The increasing interconnectedness of the world and economic ties has a significant impact on countries that are not directly participating in armed conflicts, particularly neighbouring nations. Poland, situated next to Ukraine, Russia, and Belarus, from where Russian forces initiated their assault on Ukraine during the early stages of the conflict, faces a significant geopolitical disadvantage. According to Mackinder's Heartland theory, the position of Poland – dividing Western and Eastern Europe, including Russia – holds great strategic value (Dobija, 2019: 45). This theory posits that the one who wields influence over Eastern Europe also holds sway over the Heartland and the World Island, thus having control over the entire world (Eberhardt, 2011: 252). Poland faces a potential risk due to its predominantly low-lying terrain, as this makes it an easily traversable buffer zone between Eastern and Western Europe. This holds particular significance in the ongoing conflict, as it marks the start of a modern-day Cold War, with Poland standing on the opposing side of the 'Iron Curtain'.

Recognising the influence of the war in Ukraine on the European economy is important, especially its impact on the banking sector. The smooth and efficient

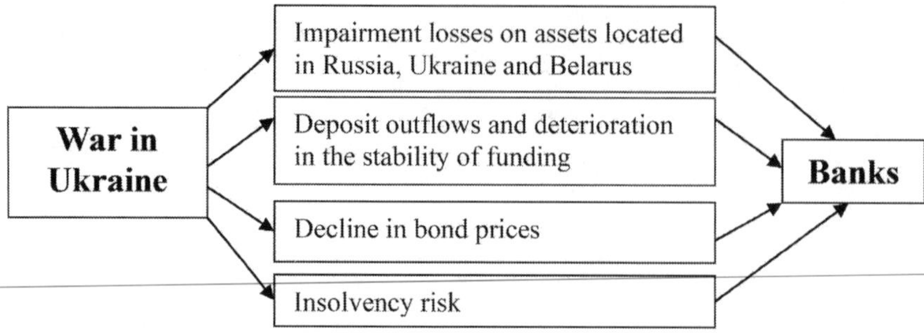

Figure 4.16 The main channels of impact of the war in Ukraine on the banking sector in Europe

Source: Own elaboration.

operation of banks plays a vital role in facilitating the movement of funds between liquidity donors and recipients contributing to the growth of consumption, production, and productivity of the economy (Mishkin, 2013: 54). Figure 4.16 illustrates the varying channels that impact the banking sector.

The initial channel of influence involves both on-balance sheet and off-balance sheet exposures to assets of countries directly engaged in the conflict, including Russia, Belarus, and Ukraine. A second direct channel is linked to heightened volatility and risk premiums, which have an impact on the valuation of bank exposures at market value. When it comes to Poland, treasury bonds play a crucial role in this context, as they hold a considerable share in banks' balance sheets in comparison to other countries within the European Union (Bańbuła & Borsuk, 2022). A decrease in bond value could lead to a reduction in the banks' capital and their own funds. Along with this, the second channel will address the effects of heightened unpredictability in the foreign exchange market and the energy, agricultural, and metals commodity markets, worsening inflation. Implementing an expansionary monetary policy in such circumstances may further exacerbate the stock market correction and heighten strain in financial markets. The third channel, meanwhile, involves supply and demand factors that affect the financial sector indirectly. Disruptions in supply chains and trade restrictions, such as sanctions, will have a significant impact on aggregate supply, while rising inflation and uncertainty surrounding socio-economic changes will affect aggregate demand. Rising inflation is mainly driven by the increased costs of grains and oils, nitrogen fertilisers, energy resources, and the depreciation of the national currency (PIE, 2022).

For instance, with food expenses making up a considerable portion of consumer expenditures in certain European countries, any rise in prices within this sector could potentially worsen the decrease in disposable income. This will lead to a decline in the willingness to spend, which has been a major driving force behind economic advancement in recent years. As time goes on, the coming together of these circumstances may prompt banks to heighten credit risk by adjusting to a decline in disposable household income, enforcing stricter credit policies, and decreasing private investment. The exceptional convergence of unfavourable factors may give rise to grave concerns in the actual economy, potentially causing a direct effect on the decline of financial institutions, including those in the banking sector, jeopardising their stability. Kichurchak (2019: 145-146) identifies another challenge for the banking sector. He believes that war, even unconventional one, leads to a loss of trust in banking institutions, which poses a significant risk to the country's economic security due to the withdrawal of deposits from the banking system. Gurgul (2010: 86) contends that a sudden depletion of deposits can have a detrimental impact on the perception of a particular financial institution, potentially causing its downfall in the future. Hence, it is crucial to determine a fourth potential channel for the effect of the Ukrainian conflict on the banking industry – specifically, the potential depletion of bank deposits. It is imperative to understand that this is not limited to nations directly impacted by armed conflicts. As affirmed by Gurgul (2010: 86), a sudden depletion of deposits can deepen the erosion of trust in a specific financial institution, potentially leading to its collapse in the long term.

Final Considerations and Conclusions

The growing geopolitical risks associated with the war in Ukraine have undoubtedly affected financial stability in Europe. Mechanisms of influence on the financial system in direct and indirect ways are diverse and complex (Figure 4.17). The immediate effects, operating through the direct channel, have already been observed in the initial weeks of the armed conflict in Ukraine. According to the

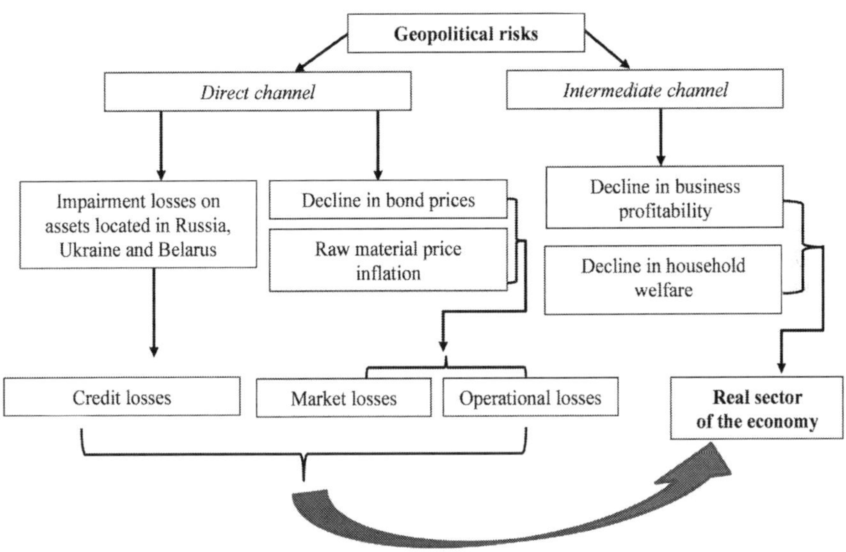

Figure 4.17 The influence of war on the financial system

Source: Own elaboration.

EBA Risk Dashboard quarterly report (2023b), "the sanctions imposed on Russia represent a high operational risk (including legal and reputational risks for banks)". As a result of geopolitical tensions and the war in Ukraine, the banking sector faced an increase in market risk. The outbreak of war has contributed to changes in the foreign exchange market and the market of agricultural, energy, and metals commodities. The currencies of Central and Eastern European countries depreciated compared to their base currencies, as a result of these countries' greater vulnerability to the direct effects of the war due to their geographic location, stronger trade relations with Russia and Ukraine, and greater dependence on energy commodity imports from Russia. Thus, geopolitical risks directly led to the bank, market, and operational losses which affect the real sector of the economy and result in the decline in business profitability and household welfare (Figure 4.20).

The economic outlook for the Eurozone has seen significant declines, with the Sentix Economic Index experiencing its lowest level in 2022 since November 2020 due to the Ukraine crisis. The macroNEXT service's indices for the Eurozone also indicate a challenging economic climate influenced by financial concerns, energy supply instability, and the increasing possibility of military conflict escalation. Despite these challenges, there are signs of improvement. The Sentix Report shows a slight increase in the overall index for the Eurozone in November and December 2023. Investors, both professional and private, are displaying decreased medium-term scepticism, leading to a recovery in economic expectations.

The short-term impact of the war on financial markets is evident, with significant disruptions observed in global indices, including STOXX® Global 1800, AEX, S&P 500, NASDAQ, Dow Jones, Euro Stoxx, FTSE 250, CAC40, and MSCI World, while Europe, being in proximity to the conflict zone, experienced a notable decline in developed-market stocks. However, despite the initial market turmoil, the EURO STOXX 50 reached its peak at the end of 2023, while projections suggest a positive trajectory in the coming months.

The ZEW Economic Sentiment Index reflects analysts' confidence in economic developments in the Euro Area. Despite obstacles, the index recorded a noteworthy surge in December 2023, exceeding market projections. The ZEW Economic Sentiment Index forecasts continued positive trends in 2024.

In the meantime, although conflicts historically do not have a lasting impact on equity markets, the future remains uncertain. Two potential scenarios include increasing tensions with negative implications for financial markets or a stable situation without adverse effects. In general, the Ukrainian war has had a diverse effect on financial markets, presenting both obstacles and potential opportunities. It is essential to continuously track important indices and indicators in order to fully comprehend the constantly changing economic situation.

References

Agyei, S. K., Owusu Junior, P., Bossman, A., Asafo-Adjei, E., Asiamah, O., & Adam, A. M. (2022). Spillovers and Contagion between BRIC and G7 Markets: New Evidence from Time-Frequency Analysis. *PLoS ONE 17*(7). https://doi.org/10.1371/journal.pone.0271088

Akhtaruzzaman, M., Boubaker, S., & Umar, Z. (2022). COVID-19 Media Coverage and ESG Leader Indices. *Finance Research Letters 45*(102170). https://doi.org/10.1016/j.frl.2021.102170

Albaity, M., Saadaoui Mallek, R., & Mustafa, H. (2023). Heterogeneity of Investor Sentiment, Geopolitical Risk and Economic Policy Uncertainty: Do Islamic Banks Differ during COVID-19 Pandemic? *International Journal of Emerging Markets*. https://doi.org/10.1108/IJOEM-11-2021-1679

Albrecht, P., Kapounek, S., & Kučerová, Z. (2022). Economic Policy Uncertainty and Stock Markets' Comovements. *International Journal of Finance & Economics 28*(4): 3471–3487. https://doi.org/10.1002/ijfe.2603

Arouri, M., Estay, C., Rault, C., & Roubaud, D. (2016). Economic Policy Uncertainty and Stock Markets: Long-Run Evidence from the US. *Finance Research Letters 18*: 136–141.

Bańbuła, P., & Borsuk, M. (2022, September 07). Wpływ wojny w Ukrainie na stabilność krajowego sektora bankowego. Obserwator Finansowy. https://www.obserwatorfinansowy.pl/-tematyka/rynki-finansowe/bankowosc/wplyw-wojny-w-ukrainie-na-stabilnosc-krajowego-sektora-bankowego/

Bedowska-Sojka, B., Demir, E., & Zaremba, A. (2022). Hedging Geopolitical Risks with Different Asset Classes: A Focus on the Russian Invasion of Ukraine. *Finance Research Letters 50*(103192). https://doi.org/10.1016/j.frl.2022.103192

Bilski, J., Janicka, M., & Miziołek, T. (2016). *Międzynarodowy System Finansowy*. Wydawnictwo Uniwersytetu Łódzkiego.

Bossman, A., & Gubareva, M. (2023). Asymmetric Impacts of Geopolitical Risk on Stock Markets: A Comparative Analysis of the E7 and G7 Equities during the Russian–Ukrainian Conflict. *Heliyon 9*(2). https://doi.org/10.1016/j.heliyon.2023.e13626

Bossman, A., Gubareva, M., & Teplova, T. (2023a). EU Sectoral Stocks Amid Geopolitical Risk, Market Sentiment, and Crude Oil Implied Volatility: An Asymmetric Analysis of the Russia–Ukraine Tensions. *Resources Policy 82*(103515). https://doi.org/10.1016/j.resourpol.2023.103515

Bossman, A., Gubareva, M., & Teplova, T. (2023b). Asymmetric Effects of Geopolitical Risk on Major Currencies: Russia–Ukraine Tensions. *Finance Research Letters 51*(103440). https://doi.org/10.1016/j.frl.2022.103440

Boungou, W., & Yatié, A. (2022). The Impact of the Ukraine–Russia War on World Stock Market Returns. *Economics Letters 215*(110516). https://doi.org/10.1016/j.econlet.2022.110516

Chowdhury, E. K., & Khan, I. I. (2023). Reactions of Global Stock Markets to the Russia–Ukraine War: An Empirical Evidence. *Asia-Pacific Financial Markets*. https://doi.org/10.1007/s10690-023-09429-4

Dobija, M. (2019). Geopolityczne czynniki innowacyjnego rozwoju Polski i krajów Trójmorza. *Nierówności Społeczne a Wzrost Gospodarczy 59*(3): 44–60. https://doi.org/10.15584/nsawg.2019.3.3

EBA. (2023a). Monitoring of Liquidity Coverage Ratio and Net Stable Funding Ratio Implementation in The EU Third Report (EBA/REP/2023/19). Publications Office of the European Union. https://www.eba.europa.eu/sites/default/files/document_library/Publications/Reports/2023/1056438/EBA%20report%20on%20LCR%20and%20NSFR%20implementation.pdf

EBA. (2023b). Risk Assessment Report of the European Banking Authority, (December 2023). Publications Office of the European Union. https://www.eba.europa.eu/sites/default/files/2023-12/ed14314d-3194-4808-935b-afc564f748ad/Risk%20Assessment%20Report%20December%202023.pdf

Eberhardt, P. (2011). Koncepcja Heartlandu Halforda Mackindera. *Przegląd Geograficzny 83*(2): 251–266.

ECB. (2023). Financial Stability Review, (November 2023). https://www.ecb.europa.eu/pub/pdf/fsr/ecb.fsr202311~bfe9d7c565.en.pdf

EPU. (2023). Monthly EPU Indices for 22 Countries. UpToDate. Retrieved November 26, 2023, from https://www.policyuncertainty.com/all_country_data.html

European Council. (2023). Impact of Russia's Invasion of Ukraine on the Markets: EU Response. https://www.consilium.europa.eu/en/policies/eu-response-ukraine-invasion/impact-of-russia-s-invasion-of-ukraine-on-the-markets-eu-response/

Google Finance. (2023). Indeks. Data. UpToDate. Retrieved December 17, 2023, from https://www.google.com/finance/

Gubareva, M. (2021). The Impact of Covid-19 on Liquidity of Emerging Market Bonds. *Finance Research Letters 41*(101826). https://doi.org/10.1016/j.frl.2020.101826

Gubareva, M., & Umar, Z. (2020). Emerging Market Debt and the COVID-19 Pandemic: A Time–Frequency Analysis of Spreads and Total Returns Dynamics. *International Journal of Finance & Economics 28*(1): 112–126. https://doi.org/10.1002/ijfe.2408

Gubareva, M., Umar, Z., Teplova, T., & Antonyuk, V. (2023a). For Whom Does It Pay to Be a Moral Capitalist? Sustainability of Corporate Financial Performance of ESG Investment. *PLoS ONE 18*(5), e0285027. https://doi.org/10.1371/journal.pone.0285027

Gubareva, M., Umar, Z., Teplova, T., & Vo, X. V. (2023b). Flights-to-Quality from EM Bonds to Safe-Haven US Treasury Securities: A Time-Frequency Analysis. *Emerging Markets Finance and Trade 59*(2): 338–362. https://doi.org/10.1080/1540496X.2022.2103399

Gulen, H., & Ion, M. (2016). Policy Uncertainty and Corporate Investment. *The Review of Financial Studies 29*(3): 523–564.

Gupta, R., Subramaniam, S., Bouri, E., & Ji, Q. (2021). Infectious Disease-Related Uncertainty and the Safe-Haven Characteristic of US Treasury Securities. *International Review of Economics and Finance 71*: 289–298.

Gurgul, G. (2010). Problemy sektora bankowego powstałe w wyniku oddziaływania światowego kryzysu gospodarczego w latach 2007–2009. *Zeszyty Naukowe Uniwersytetu Szczecińskiego. Współczesne Problemy Ekonomiczne. Globalizacja. Liberalizacja. Etyka 2*: 85–91.

Hanif, W., Mensi, W., Gubareva, M., & Teplova, T. (2023). Impacts of COVID-19 on Dynamic Return and Volatility Spillovers between Rare Earth Metals and Renewable Energy Stock Markets. *Resources Policy 80*(103196). https://doi.org/10.1016/j.resourpol.2022.103196

Hung, N. T., & Vo, X. V. (2021). Directional Spillover Effects and Time-Frequency Nexus between Oil, Gold and Stock Markets: Evidence from pre and during COVID-19 Outbreak. *International Review of Financial Analysis 76*(101730). https://doi.org/10.1016/j.irfa.2021.101730

Jakubowski, A. (2016). Społeczno-gospodarcze skutki współczesnych konfliktów zbrojnych. In E. Maj, K. Mazurek, W. Sokół, & A. Szwed-Walczak (Eds.), *Bezpieczeństwo Europy – bezpieczeństwo Polski* (pp. 71–89). UMCS.

Javaheri, B., Habibi, F., & Amani, R. (2022). Economic Policy Uncertainty and the US Stock Market Trading: Non-ARDL Evidence. *Future Business Journal 8*(36). https:// doi.org/10.1186/s43093-022-00150-8

Julio, B., & Yook, Y. (2012). Political Uncertainty and Corporate Investment Cycles. *The Journal of Finance 67*(1): 45–83. https://doi.org/10.1111/j.1540-6261.2011.01707.x

Juza, J., & Dąbrowski, B. (2021). Inwestor Europejskiego Rynku Finansowego Podczas Pandemii Covid-19. *Studia Ekonomiczne. Gospodarka. Społeczeństwo. Środowisko 2/2021*(8): 105–106.

Kichurchak, M. (2019). Bank Deposit Activity in Ukraine: Directions and Factors of Development Activation. *Journal of Eastern European and Central Asian Research 6*(1): 145–160. https://doi.org/10.15549/jeecar.v6i1.275

Klement, J. (2021). Geo-Economics: The Interplay between Geopolitics, Economics, and Investments. CFA Institute Research Foundation. https://www.cfainstitute.org//media/documents/book/rf-publication/2021/geo-economics-full.pdf

Kundu, S., & Paul, A. (2022). Effect of Economic Policy Uncertainty on Stock Market Return and Volatility under Heterogeneous Market Characteristics. *International Review of Economics & Finance 80*: 597–612. https://doi.org/10.1016/j.iref.2022.02.047

Łasak, P. (2016). Specyfika rynku finansowego w Europie. In A. Nowosad & R. Wisła (Eds.), *Zróżnicowanie rozwoju współczesnej Europy* (pp. 339–367). Wydawnictwo Uniwersytetu Jagiellońskiego.

MacroNEXT. (2023). Indeks wskaźników makroekonomicznych. UpToDate. Retrieved November 10, 2023, from https://macronext.pl/pl/wskazniki/r/1

Mallia, S., Röpke, O., & Boland, S. (2022). Rezolucja „Wojna w Ukrainie i jej skutki gospodarcze, społeczne i środowiskowe". Europejski Komitet Ekonomiczno-Społeczny. EESC.

Martins, A. M., Correia, P., & Gouveia, R. (2023). Russia-Ukraine Conflict: The Effect on European Banks' Stock Market Returns. *Journal of Multinational Financial Management 67*. https://doi.org/10.1016/j.mulfin.2023.100786

Mensi, W., Gubareva, M., Ko, H.-U., Vo, X. V., & Kang, S. H. (2023a). Tail Spillover Effects between Cryptocurrencies and Uncertainty in the Gold, Oil, and Stock Markets. *Financial Innovation 9*(92). https://doi.org/10.1186/s40854-023-00498-y

Mensi, W., Gubareva, M., Teplova, T., & Kang, S. H. (2023b). Spillover and Connectedness among G7 Real Estate Investment Trusts: The Effects of Investor Sentiment and Global Factors. *The North American Journal of Economics and Finance 66*(101919). https://doi.org/10.1016/j.najef.2023.101919

Mishkin, F. S. (2013). *The Economics of Money, Banking, and Financial Markets*. Pearson.

Naeem, M. A., Farid, S., Nor, S. M., & Shahzad, S. J. H. (2021). Spillover and Drivers of Uncertainty among Oil and Commodity Markets. *Mathematics 9*(41): 1–26.

Narayan, P. K., Devpura, N., & Wang, H. (2020). Japanese Currency and Stock Market—What Happened during the COVID-19 Pandemic? *Economic Analysis and Policy 68*: 191–198.

NBP. (2022). Raport o stabilności systemu finansowego, (June, 2022). Narodowy Bank Polski, Departament Stabilności Finansowej. https://nbp.pl/system-finansowy/raporty-o-stabilnosci-systemu-finansowego/

NBP. (2023). Raport o stabilności systemu finansowego, (December, 2023). Narodowy Bank Polski, Departament Stabilności Finansowej. https://nbp.pl/system-finansowy/raporty-o-stabilnosci-systemu-finansowego/

Pástor, Ľ., & Veronesi, P. (2012). Uncertainty about Government Policy and Stock Prices. *The Journal of Finance 67*(4), 1219–1264. https://www.jstor.org/stable/23261358

PIE. (2022). Warnomics. Gospodarcze koszty inwazji Rosji i Białorusi na Ukrainę. Polski Instytut Ekonomiczny. https://pie.net.pl/wp-content/uploads/2022/04/PIE-Raport_Warnomics.-Gospodarcze-koszty_2022.pdf

Qontigo. (2022, March 1). Ukraine Invasion: Effect on Global Stocks and Sectors [Blog posts]. https://qontigo.com/ukraine-invasion-effect-on-global-stocks-and-sectors/

Qontigo. (2023a). Indices. EURO STOXX 50® Volatility (VSTOXX®). UpToDate. Retrieved December 15, 2023, from https://qontigo.com/index/V2TX/

Qontigo. (2023b). The STOXX Eastern Europe 300 Index. UpToDate. Retrieved December 15, 2023, from https://qontigo.com/index/eebp/

Qontigo. (2023c). Stoxx Supersector Indices. UpToDate. Retrieved December 12, 2023, from https://www.stoxx.com/discovery-search?category=flagship&superType=supersector&indexFamily=standard

Rebucci, A., Hartley, J. S., & Jiménez, D. (2022). An Event Study of COVID-19 Central Bank Quantitative Easing in Advanced and Emerging Economies. In A. Chudik, C. Hsiao, & A. Timmermann (Eds.), *Essays in honor of M. Hashem Pesaran: Prediction and macro modeling*. Advances in econometrics (pp. 291–322). Emerald Publishing Limited. https://doi.org/10.1108/S0731-90532021000043A014

Sentix. (2022). Sentix Economic Index: Ukraine Crisis Causes Economy to Slump Drastically (March 06, 2022). https://www.sentix.de/

Sentix. (2023a). Sentix Economic Index: Small Ray of Hope, but No All-Clear (November 06, 2023). https://www.sentix.de/

Sentix. (2023b). Sentix Economic Index: Trend Reversal or not – That Is the Question! (December 04, 2023). https://www.sentix.de/

Sentix. (2023c). Global Investor Survey. Commentary of the Latest Results (No. 47, November 26, 2023). https://www.sentix.de/

Shaker, A., Hasan, M. M., & Kamal, M. R. (2022). Russia–Ukraine Crisis: The Effects on the European Stock Market. *European Financial Management 29*(4): 1078–1118. https://doi.org/10.1111/eufm.1238

Shen, L., & Hong, Y. (2023). Can Geopolitical Risks Excite Germany Economic Policy Uncertainty: Rethinking in the Context of the Russia–Ukraine Conflict. *Finance Research Letters 51*(103420). https://doi.org/10.1016/j.frl.2022.103420

Statista. (2023). Liquidity Coverage Ratio (LCR) of Banks in Europe as of March 2023, by Country. UpToDate. Retrieved December 11, 2023, from https://www.statista.com/statistics/909924/liquidity-coverage-ratio-in-europe-by-country/

Statistics Poland. (2023). Financial Results of Banks in 2022 (April 04, 2023) [News releases]. https://stat.gov.pl/en/topics/economic-activities-finances/financial-results/financial-results-of-banks-in-2022,6,28.html

Sun, M., Song, H., & Zhang, C. (2022). The Effects of 2022 Russian Invasion of Ukraine on Global Stock Markets: An Event Study Approach. *SSRN Electronic Journal*. https://doi.org/10.2139/SSRN.4051987

Sverdlov, M. Y., Seliverstov, S. I., Zinoviev, A. G., & Kuzmin, P. I. (2023). The Impact of Sanctions on Stock and Industry Indices of Countries that Initiated Sanctions and Countries Subject to Sanctions. In S. G. Maximova, R. I. Raikin, A. A. Chibilev, & M. M. Silantyeva (Eds.), *Advances in Natural, Human-Made, and Coupled Human-Natural Systems Research*. Lecture Notes in Networks and Systems, 234. Springer. https://doi.org/10.1007/978-3-030-75483-9_17

Trading Economics. (2023a). Euro Area Stock Market Index (EU50). UpToDate. Retrieved December 05, 2023, from https://tradingeconomics.com/euro-area/stock-market

Trading Economics. (2023b). The STOXX Europe 600 Index (EU 600). UpToDate. Retrieved December 05, 2023, from https://tradingeconomics.com/stoxx:ind

Trading Economics. (2023c). Euro Area ZEW Economic Sentiment Index. UpToDate. Retrieved December 07, 2023, from https://tradingeconomics.com/euro-area/zew-economic-sentiment-index

Umar, Z., Gubareva, M., & Sokolova, T. (2022a). Assessing the Impact of Media Sentiment on the Returns of Sukuks during the Covid-19 Crisis. *Applied Economics 55*(12): 1371–1387. https://doi.org/10.1080/00036846.2022.2097187

Umar, Z., Gubareva, M., & Teplova, T. (2021). The Impact of COVID-19 on Commodity Markets Volatility: Analyzing Time-Frequency Relations between Commodity Prices and Coronavirus Panic Levels. *Resources Policy 73*(102164). https://doi.org/10.1016/j.resourpol.2021.102164

Umar, Z., Gubareva, M., Teplova, T., & Alwahedi, W. (2022b). Oil Price Shocks and the Term Structure of the US Yield Curve: A Time-Frequency Analysis of Spillovers and Risk Transmission. *Annals of Operations Research*. https://doi.org/10.1007/s10479-022-04786-1

Wang, W., & Park, H. (2021). How Vulnerable Are Financial Markets to covid-19? A Comparative Study of the US and South Korea. *Sustainability 13*(10): 1–18. https://doi.org/10.3390/su13105587

WUI. (2024). Dataset. UpToDate. Retrieved December 11, 2023, from https://worlduncertaintyindex.com/data/

Xiao, J., Zhou, H., Wen, F., & Wen, F. (2018). Asymmetric Impacts of Oil Price Uncertainty on Chinese Stock Returns under Diferent Market Conditions: Evidence from Oil Volatility Index. *Energy Economics 74*(C): 777–786. https://doi.org/10.1016/j.eneco.2018.07.026

Yousaf, I., Nekhili, R., & Gubareva, M. (2022a). Linkages between DeFi Assets and Conventional Currencies: Evidence from the COVID-19 Pandemic. *International Review of Financial Analysis 81*(102082). https://doi.org/10.1016/j.irfa.2022.102082

Yousaf, I., Patel, R., & Yarovaya, L. (2022b). The Reaction of G20+ Stock Markets to the Russia–Ukraine Conflict 'black-swan' Event: Evidence from Event Study Approach. *Journal of Behavioral and Experimental Finance 35*(100723). https://doi.org/10.1016/j.jbef.2022.100723

Yousaf, I., Qureshi, S., Qureshi, F., & Gubareva, M. (2023). Connectedness of COVID Vaccination with Economic Policy Uncertainty, Oil, Bonds, and Sectoral Equity Markets: Evidence from the US. *Annals of Operations Research*. https://doi.org/10.1007/s10479-023-05267-9

5 Non-Military Involvement of the EU and the US in the Russian–Ukrainian War and Re-Definition of UE, UK, US Countries' Security Policy

Maryana Prokop

Introduction

The destabilisation in the region brought about by the war in Ukraine has significantly re-defined the way in which the category of state security is perceived. The global community was faced with the challenge of guaranteeing a stable and effective security policy and assistance to Ukraine. Russian actions on Ukrainian territory, especially missile attacks, led to the destruction of cities, critical infrastructure and, above all, threatened the life and health of civilians, resulting in massive migrations of Ukrainian citizens to seek refuge in other countries. The international environment has strongly condemned Russian military action and called for an end to it, and there have been discussions at the national level of many countries about the need for action to guarantee and strengthen their own security. European leaders and the US, taking a position on the side of the invaded state, pledged to provide all humanitarian, financial, and military assistance to support Ukraine. Russian actions degrade the security environment in Europe and are a direct attack on settled international norms, international order, as well as respect and promotion of international law. EU Member States, fearing for their security, have taken measures to strengthen their defence; in addition, they have actively participated in assisting Ukraine and, in particular, Ukrainian refugees leaving the country.

The aim of this is to analyse the degree of involvement of EU states, the US, and the UK in assisting Ukraine, as well as the actions of these states in the context of strengthening their own defence. The author undertook the task of answering two research questions:

- [Q1] To what extent have the EU countries, the UK, and the US been involved in assisting Ukraine?
- [Q2] Have these countries taken steps to strengthen their own security, and to what extent?

The following statements were taken as hypotheses:

- [H1] involvement in aid to Ukraine has become a significant action for EU states, the UK, and the US, thus presenting support for Ukraine and condemnation of Russian actions,

DOI: 10.4324/9781003435433-5

- [H2] the hostilities in Ukraine confirmed the need to act to guarantee its own security, and to this end the EU countries, the UK, and the US have acted on increasing their defence budget spending.

According to the European Parliament's recommendations of June 8, 2022, to the Council and the vice-president of the Commission / high representative of the Union for Foreign Affairs and Security Policy on the EU's foreign, security, and defence policy in the aftermath of Russia's aggression against Ukraine, the EU gives its strong support to the territorial integrity, sovereignty, and independence of Ukraine within internationally recognised borders; takes steps to provide all material, military, financial, and humanitarian assistance to Ukraine and to prepare to contribute as much as possible to its reconstruction after the war (Report on a European Parliament Recommendation, 2022).

Since the first days of the Russian aggression, the EU, the US, and other countries of the world have been involved in helping Ukraine in financial, humanitarian, and military terms. The aid provided is, therefore, intended to fulfil three very important objectives. Humanitarian aid is targeted at those affected by the Russian attacks, primarily food, medicine, clothing, and support for those displaced by the conflict. Military assistance is aimed at giving Ukraine support for the defence of its state and citizens through the provision of various types of military equipment, such as arms, ammunition, anti-missile systems and communications equipment. It also includes training for Ukrainian soldiers and logistical assistance. Financial assistance is aimed at sustaining the economic, financial, and social stability of the country, in the form of grant loans and development programmes. The main focus of this support is economic stabilisation, structural reforms, infrastructure modernisation, reconstruction of critical infrastructure, and reconstruction of areas affected by massive attacks.

Based on an analysis of financial, humanitarian, and military assistance to the Ukrainian state, researchers from the Kiel Institute of Economics in April 2022 included the EU and the US as the countries most strongly assisting Ukraine, while the involvement of the UK was also assessed. These actors provide support to Ukraine in the form of humanitarian aid through the provision of medicine, food, and essential materials. They also provide financial aid necessary for the functioning of the state in wartime conditions and for the housing of the country, and military aid in the form of weapons, which enables Ukraine to conduct effective defence and to counter Russian attacks on the civilian population and critical infrastructure. Accordingly, the subject of this part of the thesis is an analysis of the involvement of EU states, the UK, and the US in assisting Ukraine. The author has focused on providing a comprehensive overview of aid to Ukraine over the course of almost two years of the ongoing war and this has made it possible to identify which countries are most involved in aid policy for Ukraine (The Ukraine Support Tracker, 2023).

5.1 EU, UK, and US Aid Policy towards Ukraine

In preparing the data, the data used come from the report Ukraine Support Tracker, A Database of Military, Financial, and Humanitarian Aid to Ukraine prepared by researchers at the Kiel Institute for the world economy (Christoph Trebesch, Arianna Antezza, Katelyn Bushnell, Pietro Bomprezzi, Yelmurat Dyussimbinov, Andre Frank, Pascal Frank, Lukas Franz, Ivan Kharitonov, Bharath Kumar, Ekaterina Rebinskaya, Christopher Schade, Stefan Schramm, and Leon Weiser). The data collected include information on financial, military, and humanitarian assistance activities to Ukraine in the period from January 24, 2022, to October 31, 2023, realised by 41 countries. For the purposes of this chapter of the study, only EU countries, the UK, and the US are included. As noted in the chapter, country support data includes bilateral commitments to Ukraine. It does not include private donations, support for refugees outside Ukraine, or assistance from international organisations. Commitments were made by EU Institutions including Commission and Council, EPF and EIB, among others. Financial commitments made explicitly for military and arms purchases are counted as military assistance (The Ukraine Support Tracker, 2023).

The undisputed leader in aid to Ukraine is the US, whose aid reached over US$75.4 billion in total, of which US$ 26.37 billion was financial aid, US$ 2.71 billion humanitarian aid, and US$46.33 billion military aid (Ukraine Supplemental Appropriations Act, 2022; Additional Ukraine Supplemental Appropriations Act, 2022; Additional Ukraine Supplemental Appropriations Act, 2023; Continuing Appropriations and Ukraine Supplemental Appropriations Act, 2023).

Considering the EU's involvement in total, aid to Ukraine from the EU and Member States amounted to more than US$130.64 billion, of which financial aid was US$84.02 billion, humanitarian aid US$8.78 billion, and military aid US$37.84 billion. EU (Commission and Council) aid accounted for US$81.35 billion, where as much as US$79.69 billion was financial aid and US$2.26 billion humanitarian aid; no military aid was recorded. EU Member States' involvement in aid to Ukraine accounted for US$49.29 billion, of which financial aid accounted for US$4.93 billion, humanitarian aid was US$6.52 billion, and military aid as much as US$37.84 billion. Thus, from the perspective of the Member States, more support was given to Ukraine in the form of military aid, while the EU (Commission and Council) did not give Ukraine this aid, and there was a greater focus on financial assistance (The Ukraine Support Tracker, 2023).

Looking at the EU's involvement in supporting Ukraine on a country-by-country basis, Germany ranked first with over US$22.14 billion, the largest share of which (US$18.01 billion) was military aid, financial aid amounted to US$1.49 billion, and humanitarian aid to US$2.56 billion. In second place is Poland, whose aid accounted for US$4.59 billion, comprising military aid of US$3.21 billion, financial aid of US$1.01 billion, and humanitarian aid of US$0.37 billion. Third place is occupied by the Netherlands, by giving aid worth US$4.4 billion (US$2.62 billion military aid, US$1.16 billion financial aid, and US$0.62 billion humanitarian aid). Fourth place goes to Denmark with a total of US$4.06 billion (US$3.70 billion – military aid US$0.3 billion – humanitarian aid, and US$0.06 billion – financial aid). The top five is rounded off by Sweden providing US$3.18 billion in aid to Ukraine, where US$2.25 billion is military aid, US$0.64 billion humanitarian aid, and US$0.21 billion financial aid.

A more detailed breakdown of the assistance of all the mentioned actors is presented in Table 5.1. It is also worth noting that each of the EU countries allocated an assistance package to Ukraine; however, we can also list the countries that dominated in only one dimension of assistance. The largest dimension of assistance of a military nature was recorded by the following countries: Germany, Poland, the Netherlands, Denmark, Sweden, Finland, Czech Republic, Italy, France, Slovakia Lithuania, Estonia, Latvia, and Belgium. No military assistance was provided to Ukraine by three countries: Austria, Hungary, Malta, Ireland, and Cyprus. Aid of a

Table 5.1 Aid to Ukraine from the EU, the UK, and the US

Country	*Financial commitments billion USD*	*Humanitarian commitments billion USD*	*Military commitments billion USD*	*Total commitments billion USD*
Austria	0.68	0.11	0	0.79
Belgium	0.02	0.11	0.32	0.45
Bulgaria	0	0	0.27	0.27
Croatia	0	0.09	0.2	0.29
Republic of Cyprus	0	0	0	0
Czech Republic	0	0.4	1.17	1.57
Denmark	0.06	0.3	3.7	4.06
Estonia	0	0.03	0.45	0.49
EU (Commission and Council)	79.09	2.26	0	81.35
Finland	0.1	0.16	1.49	1.75
France	0.84	0.38	0.57	1.8
Germany	1.49	2.56	18.1	22.14
Greece	0	0	0.2	0.2
Hungary	0	0.06	0	0.06
Ireland	0.04	0.08	0	0.13
Italy	0.43	0.23	0.73	1.4
Latvia	0.03	0.01	0.39	0.43
Lithuania	0.04	0.07	0.81	0.92
Luxembourg	0	0.02	0.12	0.14
Malta	0	0	0	0
Netherlands	1.16	0.62	2.62	4.4
Poland	1.01	0.37	3.21	4.59
Portugal	0.26	0	0.09	0.36
Romania	0	0.13	0	0.13
Slovak Republic	0.01	0.01	0.72	0.74
Slovenia	0	0.01	0.07	0.07
Spain	0.55	0.08	0.36	1
Sweden	0.21	0.72	2.25	3.18
EU countries total	4.93	6.52	37.84	49.29
EU total (Commission and Council) & EU countries	84.02	8.78	37.84	130.64
United Kingdom	6.44	0.64	6.94	14.01
United States	26.37	2.71	46.33	75.4

Source: Own compilation based on the Ukraine Support Tracker (2023).

humanitarian nature was dominated by Hungary and Ireland, while a larger spectrum of financial assistance was given by Poland, Germany, the Netherlands, and France. Eleven countries did not provide financial assistance to Ukraine: Bulgaria, Croatia, Cyprus, Czech Republic, Estonia, Greece, Hungary, Luxemburg, Malta, Romania, and Slovenia. Only Greece, Malta, and Portugal did not provide humanitarian assistance. The UK, despite not being a member of the EU as of February 1, 2020, was heavily involved in assisting Ukraine by offering $14.01 billion, where financial aid accounted for $6.44 billion, military aid $6.94 billion, and humanitarian aid $0.64 billion. State aid to refugees who have left Ukraine and received all kinds of support from state governments is not included in the given summary, as the aim of this part of the work was to present targeted aid to Ukraine (The Ukraine Support Tracker, 2023).

The table above illustrates the involvement of the EU, UK, and US states for Ukraine at the time of Russia's military aggression against the country. However, despite the ranking of the most engaged states (within the EU), it is worth pointing out that a more authoritative yardstick for the engagement of states in aid policy is to indicate how much percentage of the gross domestic product (GDP) of a given state constituted the engagement in aid to Ukraine. Countries' financial capacities vary and it was, therefore, considered best to refer to the percentage of aid to GDP of each country (Table 5.2). The table shows that the highest percentage score within country GDP was achieved by the following countries: Lithuania (1.31%), Estonia (1.28%), Latvia (1.05%), Denmark (1.03%), and Poland (0.67%). Relative to the five EU Member States with the highest aid support (Germany, Poland, the Netherlands, Denmark, and Sweden), only Denmark and Poland confirmed the result with the highest percentage of GDP.

The percentage rate of the state's GDP for military assistance is as follows: Lithuania (1.15%), Estonia (1.19%), Latvia (0.95%), Denmark (0.94%), Poland (0.47%), Slovakia (0.62%), Germany (0.44%), Finland (0.53%), Czech Republic (0.40%), Netherlands (0.26%), Sweden (0.38%), Croatia (0.26%), Bulgaria (0.28%), Luxembourg (0.14%), Slovenia (0.11%), Greece (0.09%), Belgium (0.06%), Portugal (0.04%), Spain (0.04%), Italy (0.02%), and France (0.02%). The combined result for EU Member States including EU aid (Commission and Council) represents 0.26% of GDP. For the UK and the US, it represents 0.46% and 0.30%, respectively. As the aforementioned Romania, Hungary, Ireland, Malta, and Cyprus did not give military aid to Ukraine, therefore, the score in this case is zero. In the case of the US, military aid represented 0.18% and the UK 0.23% of GDP.

Looking at aid of a financial nature, the percentage result is as follows in relation to GDP: EU (Commission and Council), where this aid represents 0.48% of EU GDP, the UK with 0.21%, Austria 0.14%, and Poland with 0.15%, the Netherlands (0.12%), Portugal (0.10%), Latvia (0.08%), Lithuania (0.06%), Spain (0.04%), Sweden (0.04%), Finland (0.03%), Germany (0.04%), France (0.03%), Italy (0.02%), Denmark (0.02%), and Ireland (0.01%). For Estonia, Belgium, Slovakia, Slovenia, Romania, Hungary, the Czech Republic, Luxemburg, Bulgaria, Croatia, and Cyprus, the commitment was zero. It is worth adding that financial aid represented 0.10% of US GDP and 0.21% of the United Kingdom.

Table 5.2 EU, UK, and US aid to Ukraine in relation to GDP

Country	*finan in GDP %*	*hum in GDP %*	*milit in GDP %*	*total in GDP %*
Austria	0.14%	0.02%	0.00%	0.16%
Belgium	0.00%	0.02%	0.06%	0.08%
Bulgaria	0.00%	0.00%	0.30%	0.30%
Croatia	0.00%	0.13%	0.28%	0.41%
Republic of Cyprus	0.00%	0.01%	0.00%	0.01%
Czech Republic	0.00%	0.14%	0.40%	0.54%
Denmark	0.02%	0.08%	0.94%	1.03%
Estonia	0.00%	0.09%	1.19%	1.28%
Finland	0.03%	0.06%	0.53%	0.61%
France	0.03%	0.01%	0.02%	0.06%
Germany	0.04%	0.06%	0.46%	0.56%
Greece	0.00%	0.00%	0.09%	0.09%
Hungary	0.00%	0.03%	0.00%	0.03%
Ireland	0.01%	0.02%	0.00%	0.03%
Italy	0.02%	0.01%	0.04%	0.07%
Latvia	0.08%	0.02%	0.95%	1.05%
Lithuania	0.06%	0.10%	1.15%	1.31%
Luxembourg	0.00%	0.02%	0.14%	0.16%
Malta	0.00%	0.01%	0.00%	0.01%
Netherlands	0.12%	0.06%	0.26%	0.44%
Poland	0.15%	0.05%	0.44%	0.64%
Portugal	0.10%	0.00%	0.04%	0.14%
Romania	0.00%	0.04%	0.00%	0.04%
Slovak Republic	0.00%	0.01%	0.62%	0.63%
Slovenia	0.00%	0.01%	0.11%	0.12%
Spain	0.04%	0.01%	0.03%	0.08%
Sweden	0.04%	0.12%	0.38%	0.54%
EU (Commission and Council)	0.48%	0.01%	0.00%	0.49%
EU TOTAL	0.53%	0.05%	0.26%	0.84%
United States	0.10%	0.01%	0.18%	0.29%
United Kingdom	0.21%	0.02%	0.23%	0.46%

Source: Own compilation based on the Ukraine Support Tracker (2023).

Humanitarian aid to Ukraine takes up 0.14% of the GDP of the Czech Republic, Sweden (0.12%), Lithuania (0.09%), Croatia (0.13%), Denmark (0.08%), the Netherlands (0.06%), Germany (0.06%), Poland (0.05%), Romania (0.04%), Hungary (0.03%), Finland (0. 06%), Estonia (0.09%), Austria (0.02%), Luxembourg (0.02%), Belgium (0.02%), France (0.01%), Latvia (0.02%), Ireland (0.02%), Malta (0.01%), Italy (0.01%), Cyprus (0.01%), Slovakia (0.01%), Slovenia (0.01%), Spain (0.01%). The countries that did not provide humanitarian assistance were Bulgaria, Portugal, and Greece. For the US the result was (0.01%) and for the UK (0.02%).

In addition to strictly financial support, these countries also provide Ukraine with military equipment and weapons. The estimated values of heavy weapons commitments for Ukraine (January 2022–October 2023) show the largest donors in billion euros. The result for the EU represents €11.85 billion, while the US accounts for €10.95 billion. The figure does not include ammunition of any kind, smaller arms or equipment, or funds earmarked for future arms purchases. Among EU countries, the largest contributors to this plan were Germany with €5.21 billion, Poland with €1.40 billion, the Netherlands with €1.24 billion, the Czech Republic with €0.74 billion, and Italy with €0.54 billion.

In 2022, the supporting states provided the armed forces of Ukraine with some 4,300 units of armoured vehicles (mainly light vehicles) and 750 artillery systems. In 2023, the allies promised Ukraine more than 1,250 units of armoured vehicles (including tanks) and an unspecified amount of artillery (mainly to repair and replace damaged weapons). Another summary in Table 5.3 includes bilateral commitments for tanks delivered to Ukraine in 2022 and 2023 (by February 24, 2023). It includes 110 Leopard-1A5 tanks for which Germany has issued an export licence and plans to deliver them jointly with the Netherlands and Denmark. The shares in this cooperation are distributed equally. The Belgian promise of 50 Leopard 1 tanks is not on the list, as the announcement has been withdrawn. The US and Dutch donations include 45 T-72 tanks each, which were purchased from Czech industry stocks, refurbished, and then transferred to Ukraine. As these tanks were purchased by the US and the Netherlands, they are not considered a Czech contribution to Ukraine. The largest number of tanks for Ukraine was delivered by Poland in 2022 – 250 units (240 T-72, 10 PT-91), and in 2023 – 74 (30 T-72, 14 Leo 2, 30 PT-91). In second place is the Czech Republic, with 66 in 2022 and 2023 – 24 (90 T-72), the Netherlands in 2022 – 45, and 2023 – 44 (45 T-72, 37 Leopard 1A5, 7 Leopard 2A4), Germany delivered 80 tanks in 2023 (62 Leopard 1A5, 18 Leo), the US in 2022 – 45 and in 2023 – 31 (45 T-72, 31 Abrams M1A2), Denmark in 2023 – 44 (37 Leopard 1A5, 7 Leopard 2A4), Slovenia – 28 (28 M-55S) in 2022, the UK – 14 (14 Challenger 2) in 2023, Sweden – 10 (10 Leopard 2A6), Spain (10 Leopard 2A4) – 10 in 2023, and Portugal in 2023 – 3 (3 Leopard 2A6). Countries, such as Finland, Latvia, Estonia, Lithuania, Bulgaria, Slovakia, Croatia, Austria, Greece, Belgium, France, Hungary, Italy, Luxembourg, Cyprus, Romania, and Ireland have not delivered any tanks (Statista, 2023a).

The presented breakdowns show that the highest score in aid to Ukraine (within the EU countries) went to Germany, which gave Ukraine more than US$23.07 billion, followed by Poland, whose aid accounted for US$4.72 billion, and in third place on the list was the Netherlands, by giving aid worth US$4.52 billion. The fourth place was occupied by Denmark with a total of US$4.22 billion, and fifth place went to Sweden by giving US$2.61 billion worth of aid. The UK supported Ukraine by offering US$15.22 billion in total aid. The leader in the breakdown of aid to Ukraine was the US, whose aid reached over US$76.83 billion in total. However, when we relate the countries' support data to the percentage score in relation to GDP, it emerges that the highest aid percentage score in relation to the country's GDP framework was achieved by the following countries: Lithuania (1.31%), Estonia (1.28%), Latvia (1.05%), Denmark (1.03%), and Poland (0.67%). Comparing the results of the five EU Member States that gave the largest support to

Table 5.3 Commitments of Main Battle Tanks in 2022 and 2023 (the UE, the UK, and the US)

Country	*Tanks in 2022*	*Tanks in 2023*	*Total tanks*
Poland	250	74	324
Czech Republic	66	24	90
Netherlands	45	44	89
Germany	0	80	80
United States	45	31	76
Denmark	0	44	44
Slovenia	28	0	28
United Kingdom	0	14	14
Sweden	0	10	10
Spain	0	10	10
Portugal	0	3	3
Finland	0	0	0
Latvia	0	0	0
Estonia	0	0	0
Lithuania	0	0	0
Bulgaria	0	0	0
Slovak Republic	0	0	0
Croatia	0	0	0
Austria	0	0	0
Greece	0	0	0
Belgium	0	0	0
France	0	0	0
Hungary	0	0	0
Italy	0	0	0
Luxembourg	0	0	0
Republic of Cyprus	0	0	0
Romania	0	0	0
Ireland	0	0	0

Source: Own compilation based on: Statista (2023a), The Ukraine Support Tracker (2023).

Ukraine in real terms (Germany, Poland, the Netherlands, Denmark, and Sweden) with the result of the percentage of GDP, only Denmark and Poland confirmed the result with the largest share of aid and percentage of GDP. Considering the delivery of tanks and heavy weapons, Poland, the Czech Republic, Germany, the Netherlands, Denmark, the US, and the UK provided the greatest support to Ukraine.

5.2 EU, US, and UK Security Policy after the Russian Aggression against Ukraine

After Russia's attack on Ukraine, the EU took decisive steps in the field of security policy, the main task of the organisation being to strive for regional and global stability and to develop all kinds of mechanisms to prevent, respond to, and mitigate the consequences of the resulting threats and conflicts. In this regard, a number of measures have been taken, such as strengthening defence, strengthening information intelligence cooperation, efforts to ensure cyber security and diplomatic efforts to continue dialogue and negotiations with Russia in order to restore stability and peace in the region. For many states, an important action was to increase defence spending from the state budget in order to modernise, increase, and improve their military. This part of the thesis undertakes the task of analysing whether, and to what extent, EU states, UK and US defence spending has changed following the Russian aggression against Ukraine.

The key document for the EU in the field of security is the 2003 *European Security Strategy*. The strategy encompasses the joint responsibility of the Member States for security, which implies the need for cooperation and solidarity in solving security problems. The strategy takes a multifaceted view of security, covering not only traditional military aspects but also economic, environmental, and social aspects. The ESS includes dialogue and diplomacy as an important instrument for conflict prevention (European Security Strategy, 2003).

In the Versailles Declaration of March 10–11, 2022, EU leaders reaffirmed that an important task for the European Union is to take greater responsibility for its own security and to work towards increasing its capacity to act independently in this regard. The importance of EU cooperation with NATO was also identified as an important point. The consensus approach of the Member States was to increase the scope of investment in defence capabilities and innovative technologies through increased defence spending, joint investments, such as joint procurement, investment in military capabilities, and strategic factors for their development, strengthening synergies in research and innovation, and the development of the EU defence industry (The Versailles Declaration, 2022). In March 2022, the Strategic Compass – an action plan to strengthen the EU's security and defence policy until 2030 – was approved. This plan included processes for joint action, securing, investing, and partnership. The action process included: developing a rapid and comprehensive response to crises by creating the capacity to rapidly deploy up to 5,000 troops for different types of crises, increasing military mobility, conducting regular tactical exercises on land and at sea, and strengthening EU Common Security and Defence Policy (CSDP) missions and operations. In the securing phase, the EU will take action to enhance intelligence analysis capabilities, establish an EU cyber defence policy to counter cyber attacks, and take action to counter foreign information manipulation. The investment process boils down to increasing defence spending by Member States, conducting exchanges on state defence spending targets, and supporting technological innovation in the area of defence. The partnership includes strengthening cooperation with strategic partners, such as NATO, UN, OSCE, ASEAN, among others, and through bilateral relations with countries, such as the US, Canada, Norway, the UK, Japan, Western Balkans, Africa, Asia, and Latin America (Strategic Compass, 2022).

In October 2022, the US administration unveiled a new *National Security Strategy for the United States of America*. The document contained two fundamental strategic challenges from the US perspective: the issue of great power rivalry over the shape of the international order and the issue of transnational common threats, such as climate change, food security threats, infectious diseases, terrorism, etc.

In the case of rivalry over the shape of the international order, China was identified as the most important rival according to the strategy, as the only state that can change the international order, and Russia, which does not pose as strong a threat to the international system as China, although the Russian Federation poses a direct and constant threat to international peace and stability. Thus, the chapter outlines the challenge of countering China and containing Russia. Given the Russian aggression against Ukraine, the strategy mentions Ukraine thirty-two times, condemning the brutal actions of Russian aggression in the country and violations of international law. Russia's pursuit of an imperial policy in the Eastern European region culminated in its assault on independent Ukraine (National Security Strategy of U. S., 2022).

The Integrated Review 2021 (IR21) document sets out the UK government's national security and international policy. It sets out core foreign policy values, assesses threats, and how to prevent and address them. It is the overarching strategy for security aims to inform and guide national, international, and domestic security policy (*The Integrated Review 2021*). *The Integrated Review Refresh 2023* (IR23) is an update of the government's security, defence, development, and foreign policy priorities to adapt to the threats that have occurred and changes in the international arena since the 2021 strategy was adopted.

> Since then, Russia's illegal invasion of Ukraine, weaponisation of energy and food supplies and irresponsible nuclear rhetoric, combined with China's more aggressive stance in the South China Sea and the Taiwan Strait, are threatening to create a world defined by danger, disorder and division – and an international order more favourable to authoritarianism.
>
> (The Integrated Review Refresh, 2023: 2)

Ukraine is mentioned as many as 68 times in the IR23 document. It identifies the promotion of self-defence and the restoration of Ukraine's sovereignty and territorial integrity as a priority. The Russian occupation of Ukraine poses a threat to GB security while attempts to destroy Ukraine are attacks on European security. The government is, therefore, committed to providing at least £2.3 billion in support to Ukraine. An important point in the document is the long-term efforts to strengthen the security of the country. As a result, defence will receive £5 billion of additional funding over two years – primarily in the areas of nuclear resilience and conventional stockpiles. Building on the record investment announced in 2020, overall UK defence spending is expected to reach 2.2% of GDP this year (2.29% when including the military support to Ukraine) (The Integrated Review Refresh, 2023: 3).

As presented in the first part of this chapter, the US, the UK, and EU countries declare their support for Ukraine in financial, humanitarian, and mainly military terms. From the US perspective, a very important activity is the work on strengthening defence in the neighbouring NATO countries with Russia (the so-called NATO Eastern Flank). From an EU perspective, it is important to protect its external borders. A clear signal presenting the fear of the Russian Federation was the creation in 2014, on the initiative of the presidents of Poland and Romania, of the Bucharest

Nine, which includes the countries on NATO's eastern border: Lithuania, Latvia, Estonia, Poland, the Czech Republic, Slovakia, Hungary, Romania, and Bulgaria. Already at that time, after the events of 2014 in Ukraine, it was understood that Russia posed a significant threat to the international order. The most important goals set by the associated states are to strengthen the eastern flank of NATO, to ensure the stability and security of the countries of Central and Eastern Europe, and to develop the military cooperation of the states (Pawłowski, 2020: 17–18).

The leaders of the Bucharest Nine adopted a joint declaration at the June 2022 summit, in which they condemned, among other things, Russia's unprovoked aggression against Ukraine and brutal violations of international law, expressed the expectation that those responsible for war crimes would be held accountable and declared support for Ukraine's Euro-Atlantic and European aspirations. The maintenance of the allied open-door policy and support for the accession of Sweden and Finland to NATO, support for the independence and territorial integrity of Moldova and Georgia, and the declaration of defence spending from national budgets at no less than 2% of GDP by 2024 (Declaration, 2022) were also important agreements.

The year of the outbreak of war in Ukraine has shown that defence spending has become very important for the countries of the world. According to the Stockholm International Peace Research Institute SIPRI Report, 2022 was the year of the highest spending in the world with US$2.24 billion spent, taking into account the defence spending in Europe increased by 13%, a record high. US$345 billion was spent by Central and Western European countries on the military (SIPRI Yearbook, 2023). According to the European Defence Agency (EDA) report for 2022, defence spending from all EU Member States was a record EUR 240 billion, an increase of 6% compared to the previous year (The Annual Report, 2022).

The Baltic States began to work most intensively on strengthening their own security, as they had identified Russia as a real threat since 2014, when the annexation of Crimea took place and the fight against separatist movements in the eastern part of the country began after the formation of the LPR and DPR. Securing the rebels with weapons by Russia became a reason to destabilise the eastern part of Ukraine. The Ukrainian side, therefore, took up arms against the separatists in order to regain control of the occupied territory. The situation escalated into an armed conflict that lasted until the Russian aggression against Ukraine on February 24, 2022. The international community including the US and the EU condemned Russia's actions and applied a series of diplomatic financial and economic sanctions against the Russian state (Tomala & Prokop, 2021: 50–55).

This invasion has only reinforced in these countries that it is worthwhile to take all kinds of measures to strengthen their own security. As presented earlier, it is Lithuania, Latvia, and Estonia that are among the leading states supporting Ukraine in terms of the percentage of this aid in their GDP. The war in Ukraine has contributed to increased defence spending by the Baltic governments. When analysing defence spending, the caesura 2021–2023 was used. The starting caesura is determined by the year before Russian aggression and it is the benchmark for defence spending after the outbreak of war. The end caesura is determined by 2023, as it represents the results of a full calendar year. The year 2024 at the stage of preparation of the given work has only just begun and many countries present some preliminary estimates of the planned expenditure for a given calendar year; however, taking into account the fact that very often the preliminary estimates differ from the final expenditure, it has been decided not to take into account the 2024 estimates. It is important to point out that, depending on the sources used, the amounts of defence expenditure may differ slightly in both percentage and numerical terms and this is because for some countries the expenditure for 2023 is an estimated amount, which may differ slightly from each other.

The year before the war in Ukraine, Lithuania's (78 place in Military Strength Ranking 2024 [MSR]) defence spending was US$1.31 billion, which accounted for approximately 2% (1.91%) of the country's GDP. In 2022, US$1.73 billion (2.5% of GDP) was spent on defence. In 2023, the amount was already 2 billion, which is estimated to be 2.75% of GDP. In December, the Parliament of the Republic of Lithuania adopted the government's draft budget for 2024, which allocates €2.91 billion for national defence. The defence budget will amount to 2.75% of GDP, and most of it will be allocated to strengthening the capabilities of the Lithuanian Armed Forces. Lithuania's goal in the defence plan is to acquire state-of-the-art weapons systems, increase combat capabilities, airspace surveillance and defence (Ministry of National Defence Republic of Lithuania; Worldbank: Military expenditure – Lithuania, Statista. Defence expenditures of NATO countries, 2023).

Latvia's (99 place in MSR) defence budget in 2024 envisages €1.13 billion, or 2.4% of GDP, and an increase in defence spending to 3% of GDP the country plans to meet by 2027. The Ministry of Defence's assumptions for 2024 include improving the combat capabilities of the National Armed Forces by developing medium-range air defence, coastal defence and acquiring a long-range rocket artillery system, improving the National Armed Forces Reserve System, developing military infrastructure, developing a comprehensive national defence system. It is also planned that an additional €200 million will be invested in the defence budget between 2023 and 2027 to increase air defence capabilities. Defence spending accounted for 2.07% in 2021 and 2.05% in 2022 and 2.25% in 2023 (Ministry of Defence Republic of Latvia; Statista. Statista. Defence expenditures of NATO countries, 2023b).

In response to Russian military aggression against Ukraine, on March 24, 2022, the Government of the Republic of Estonia (77 in MSR) approved a package of measures for Estonia's military defence totalling €476.77 million, of which €15.44 million was allocated in the 2022 supplementary budget. Estonia's defence spending in 2021 was US$748.58 million (2% of GDP) and in 2022 US$810.92 billion (2.10% of GDP), and in 2023 – US$1.1 billion (2.73%). In 2024, it is assumed to exceed 3% for the first time, confirming the upward trend, as assumed by this country. Additional defence funding has been earmarked for deployment of short-range air defence systems, modernisation of anti-tank capabilities, improvement of indirect fire capabilities, increased situational awareness, construction of additional infrastructure for allies. The main task for the coming years, taking into account the financial breakdown of military expenditure for 2023–2026, is that 54% of the military budget will be allocated to the purchase of new military equipment (Ministry of Defence Republic of Estonia; Worldbank: Military expenditure – Estonia; Statistista, Defence expenditures of NATO countries, 2023b).

In the case of Bulgaria (62 in MSR), we can note that in 2021 and 2022, defence spending accounted for US$1.28 billion and US$1.34 billion, which corresponded to only 1.5% of GDP, meaning that the warfare in Ukraine did not affect the process of increasing this spending, only reaching 1.83% in 2023. The Bulgarian authorities emphasise that the difficulty in reaching the 2% level is due to the fact that Bulgaria, like other countries, is suffering the consequences of the crisis caused by the pandemic and the situation in Ukraine, so it cannot even afford such a ceiling due to other more important state expenditures while, interestingly, in 2019 military spending accounted for US$2.16 billion (3%). Another serious problem is that 20% of posts in the Bulgarian armed forces remain unfilled. In 2017, the *National Plan for Increasing the Defence Spending to 2% of the Gross Domestic Product until 2024* was enacted, according to which the result in 2021 should be 1.64%, in 2021 – 1.70%, in 2023 – 1.85%, and in 2024 – 2%. The results presented show that only in 2023 did Bulgaria manage to come close to meeting the set target (Military expenditure Bulgaria, Worldbank; Bulgaria, 2017, National Plan, 2017; Ministry of Defence The Republic of Bulgaria; Statista. Defence expenditures of NATO countries, 2023b).

The Czech (46 in MSR) government adopted a defence strategy in October 2023, which, against the backdrop of the prolonged intensification of Russian aggression against Ukraine, assumes that the state must be prepared for a long-term defensive war against an opponent equipped with nuclear defence (Obranná Strategie České Republiky, 2023). This strategy is a continuation of the security policy assumptions of the Security Strategy of June 2023, according to which Russia's war against Ukraine put an end to the peace, stability, and cooperation that Europe enjoyed after the end of the Cold War. It recognised Russia's actions as a threat to the economic, social stability of the Czech Republic as well as to state security. Based on the example of Russian aggression against Ukraine, the document assumes the necessity of the state's engagement with NATO. The most important assumption according to the strategy is to increase defence spending in order to achieve the required 2% of GDP by 2024 (Security Strategy of the Czech Republic 2023: 6–15, 27). The Czech Republic's defence spending in 2021 amounted to US$3.94 billion, which represented only 1.4% of the country's GDP, a percentage that was also maintained in 2022, when it amounted to US$4.01 billion. On the other hand, in 2023, according to estimates, CZK 111.8 billion (US$4.92 billion) will be spent on defence, representing 1.5% of GDP. The results data present that the state failed to achieve the 2% result despite the government's announcement in 2022 to change the funding of projects of strategic importance to the army in order to achieve the NATO indicator (Ministry Defence & Armed Forces of the Czech Republic; World bank, military expenditures, Statista. Defence expenditures of NATO countries, 2023).

The unquestionable leader in terms of defence expenditure growth in 2023 among NATO's eastern flank countries (as well as NATO as a whole) is Poland (21 in MSR) with 3.9% of GDP, achieving a higher result than estimated in the provisions of the Budget Act for that year, where the planned indicator was 3%. In 2021, US$15.11 billion (2.2 GDP) will be spent on defence, and in 2022 – US$16.57 billion (2.4% of GDP) (Statista. Defence expenditures of NATO countries, 2023). The activities of the current Polish security policy are based on the assumptions of the National Security Strategy of 2020 which included assumptions regarding the threat from the Russian Federation to the security of the state. It recognises that the most serious threat is posed by the neo-imperialist policy of the Russian Federation authorities, realised through the use of military force. This is exemplified by the aggression against Georgia, the illegal annexation of Crimea, and actions in eastern Ukraine, which constitute violations of the fundamental principles of international law and undermine the pillars of the European security system (National Security Strategy of the Republic of Poland, 2020: 4). Poland, as a state bordering Russia (from the Kaliningrad region) and Ukraine, has felt a particular need to strengthen its security also through the presence of NATO forces on its territory, with an estimated 12,000 NATO troops stationed in Poland. After the tragic accident (two fatalities) in November 2022 due to the downing of two missiles in Przewodów in the Lublin Province, the protection of its own territory and airspace has become extremely important (Żaryn, 2023).

Similar results for defence spending in 2023 were achieved by Romania (2.44%) – 47 place in MSR 2024 and Hungary (2.43%) – 54 place in MSR 2024, the required 2% was also achieved by Slovakia (2.02%) – 54 place in MSR 2024. Taking into account the year before Russian aggression (2021) and the first year of aggression (2022), Romania achieved 1.86% and 1.72% of GDP. In contrast, Hungary's expenditure in 2021 amounted to 1.68% and in 2022 recorded a decrease to 1.53% of GDP. Slovakia, on the other hand, reached 1.76% and 1.74% of GDP (Statista; Defence expenditures of NATO countries, 2023; Statista. Hungary; Statista, Romania. Statista, Slovakia). The data presented shows that these countries have successfully met the target of achieving 2% of GDP in defence spending in 2023. An undoubted factor implying a significant increase in spending is the location of these countries at the border between the EU and NATO and non-members (Table 5.4).

Considering countries that are not directly an external border of either the EU or NATO, we can observe that, according to the 2023 data, most of them failed to achieve a defence spending score of 2% of GDP. These countries include France – 1.9% (2021 – 1.04%, 2022 – 1.18%) – 11 place in MSR 2024, Croatia – 1.74% (2021 – 2.1%, 2022 – 2.2%) – 66 place in MSR 2024, the Netherlands – 1.7% (2021 – 1.38%, 2022 – 1.58%) – 40 place in MSR 2024, Denmark – 1.65% (2021 – 1.32%, 2022 – 1.42%) – 48 place in MSR 2024, Germany – 1.57% (2021 – 1.33%, 2022 – 1.39%) – 19 place in MSR 2024, Italy – 1.46% (2021 – 1.72%, 2022 – 1.68%) – 10 place in MSR 2024, Portugal – 1.45% (2021 – 1.54%, 2022 – 1.35%) – 21 place in MSR 2024, Slovenia – 1.35% (2021 – 1.24%, 2022 – 1.19%) – 91 place in MSR 2024, Spain – 1.26% (2021 – 1.37%, 2022 – 1.47%) – 20 place in MSR 2024, Belgium – 1.13% (2021 – 1.05%, 2022 – 1.18%) – 90 place in MSR 2024, and

Table 5.4 EU states, UK, and US defence spending % GDP

	Country	*NATO*	*2021 % GDP*	*Mld*	*2022 % GDP*	*Mld usd*	*2023 % GDP*	*RESULTS*	*Military Strength Ranking (MSR) Position 2024*
1.	Austria		0.87	32.72	0.77	32.30	NA		71
2.	Belgium	+	1.05	6.3	1.18	6.87	1.13		70
3.	Bulgaria	+	1.5	1.28	1.5	1.34	1.83		62
4.	Croatia	+	2.1	1.36	2.2	1.31	1.74	++	66
5.	Republic of Cyprus		1.91	0.542	1.81	0.494	NA		---
6.	Czech Republic	+	1.4	3.94	1.4	4.02	1.5		46
7.	Denmark	+	1.32	5.27	1.42	5.47	1.65		48
8.	Estonia	+	2.0	0.749	2.10	0.811	2.73	+++	77
9.	Finland	+	1.40	3.75	1.68	4.82	2.45	+	50
10.	France	+	1.04	56.65	1.18	53.64	1.9		11
11.	Germany	+	1.49	56.51	1.33	55.76	1.39		19
12.	Greece	+	3.70	8.30	3.76	8.10	3.01	+++	32
13.	Hungary	+	1.68	3.06	1.53	2.57	2.43	+	54
14.	Ireland		0.25	1.27	0.23	1.16	NA		94
15.	Italy	+	1.72	36.25	1.68	33.45	1.46		10
16.	Latvia	+	2.07	0.823	2.05	0.848	2.25	+++	99
17.	Lithuania	+	2.0	1.31	2.5	1.73	2.75	+++	78
18.	Luxemburg	+	0.47	0.403	0.70	0.565	0.72		109
19.	Malta		0.5	0.088	0.5	0.087	NA		---
20.	Netherlands	+	1.38	13.94	1.58	15.61	1.7		40
21.	Poland	+	2.2	15.11	2.4	16.57	3.9	+++	21
22.	Portugal	+	1.54	3.90	1.35	3.50	1.45		38
23.	Romania	+	1.86	5.30	1.72	5.19	2.44	+	47
24.	Slovak Republic	+	1.76	2.06	1,73	5.19	2.02	+	69
25.	Slovenia	+	1.24	0.763	1.19	0.735	1.35		91
26.	Spain	+	1.37	19.54	1.47	20.30	1.26		20
27.	Sweden		1.19	7.58	1.31	7.72	NA		29
28.	United Kindom	+	2.16	67.50	2.23	68.46	2.07	+++	6
29.	United States	+	3.46	806.23	3.45	876.94	3.49	+++	1
30.	Ukraine		3.23	5.94	33.55	43.99	18.2		18
31.	Russia		3.72	65.91	4.06	86.37	4.1		2

Source: Own compilation based on collected data.

Luxembourg – 0.72% (2021 – 0.47%, 2022 – 0.70%) – 109 place in MSR 2024 (Defence Expenditures of NATO Countries (2014 – 2022); Statista, Defence expenditures of NATO countries, 2023; SIPRI Milex Data 1949 – 2022).

Greece and Finland managed to score above the 2% indicator. For Greece, in 2023, it represented 3.01% (2021 – 3.70%, 2022 – 3.76%) – 32 place in MSR

2024. Finland, on the other hand, as a NATO applicant country (obtained in April 2023), the result represented 2.45% (2021 – 1.40%, 2022 – 1.68%) – 50 place in MSR 2024. We can observe a significant increase in relation to previous years, where the defence budget represented US$3.75 billion, and a year later already US$4.82 billion, and in turn in 2023 the budget was already US$6.4 billion. This result shows a significant increase, as the budget nearly doubled as compared to 2021. On the one hand, the reason for the increase is the fact that the country is a neighbour of Russia, which, against the backdrop of the situation in Ukraine, causes a change in security policy; on the other hand, given its membership of NATO, significant financial resources are required to bring the country in line with NATO rules and standards, as according to the Global Firepower ranking(2024), Finland's military potential ranks 50 out of 145 countries worldwide. Therefore, a number of activities related to modernisation, improvement, and development of the state's military potential will be important in this situation (Statista, Defence expenditures of NATO countries, 2023; SIPRI Milex Data 1949–2022; Ministry of Defence, Finland).

Five EU states are not members of NATO, in which case it would seem that for them the issue of defence spending may be crucial. In the case of Austria (71 in MSR), in 2023, defence spending from the state budget was only 1%, in 2022 – 0.87%, and in 2021 – 0.77%. In contrast, the Republic of Cyprus'(n/a in MSR) expenditure reached 1.91% in 2021 and 1.81% in 2022, comprising 1.81% of GDP. According to the Cyprus government's announcement, the authorities' target is to achieve a result of 2% of GDP; however, it was not possible to find information on how much defence spending was in 2023. Malta's (n/a in MSR) military expenditure in 2021 and 2022 reached only 0.5% of GDP. Sweden in 2021 and 2022 recorded 1.19% and 1.31% of GDP, respectively. As with Cyprus, it was not possible to find information on the year 2023. Sweden (29 in MSR) became a NATO member on March 7, 2024. The Swedish government has announced that the budget for the country's armed forces in 2024 will be 119 billion kronor (approximately $184 billion), meaning that it will be 27 billion kronor ($40 billion) larger than 2023, an increase of approximately 28% compared to the previous year. According to the Government Offices of Sweden website, the 2% of GDP ceiling is expected to be reached in 2024. Ireland's (94 in MSR) spending in 2021 and 2022 is estimated at 0.25% and 0.23% of GDP and no information was found for the last year. The most recent reports tend to refer to the defence expenditure of NATO countries (SIPRI Milex Data 1949–2022); Defence Expenditures of NATO Countries (2014–2022); (Government Offices of Sweden).

The result for defence spending for the US (1 in MSR), in 2023, was 3.49% of GDP (2021 – 3.46%, 2022 – 3.45%) and for the UK 2.07% (2021 – 2.16%, 2022 – 2.23%). It is important for the two entities not only to take care of strengthening their own security but also to permanently support Ukraine in its fight against Russia (SIPRI Milex data 1949–2022; Defence Expenditures of NATO Countries (2014–2022)). Ukraine's (18 in MSR) defence against Russian aggression required significant financial outlays and the state budget for expenditure in 2022 in relation to 2021 increased tenfold from 3.23% to 33.55% of GDP; in 2023, it accounted for almost 20% of the state budget. The Russian state (2 in MSR) is also aiming to increase defence spending, having managed to exceed the 4% of GDP ceiling in 2023 in relation to 3.72% the year before the attack on Ukraine (SIPRI Milex data 1949–2022). This part of the thesis focuses on an analysis of the defence spending of individual states, following the Russian aggression against Ukraine in order to verify whether and to what extent the military aggression of one state against another has contributed to an intensification in the conduct of other states' defence policies, thus enabling the research hypothesis set out in the introduction to be resolved.

Conclusion

In the face of dynamically emerging threats and challenges of a military nature, states have been faced with the challenge of guaranteeing and strengthening their own security. Focusing on strengthening and securing their borders, modernising their armed forces, and strengthening their position in the international arena are among the many tasks that states face in order to implement an effective national policy. The international response to Russia's aggression against Ukraine has been robust, with the European Union (EU), the United States (US), and other nations providing substantial financial, humanitarian, and military assistance to Ukraine. The Russian–Ukrainian war has shown many states how important it is to guarantee their own security. Furthermore, the international community has continuously supported Ukraine in resisting Russian aggression. In answering the first research question posed [P1]: "To what extent have the EU, UK, and US states engaged in assistance to Ukraine?", it should be noted that in this case the research hypothesis [H1] that engagement in assistance to Ukraine has become a significant factor for the EU states, the UK, and the US, thus presenting support for Ukraine and condemnation of Russian actions, was confirmed positively. The analysis carried out concluded that the involvement of EU member states, the UK, and the US in aiding Ukraine has been analysed, revealing substantial contributions in various forms. Notably, the US emerged as the largest contributor, followed by the EU and its member states. Germany, Poland, and the Netherlands were among the top contributors, providing extensive military aid alongside financial and humanitarian assistance.

Assessing the aid provided in relation to each country's gross domestic product (GDP) underscores the significant commitment of certain nations like Lithuania (1.31%), Estonia (1.28%), and Latvia (1.03%), which allocated a notable percentage of their GDP to support Ukraine. Denmark (1.03%) and Poland (0.64%) stood out as consistent contributors, both in absolute terms and relative to their GDP. Furthermore, the provision of heavy weapons and military equipment, particularly tanks, by several countries including Poland, the Czech Republic, and Germany, underscores the collective effort to bolster Ukraine's defence capabilities against Russian aggression.

The second research question [P2] was: "Have these countries taken steps to strengthen their own security, and to what extent?" By verifying hypothesis [H2], the hostilities in Ukraine confirmed the necessity to take measures to guarantee their own security, to this end, the EU states, the UK, and the US have taken measures to increase defence budget spending. Thus, also the research hypothesis was confirmed. It is noteworthy that almost all EU countries expressed that they would make every effort to increase their military capabilities, which entails an increase in defence spending. European NATO Member States, especially those on the eastern flank, have demonstrated a commitment to bolstering their defence capabilities in response to perceived threats from Russia. Countries like Poland, Romania, and the Baltic States have significantly increased defence spending, reflecting a growing concern over regional security. Analysing the period 2021–2023, an upward trend in expenditure in relation to a country's GDP was recorded by most countries; however, only a few managed to reach a figure of 2% of GDP. Notable among these are Estonia, Greece, Latvia, Lithuania, and Poland, as well as the UK and the US, all of which achieved the required figure within three years. The US and the UK, as key allies, have reaffirmed their commitment to supporting Ukraine and countering Russian aggression. Both countries have maintained substantial defence budgets and have pledged military support to Ukraine, underscoring their role as global security actors. The commitments following Russia's aggression against Ukraine have underscored the importance of robust defence policies and international cooperation in maintaining regional and global stability. The increase in defence spending, coupled with efforts to strengthen alliances and partnerships, reflects a collective commitment to deterring aggression and promoting peace and security in the face of evolving geopolitical challenges.

References.

Additional Ukraine Supplemental Appropriations Act 2022. (May 2022). https://appropriations.house.gov/sites/democrats.appropriations.house.gov/files/Additional%20Ukraine%20Suplemental%20Appropriations%20Act%20Summary.pdf

Additional Ukraine Supplemental Appropriations Act 2023. (December 2022). https://appropriations.house.gov/sites/democrats.appropriations.house.gov/files/Ukraine%20Supplemental%20Summary%20FY23.pdf

Bulgaria, (2017). National Plan for Increasing the Defense Spending to 2% of the Gross Domestic Product until 2024. https://www.mod.bg/en/doc/programi/20180202_National_Plan_EN.pdf

Christoph, T., Antezza, A., Bushnell, K., Bomprezzi, P., Dyussimbinov, Y., Frank, A., Frank, P., Franz, L., Kharitonov, I., Kumar, B., Rebinskaya, E., Schade, C., Schramm, S., & Weiser, L. (2023). The Ukraine Support Tracker: Which Countries Help Ukraine and How? Kiel Working Paper, No. 2218, 1–75

Continuing Appropriations and Ukraine Supplemental Appropriations Act 2023. (September 2022). https://appropriations.house.gov/sites/democrats.appropriations.house.gov/files/Summary%20Continuing%20Appropriations%20and%20Ukraine%20Supplemental%20Appropriations% https://en.bbn.gov.pl/en/news/832,Declaration-of-the-heads-of-state-Bucharest-9-meeting.html 20Act%202023.pdf

Defence Expenditures of NATO Countries (2014–2022). https://www.nato.int/cps/en/natohq/news_197050.htm

European Security Strategy (2003). A Secure Europe in a Better World. https://www.consilium.europa.eu/en/documents-publications/publications/european-security-strategy-secure-europe-better-world/

Federal Government of Germany. Retrieved December 2023, https://www.bundesregierung.de/breg-en/news/military-support-ukraine-2054992

Goverment of Canada. https://www.canada.ca/en/department-national-defence/news/2023/01/defence-minister-anita-anand-announces-air-defence-system-donation-to-ukraine.html

Goverment Offices of Sweden. https://www.government.se/articles/2023/09/military-budget-initiatives-for-2024/

Global Firepower Ranking (2024). https://www.globalfirepower.com/countries-listing.php

Military Expenditure-Lithuania. https://data.worldbank.org/indicator/MS.MIL.XPND.GD.ZS?locations=LT&most_recent_value_desc=true

Military Expenditure Bulgaria, Worldbank. https://data.worldbank.org/indicator/MS.MIL.XPND.CD?locations=bg

Ministry of Defence & Armed Forces of Czech Republic. https://www.army.cz/en/ministry-of-defence/newsroom/news/successful-six-months-at-the-mod:-2-gdp--modernisation--cooperation-with-the-u-s---and-efficient-help-to-ukraine-245605/

Ministry of Defence & Armed Forces of the Czech Republic - Defence Budget. https://www.army.cz/en/facts-file/defence-budget/defence-budget-130198/

Ministry of Defence, Finland, https://www.defmin.fi/en/ministry_of_defence#787374ea

Ministry of Defence Netherlands. https://www.defensie.nl/actueel/nieuws/2022/11/04/nederlands-militair-steunpakket-voor-oekraine

Ministry of Defence Republic of Estonia. https://kaitseministeerium.ee/en/objectives-activities/defence-budget

Ministry of Defence Republic of Latvia. https://www.mod.gov.lv/en/about-us/defence-budget

Ministry of Defence The Republic of Bulgaria. https://www.mod.bg/en/

Ministry of National Defence Republic of Lithuania. https://kam.lt/en/lithuanian-defence-budget-to-strengthen-lithuanian-armed-forces-fighting-power-and-further-modernization/

National Security Bureau (2022, 10 July). Declaration of the Heads of state Bucharest 9 Meeting. https://en.bbn.gov.pl/en/news/832,Declaration-of-the-heads-of-state-Bucharest-9-meeting.html

National Security Strategy of U. S. (2022). https://www.whitehouse.gov/wp-content/uploads/2022/11/8-November-Combined-PDF-for-Upload.pdf

Obranná strategie České republiky (2023). https://mocr.army.cz/assets/informacni-servis/zpravodajstvi/obranna__strategie_c_r_2023_final.pdf

Pawłowski, K. (2020). *Bukareszteńska Dziewiątka: współpraca państw wschodniej flanki NATO*. Instytut Europy Środkowej.

Report on a European Parliament recommendation to the Council and the Vice- President of the Commission / High Representative of the Union for Foreign Affairs and Security Policy on the EU's Foreign, Security and Defence Policy after the Russian invasion of Ukraine, 2022/2039(INI). https://www.europarl.europa.eu/doceo/document/A-9-2022-0164_EN.html

Security Strategy of the Czech Republic 2023. https://mzv.gov.cz/jnp/en/foreign_relations/security_policy/security_strategy_of_the_czech_republic/

Statista (2023a). Number of Disclosed Main Battle Tanks Committed to Ukraine as of July 2023, by Type and Donor Country Ukraine Tanks Committed. https://www.statista.com/statistics/1364974/ukraine-military-aid-tanks/

Statista. (2023b) Defense Expenditures of NATO Countries as a Percentage of Gross Domestic Product in 2023. https://www.statista.com/statistics/584088/defense-expenditures-of-nato-countries/

Strategia Bezpieczeństwa Narodowego Rzeczypospolitej Polskiej (2020). https://www.bbn.gov.pl/ftp/dokumenty/Strategia_Bezpieczenstwa_Narodowego_RP_2020.pdf

Strategic Compass (2022). For a Stronger EU Security and Defence in the Next Decade. https://www.consilium.europa.eu/en/press/press-releases/2022/03/21/a-strategic-compass-for-a-stronger-eu-security-and-defence-in-the-next-decade/

The Integrated Review (2021). https://www.gov.uk/government/collections/the-integrated-review-2021

The Integrated Review Refresh (2023). https://assets.publishing.service.gov.uk/media/641d72f45155a2000c6ad5d5/11857435_NS_IR_Refresh_2023_Supply_AllPages_Revision_7_WEB_PDF.pdf

The Ukraine Support Tracker (2023). A Database of Military, Financial and Humanitarian aid to Ukraine. https://www.ifw-kiel.de/topics/war-against-ukraine/ukraine-support-tracker/

The Versailles declaration (2022). 10 and 11 March 2022. https://www.consilium.europa.eu/en/press/press-releases/2022/03/11/the-versailles-declaration-10-11-03-2022/

Tomala, M., & Prokop, M. (2021). Zagrożenia militarne i wojenne a bezpieczeństwo gospodarcze państwa. Case study: Konflikt zbrojny między Ukrainą a Rosją w 2014 roku. Annales Universitatis Pedagogicae Cracoviensis. *Studia de Securitate 11*(2): 40–59.

U. S. Department of Defence. https://search.usa.gov/search?query=ukraine&affiliate=defensegov&utf8=%26%23x2713%3B

Ukraine Supplemental Appropriations Act 2022. (March 2022). https://appropriations.house.gov/sites/democrats.appropriations.house.gov/files/Ukraine%20Supplemental%20Summary.pdf

World Bank, Military Expenditures. https://databank.worldbank.org/reports.aspx?source=2&series=MS.MIL.XPND.CD&country=

Worldbank: Military expenditure - Estonia https://data.worldbank.org/indicator/MS.MIL.XPND.CD?locations=ee

SIPRI Yearbook (2023). *Armanents, Disarmament and International Secuirity.* Oxford University Press. https://www.sipri.org/yearbook/2023

SIPRI Milex data 1949–2022. https://view.officeapps.live.com/op/view.aspx?src=https%3A%2F%2Fwww.sipri.org%2Fsites%2Fdefault%2Ffiles%2FSIPRI-Milex-data-1949-2022.xlsx&wdOrigin=BROWSELINK

Statista. Hungary: Ratio of Military Spending to Gross Domestic Product (GDP) from 2012 to 2022. https://www.statista.com/statistics/810417/ratio-of-military-expenditure-to-gross-domestic-product-gdp-hungary/

Statista, R. Defense Expenditure as a Share of Gross Domestic Product (GDP) in Romania from 2000 to 2023. https://www.statista.com/statistics/1112233/expenditure-on-defense-as-a-share-of-gdp-romania/

Statista, S. Defense Expenditure as a Share of Gross Domestic Products (GDP) in Slovakia from 2012 to 2023. https://www.statista.com/statistics/1401319/slovakia-military-expenditure-share-of-gdp/

The Annual Report 2022, European Defence Agency. https://eda.europa.eu/publications-and-data/all-publications/annual-report-2022

Żaryn, S. (2023). Działania ABW po rozpoczęciu rosyjskiej inwazji na Ukrainę. Serwis Rzeczypospolitej Polskiej. https://www.gov.pl/web/sluzby-specjalne/dzialania-abw-po-rozpoczeciu-rosyjskiej-inwazji-na-ukraine

6 Ukraine's Economic Recovery

Key Priorities for the Future

Nataliya Struk

Introduction

Analysing Ukraine's economic recovery during the ongoing war is a critical task amid the challenges posed by Russia's full-scale invasion. The Ukraine Recovery Conference (URC) 2023, held in London, has become a key platform for international cooperation, highlighting the need for a sustainable economic future. Despite the continuation of martial law, the conference focused on mobilising global support for Ukraine's stabilisation and recovery.

The estimated cost of rebuilding Ukraine over a decade, estimated at US$ 411 billion, underscores the monumental financial needs for post-war reconstruction. The allocation of substantial funds, including during the World Bank Group and International Monetary Fund meeting in Morocco, underscores the urgent need for transparent and well-managed investment procedures.

The Third Rapid Damage and Needs Assessment of Ukraine (RDNA3), which is being conducted by the government, the World Bank, the European Commission, the United Nations and other partners, aims to assess the impact of the Russian invasion between February 2022 and December 2023. This assessment is crucial for identifying recovery needs and coordinating financial assistance to Ukraine.

The EU-funded Ukraine Recovery and Reconstruction Monitoring no.4 project provides additional information on the current state of recovery, with a focus on economic spending and development projects. Despite the difficulties in obtaining official statistics during the war, the project provides valuable data through its analytical tool that sheds light on approved projects, funding allocation, and financial coverage.

A detailed breakdown of approved projects by region, funding source and sector, such as transport services and agriculture, reveals the complex landscape of Ukraine's recovery and reconstruction efforts. An analysis of the financial coverage of budget expenditures on projects reveals both successes and gaps in their financing, highlighting the importance of coordinated efforts by business partners to ensure a comprehensive economic recovery.

Amidst the myriad of challenges, construction waste management is becoming a critical issue that requires strategic solutions to responsibly address the consequences of destruction. As Ukraine grapples with the unprecedented destruction

DOI: 10.4324/9781003435433-6

of buildings and infrastructure, the need to harmonise international procurement approaches, as reflected in the Memorandum of Understanding signed by development banks, is becoming increasingly apparent.

This chapter provides an insight into the complex process of rebuilding Ukraine's economy during the war, examining financing mechanisms, project implementation, regional differences, and environmental considerations. As the country moves along the complex path of reconstruction, this analysis aims to provide a comprehensive framework for understanding the multifaceted dynamics shaping the post-war economic environment for sustainable development in Ukraine.

Achieving an acceptable degree of completeness in addressing the key priorities for Ukraine's economic recovery will enable the following questions to be explored:

1 Progress in economic recovery: What is the current state of Ukraine's economic recovery, given the damage caused by Russia's full-scale invasion? How effective have the initiatives of the Ukraine Recovery Conference (URC) 2023 been in stabilising and reviving the economy?
2 Financial management and transparency: How transparent and effective are Ukraine's investment management procedures, especially with regard to the substantial funds allocated and the need for additional financing during the post-war reconstruction? What measures are in place to ensure fiduciary oversight of the use of funds from international partners?
3 International cooperation and procurement: To what extent do international organisations, including the Council of Europe Development Bank (EBRD), the European Bank for Reconstruction and Development (EBRD), the European Investment Bank (EIB) and the World Bank, coordinate and streamline procurement procedures for public sector investments in Ukraine? How does this coordination increase the effectiveness of financial support?
4 Rapid Damage and Needs Assessment (RDNA): What are the key findings of the Third Rapid Damage and Needs Assessment of Ukraine (RDNA3), covering the period from February 24, 2022, to December 31, 2023? How has this assessment influenced the planning and implementation of early recovery projects, especially those aimed at economic recovery and job creation?
5 Distribution of projects by region: What is the regional distribution of approved projects for economic recovery and development in Ukraine? How does the distribution of funding correlate with the severity of the damage in different regions, and what factors contribute to regional differences in project funding?
6 Financial coverage and sectoral priorities: What is the overall financial coverage of the total expected project budget, and how does it vary across different sectors of the Ukrainian economy? What factors contribute to the differences in financial coverage between sectors, and what are the implications for the overall recovery?
7 Public and international financing: How are project budgets split between public sources and international partners? In which key sectors are public funds

dominant, and in which are international support more significant? What are the challenges and opportunities arising from this distribution?

8 Financial aspects of projects and investments: Who are the main investors in recovery and development projects in Ukraine, and what are the agreed levels of funding provided by these investors? How does the type of financing (public or international) affect project initiation, implementation, or cancellation?
9 Project progress and cancellation: What is the status of project implementation, and how many projects have been started, are in progress, or have been cancelled? What factors contribute to the success or cancellation of projects, especially in key sectors, such as industry, trade, services, education, and health?
10 Restoration of infrastructure and social facilities: How has the recovery process addressed the destruction and reconstruction of social infrastructure, such as healthcare and educational facilities? What progress has been made in restoring damaged facilities and what challenges remain in this regard?
11 Compensation and support programmes: How effective are the compensation and support programmes for conflict-affected people, including emergency repair funds, housing certificates, and increased funding for destroyed property? What impact have these programmes had on overall recovery efforts?
12 Construction waste management: What measures and policy instruments are in place to manage the significant amount of construction waste generated during the war? How effective are these measures in terms of recycling and reuse, and what are the challenges faced in disposing of hazardous materials contained in construction waste?
13 Environmental impact and demining: How has the war affected the environment in terms of waste accumulation and environmental crime? What initiatives exist in the field of demining and mine clearance, and what progress has been made in securing the de-occupied territories?
14 Return of migrants: What measures are being taken to facilitate the return of migrants, including those who fled Ukraine due to the conflict? How is the government responding to the needs and concerns of returning migrants and what policies are in place to reintegrate them into society and the labour market?
15 Post-war development prospects: Given the ongoing war, what are the main priorities for the recovery and development of Ukraine's economy in the post-war period? How can the government and international partners strategically plan for long-term economic growth and stability?

The theoretical and methodological basis of the study is based on general scientific and philosophical methods of scientific knowledge, dialectical, systematic, and empirical approaches to the study of problems of recovery and development of the Ukrainian economy. Statistical and mathematical methods were used to analytically assess the implementation of projects for the restoration and development of Ukraine's economy according to various criteria. The bibliographic method of the study made it possible to systematise and summarise the work of scientists and experts to identify unresolved scientific and applied problems.

The information base of the study is formed by legislative and regulatory documents of the state authorities of Ukraine and international institutions, materials of the State Statistics Service, the NBU, Eurostat, the World Bank, the EU, the UN, etc.; scientific works (monographs, articles, reports of scientists on the subject of the study), and Internet resources.

6.1 Analysis of the State of Economic Recovery in Ukraine during the War

Despite the continuation of martial law in Ukraine, the country's recovery must continue. As a reminder, the Ukraine Recovery Conference (URC) 2023 was held in London on June 21–22, 2023, under the joint chairmanship of the United Kingdom and Ukraine (URC, 2023). The conference continued the series of annual meetings that began in London in 2017 as the URC.

> URC 2023 brought together the international community to help secure Ukraine's long-term economic future – one that is more modern, open, and resilient. The conference focused on mobilising international support for Ukraine's economic and social stabilisation and recovery from the effects of war, including through emergency assistance for immediate needs and financing private sector participation in the reconstruction process.
>
> (URC, 2023)

Taking into account the damage caused in the first year of the war alone (from February 2022), the World Bank estimated the cost of rebuilding Ukraine at $411 billion over ten years (World Bank Group, 2023a). Ukraine has already been allocated significant funds, and even more will be needed when the post-war reconstruction begins. That is why it is important to ensure transparency and proper procedures for investment management.

During the annual meeting of the World Bank Group and the International Monetary Fund (October 16, 2023) in Morocco, the heads of four development banks, the Council of Europe Development Bank (EBRD), the European Bank for Reconstruction and Development (EBRD), the European Investment Bank (EIB), and the World Bank) signed a Memorandum of Intent. It states that international organisations in Ukraine will harmonise and streamline procurement procedures for public sector investment as much as possible. In particular, EBRD President Odile Renaud-Basso said:

> Ukraine's financing needs are enormous, and to ensure maximum effectiveness, clear coordination between Ukraine's partners is vital. The EBRD, which is approaching €3 billion in financing for Ukraine during the war, considers this agreement an important step forward. Deeper cooperation among multilateral development banks to harmonise procurement approaches will

> support Ukraine and its people. The MoU reflects the current procurement context and an agreed development path, while not losing sight of the need for fiduciary oversight.
>
> (World Bank Group, 2023a)

Oleksandr Kubrakov, vice prime minister for Reconstruction of Ukraine, Minister of Communities, Territories and Infrastructure Development, announced the launch of the Third Ukraine Rapid Damage and Needs Assessment (RDNA3) by the Government of Ukraine, the World Bank, the European Commission, the UN, and other partners. This will be an updated assessment of the consequences of Russia's invasion for the period from February 24, 2022, to December 31, 2023. In particular, he noted:

> Thanks to the first and second RDNAs, we were able to compile, structure and start implementing rapid recovery projects in priority areas for 2023, as well as create a framework and the ability to plan for further recovery of Ukraine in the medium term. In 2024, we want to focus on projects that will contribute to economic recovery and create jobs. This report will allow us to clearly identify recovery needs and coordinate financial assistance.
>
> (Kubrakov, 2023)

It is worth noting that according to the World Bank's updated RDNA2 report (23 March 2023), in the first year of Russia's war in Ukraine, the direct destruction of buildings and infrastructure amounted to more than $135 billion (Figure 6.1), and the damage caused was about $290 billion (Figure 6.2) (World Bank Group, 2023b).

Since official statistics for the war period are not often updated, and many data are deliberately withheld for state security reasons; it is interesting to review and analyse the input data and research results of the EU-funded project "Monitoring of Ukraine's Recovery and Reconstruction №4" (The recovery spending watchdog, 2023) to assess the current state of Ukraine's recovery from Russia's full-scale invasion. The project is a joint effort of the Centre for Economic Strategy, the Institute for Economic Research and Policy Consulting, and the NGO Technologies of Progress.

The main objective of the project is to control the costs of economic recovery and development in Ukraine as of the end of 2023. At the pilot project stage, the results of the analysis are not official statistics and may be somewhat inaccurate, but are as close as possible to the actual data.

Since the RDNA1 report, the energy, housing, and transport sectors have seen the greatest increase in damage. The damage to agriculture is also quite significant.

First of all, a total of 1,908 projects have been approved for the recovery and development of various sectors of Ukraine's economy: 1,372 for economic recovery and 536 for development. The implementation of the projects requires funding of approximately UAH 121.97 billion, and the total amount of confirmed project funding is UAH 75.98 billion.

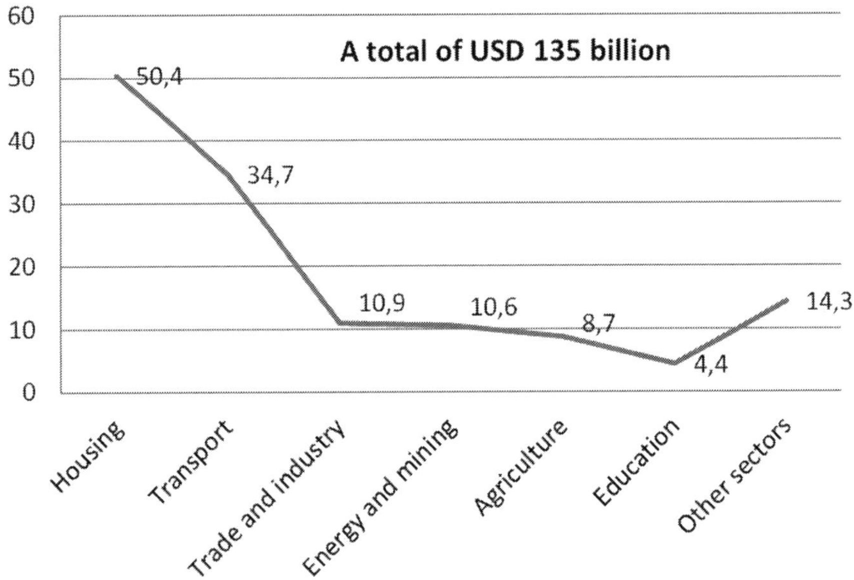

Figure 6.1 Indicators of direct damage by major sectors of Ukraine's economy caused by Russia's full-scale invasion (by the end of 2022), billion US$

Source: Own elaboration based on data from World Bank Group (2023b).

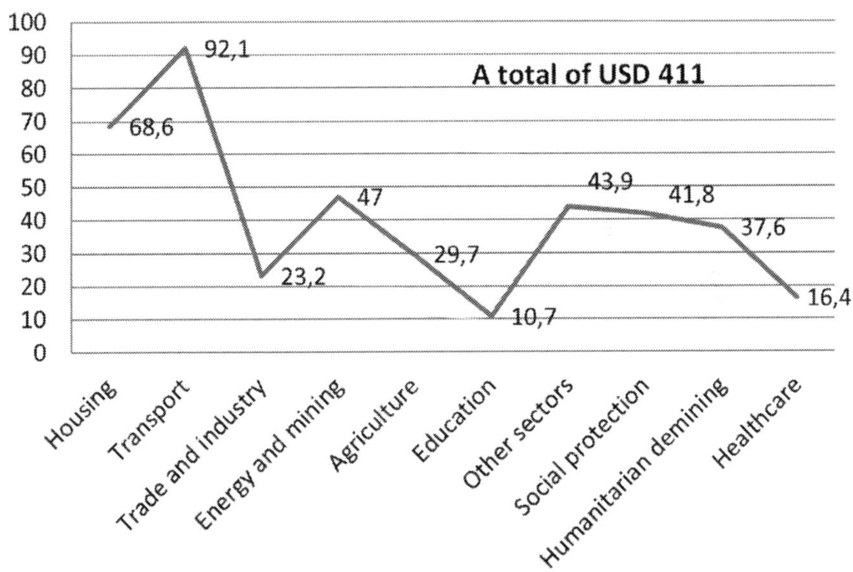

Figure 6.2 Indicators of recovery needs by major sectors of Ukraine's economy as a result of Russia's war in Ukraine (by 2022), US$ billion

Source: Own elaboration based on data from World Bank Group (2023b).

Figure 6.3 Breakdown of the number of approved projects for the recovery and development of Ukraine's economy by region (as of 01.01.2024)

Source: Own elaboration based on data from DREAM Analytics Module; The recovery spending watchdog, 2023.

Figure 6.3 illustrates the distribution of approved projects across different regions of Ukraine, while Figure 6.4 provides insights into the confirmed funding amounts. These figures were generated using data from the Monitoring of Reconstruction and Recovery of Ukraine №4, utilising the freely available analytical tool on the Internet known as the "DREAM Analytics Module".

The undisputed leader in terms of confirmed project funding is Sumy region – UAH 3,185.3 billion, although it ranks 11th in terms of the number of projects (57 projects). All projects are financed by public funds.

Kyiv region is the leader in terms of the number of approved projects (594) and the second in terms of their confirmed funding (UAH 10,950.2 billion). Moreover, 220 projects are funded by the state (the largest number among other regions), while the rest are funded by international partners.

Kharkiv region ranks second in terms of the number of projects (244) and fourth in terms of confirmed funding (UAH 5,983.5 billion). Almost all of the funding comes from public funds (UAH 5,789 billion).

Chernihiv region ranks third in terms of the number of projects (140) and confirmed funding (UAH 7,545.5 billion). Like Kharkiv region, it is mainly funded by public funds (UAH 7,350.1 billion). Chernihiv region has the highest amount of confirmed funding from public funds compared to other regions.

Kyiv (UAH 2 848.3 billion), Dnipro (UAH 6 052.9 billion), and Mykolaiv (UAH 1 452.9 billion) regions are the most heavily financed by international partners.

Figure 6.4 Amounts of confirmed project financing by regions of Ukraine (as of 01.01.2024), billion UAH

Source: Own elaboration based on data from DREAM Analytics Module; The recovery spending watchdog, 2023.

Luhansk (1), Ivano-Frankivsk (2), and Volyn (2) regions are at the bottom of the ranking of approved projects. The city of Kyiv ranks last in terms of confirmed funding (UAH 1.1 billion).

The financial coverage of the total expected budget is 62% for 1908 projects. Figure 6.5 shows that only the transport services sector has 100% financial coverage. The agriculture, fisheries, and forestry sector is not funded at all.

The total expected budget of projects is covered by two types of funding: from public funds (Figure 6.6) or from international partners (Figure 6.7).

A total of 844 projects are being implemented at the expense of public funds, with a total budget of UAH 101.11 billion. Of this, UAH 96,121.1 million is planned for capital expenditures.

Confirmed funding totalled UAH 64.88 billion, which is 64% of the financial coverage of the total budget. Not a single project is 100% funded. The highest financial coverage rates are observed in the sector of transport services recovery (91%) and in industry, trade, and services (90%). The lowest coverage (1%) is in the information technology and communications segment. The agriculture, fisheries, and forestry sector is not funded at all.

International partners are funding 225 projects with a total budget of UAH 18.57 billion. Of this, UAH 16,512.5 million is planned for capital expenditures. Confirmed funding is UAH 11.10 billion, which is 60% of the total budget. As we can see, 100% financial coverage of the total expected budget can be traced only to

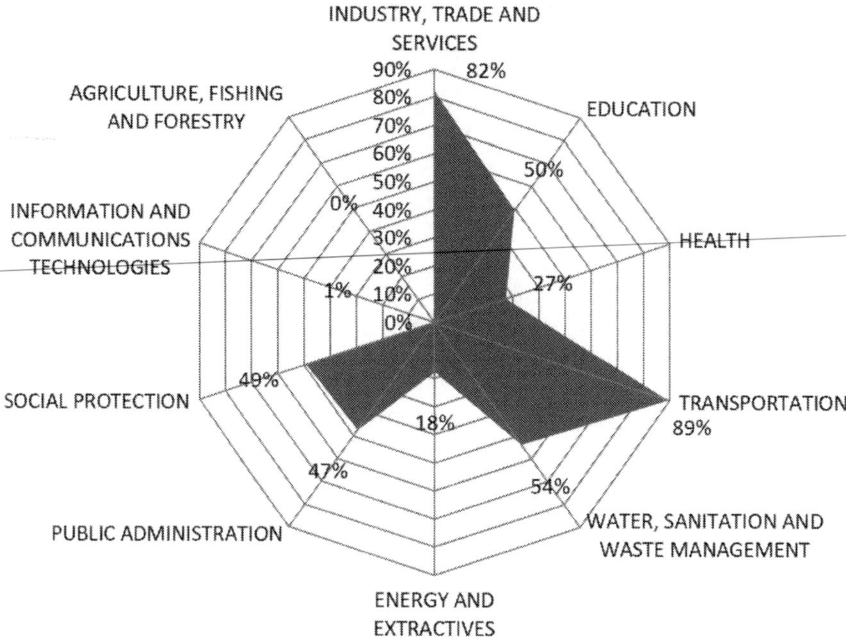

Figure 6.5 Financial coverage of project budgets by sectors of the Ukrainian economy (% of the total expected budget)

Source: Own elaboration based on data from DREAM Analytics Module; The recovery spending watchdog, 2023.

the sector of restoration of transport services. The lowest coverage (40%) is in the segment of water supply, sanitation, and waste management.

So, regardless of the type of financing, the main share of project costs is related to construction works (capital expenditures). And this is predictable. After all, due to frequent bombardments and rocket attacks on the territory of Ukraine, buildings, structures, and transmission devices are destroyed first and foremost.

Among the 205 financing parties, we identified those with confirmed investments of more than UAH 100 million and project co-financing above 45% (Table 6.1; Figure 6.8). The first six project financiers listed in Table 6.1 are investors with an agreed amount of funding of more than UAH 1 billion. Three of them are publicly financed and three are financed by international partners.

In terms of agreed funding amounts, the largest amounts were provided by: Liquidation Fund (UAH 44.6 billion) and Other Specific (UAH 12 billion). Both are state budget funds. It is worth noting that of all the projects to restore Ukraine's economy, 46.1% were initiated, 45.8% are being implemented, and 7.3% have been cancelled. Most recovery projects are being implemented in the following segments: Industry, trade and services (housing construction subsection – 426), education (higher education – 159, primary education – 118, pre-school education – 82, other education – 28), and healthcare (153).

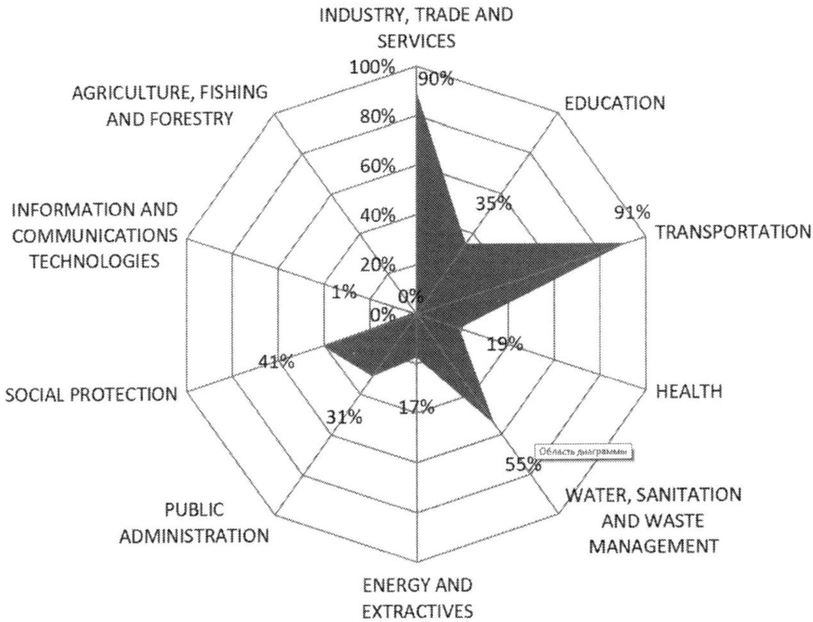

Figure 6.6 Financial coverage of the project budget by public funds by economic sector (% of the total expected project budget)

Source: Own elaboration based on data from DREAM Analytics Module; The recovery spending watchdog, 2023.

As for development projects: 40.5% were initiated, 51.9% are being implemented, and 7.1% were cancelled. Most development projects are being implemented in the following sectors: education (79 in higher education and 32 in primary education) and healthcare (92).

Of all the projects, 307 are new construction projects. Moreover, 49.5% of them have been initiated, and the remaining 50.5% are already underway. Most of these projects are in Kyiv (47), Lviv (24), and Kherson (23) regions (DREAM Analytics Module; The recovery spending watchdog, 2023).

As for reconstruction and modernisation projects, there are a total of 1,433 of them: 48.4% have been initiated and the remaining 51.6% are being implemented. The largest number of such projects is in Kyiv (425), Kharkiv (213) and Chernihiv (121) regions. The highest percentage of implementation is in Chernihiv region (71.7%).

Today, the reality is that "the destruction and reconstruction of social infrastructure go hand in hand" (BRP, 2024). It is worth noting that as of the beginning of 2024, 1,497 healthcare facilities were damaged and 195 facilities were completely destroyed. Most of them were damaged in Kharkiv, Donetsk, Dnipro, Mykolaiv, Kherson, Zaporizhzhia, Kyiv, and Chernihiv regions.

On a positive note, 451 facilities have been fully restored and 406 partially restored. Most of the restored facilities are in Mykolaiv, Dnipro, Kyiv, Kharkiv, and Chernihiv regions (BRP, 2024).

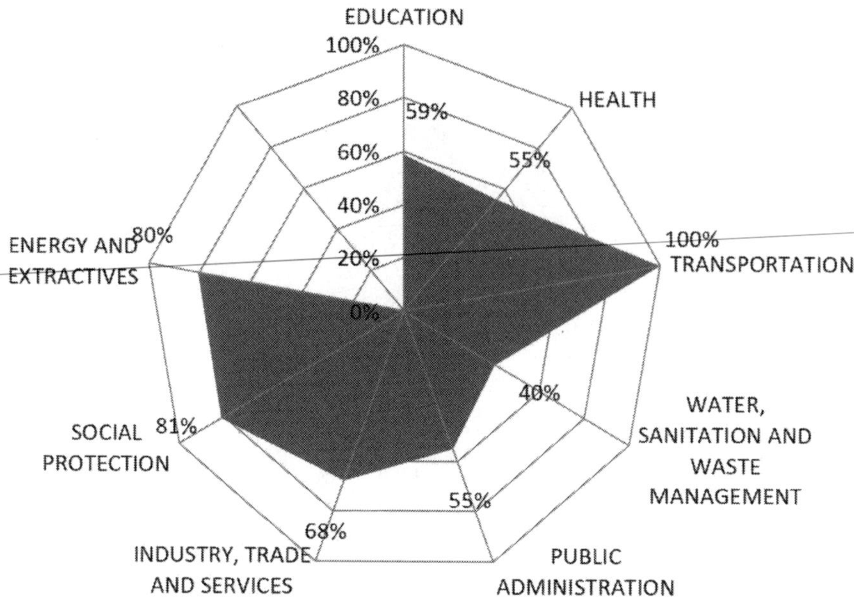

Figure 6.7 Financial coverage of projects by international partners by economic sectors (% of the total project budget)

Source: Own elaboration based on data from DREAM Analytics Module; The recovery spending watchdog, 2023.

Table 6.1 List of entities, types, and sources of funding for projects of economic recovery and development of Ukraine, the amount of confirmed investment of which is more than UAH 100 million and co-financing of projects exceeds 45%

№	*Financing party*	*Funding type*	*Funding source*
1	Liquidation Fund	State Funds	Central Budget
2	Other Specific	State Funds	Central Budget
3	Ukraine Recovery Programme (URP)	International Partners	International Organisation
4	European Investment Bank (EIB)	International Partners	International Organisation
5	Ukraine Early Recovery Programme (UERP)	International Partners	International Organisation
6	Subsidiaries	State Funds	Central Budget
7	Roads State Fund	State Funds	Central Budget
8	Other	State Funds	Charity Funds
9	Lithuania	International Partners	Bilateral Support
10	Irpin, Kyivska	State Funds	Local Budget
11	Reserve Fund	State Funds	Central Budget
12	EIB	International Partners	Technical Assistance
13	United24	State Funds	Fundrasing Platforms
14	Howard G. Buffett Foundation	International Partners	Donor Funds

Source: Own elaboration based on DREAM Analytics Module; The recovery spending watchdog, 2023.

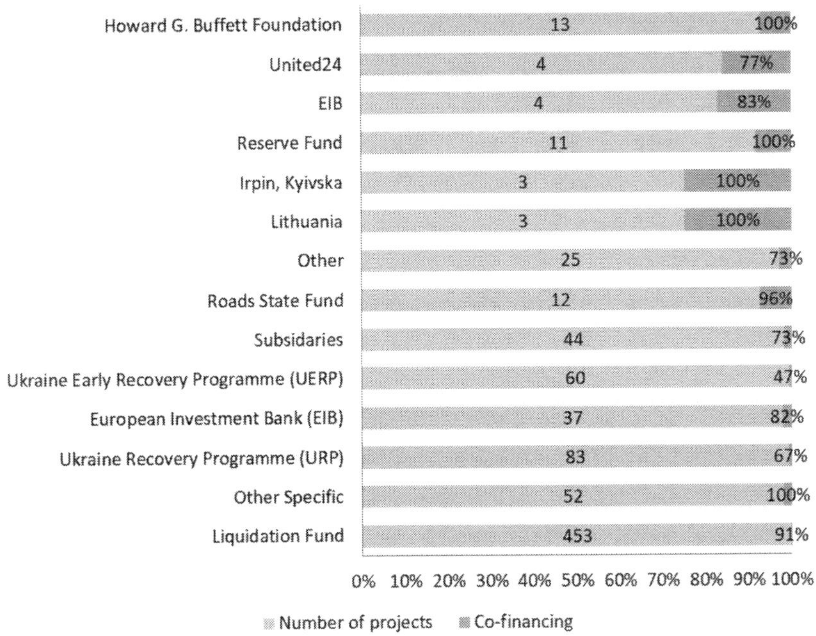

Figure 6.8 Number of economic recovery projects in Ukraine with confirmed financing (investment amount exceeding UAH 100 million and co-financing of projects exceeding 45%)

Source: Own elaboration based on DREAM Analytics Module; The recovery spending watchdog, 2023.

In the education sector, 3,428 educational institutions were damaged and 365 were completely destroyed. Nevertheless, 500 institutions have been restored.

In 2023, the Fund for Elimination of the Consequences of Armed Aggression spent UAH 61.8 billion out of the planned UAH 61.8 billion: UAH 8.5 billion for the construction of a main water pipeline that will provide water to more than a million residents in communities affected by the explosion of the Kakhovka hydroelectric power station; UAH 3.3 billion for the restoration of five settlements destroyed by Russian troops in Borodyanka, Trostianets, Tsirkuny, Posad Pokrovsky, Yahidne; UAH 3.5 billion for the restoration of 46 facilities in nine regions of Ukraine.

According to the Ministry of Reconstruction, 35,000 Ukrainians have received funds for urgent and major repairs worth over UAH 3 billion, 60 families have concluded purchase and sale agreements using housing certificates, and over 8,000 applications are in the process of being processed (Kubrakov, 2024).

Funding for compensation for destroyed real estate was increased from UAH 2.5 billion to UAH 5.8 billion (from the Liquidation Fund) (Resolution of the Cabinet of Ministers of Ukraine, 2023).

In total, more than 670,000 tonnes of demolition waste have accumulated in Ukraine since the start of the full-scale invasion. According to the regional military administrations, as of October 31, 2023, the largest amount of demolition waste was recorded in Kyiv, Kherson, Kharkiv, Mykolaiv, Donetsk, and Zaporizhzhia regions (Popovych, 2023). Much of it is construction waste generated after artillery and rocket attacks.

Rebuilding the economy during the war is not only about building new facilities, but also a huge problem of using construction waste. The Law of Ukraine "On Waste Management" (2023) states that construction waste must be ready for reuse and recycling. Recycling is

> a recovery operation whereby waste is converted into products, materials or substances for their original or other use. This operation includes the processing of organic material, but does not include the production of energy or the conversion of waste into materials that can be used as fuel or as materials for backfilling.
>
> (Law of Ukraine, 2023)

By 2025, it is predicted that local governments could reach a target of at least 10% of the weight of recycled household waste (BRP, 2024).

The adopted Resolution of the Cabinet of Ministers of Ukraine

> On Approval of the Procedure for Waste Management Generated Due to Damage (Destruction) of Buildings and Structures as a Result of Hostilities, Terrorist Acts, Sabotage or Works to Eliminate Their Consequences and Amendments to Certain Resolutions of the Cabinet of Ministers of Ukraine.
>
> (2023)

covers the following issues: classification and accounting of waste; requirements for waste management, storage, and reuse; procedure for temporary storage of waste in designated places if there are no landfills or insufficient.

It is worth noting that before Russia's war in Ukraine, part of the construction waste from Ukraine was sent to a processing plant in Belarus. And the rest was accumulated at landfills. This approach is not correct. After all, construction waste contains hazardous materials. In particular, 30% of all municipal buildings in Ukraine have asbestos-containing materials, and the level of slate used as a roofing material in the private sector can reach 60–70% (BRP, 2024).

Most territorial communities in Ukraine solve the problem of construction waste disposal on their own. It is important to organise the right approach to this process at the state level. To stimulate the recycling of construction waste, it is advisable to raise the cost of its disposal in Ukraine. After all, the disposal of one cubic metre of such waste costs from 30 to 150 UAH (BRP, 2024).

Kyiv region has 50 landfills for construction waste. This is despite the fact that in some countries, construction landfills are banned altogether.

> Globally, construction waste recycling is a very profitable industry. In most European countries, the level of recycling is quite high. For example, in the

> Netherlands, about 90% of construction waste is recycled, in Belgium – 87%, in Denmark – 81%, in the UK – 45%, in Finland – 43%, in Austria – 41%. In European countries and the United States, the problem of waste disposal has long been addressed at the state level: some countries have banned construction landfills altogether, while in the United States and Canada they still exist, but the cost of transporting such waste there is much higher than the cost of recycling it. Depending on the country, the type of scrap and the location of the landfill, the cost of removing 1 tonne of construction waste ranges from 4 to 150 euros. Therefore, it is more profitable for many developers to spend money, time and effort on recycling and disposal of construction waste than to take it to a landfill.
>
> (Orekhanova et al., 2023)

Having analysed the state of recovery of Ukraine's economy during the war, it is appropriate to consider the prospects for its development in the post-war period.

6.2 Priority Areas for the Reconstruction and Development of Ukraine's Economy after the War

At a time when Russia's full-scale war against Ukraine is still ongoing, it is almost impossible to outline all the directions for the reconstruction and development of Ukraine's economy in the post-war period. Taking Peter Drucker's famous phrase as a motto: "The best way to predict the future is to create it", we will consider only the main, priority areas.

The first thing we need to pay attention to today so that we can continue to work on economic development is people and the environment. After all, development is impossible without these components.

The war started by Russia has forced millions of Ukrainians to leave either their regions or the country in search of safety. Some have returned or are planning to return. Some will never return. The demographic situation in Ukraine is changing rapidly. This affects the socio-economic environment and the country's defence capability. Most migrants are in European countries. Despite the slowdown in migration in 2023 compared to 2022, the continuation of the war may lead to further emigration of Ukrainians. Internally displaced persons risk losing the opportunity to return to their territory of permanent residence even after the cessation of intense hostilities. It is time to create favourable conditions for the employment of internally displaced persons. At the state level, it is important to skilfully coordinate relations with relocated enterprises regarding the need for skilled workers.

Before the full-scale invasion, there were about 2.5–3 million Ukrainian labour migrants abroad. Therefore, the total number of Ukrainians abroad (excluding the diaspora) is estimated to be between 4 and 7 million.

According to Eurostat, as of August 31, 2023, almost 4.2 million non-EU nationals who fled Ukraine as a result of the Russian invasion on February 24, 2022, had temporary protection status in EU countries. The main EU countries that accepted Ukrainians for temporary protection

> were Germany (1,175,695 people; 28% of the total), Poland (960,550; 23%), Czech Republic (365,085; 9%)… Since the end of July 2023, the number of beneficiaries of temporary protection from Ukraine in the EU has increased by 41,275 (+1.0%). The largest absolute increase was observed in Germany (+21,830; +1.9%), the Czech Republic (+7,545; +2.1%) and the Netherlands (+2,635; +1.7%).
>
> (Eurostat, 2023)

As a result of Russia's war of aggression against Ukraine. On September 19, the European Commission proposed to extend temporary protection for people fleeing Russia's aggression against Ukraine until March 3, 2025 (EU Solidarity with Ukraine, 2023).

As a result of the study, the experts of the Centre for Economic Recovery cite the following facts (Livch, 2023):

- 10% of forced migrants do not plan to return, 16% are undecided. That is, up to 2.7 million people plan to stay abroad.
- 83% of adult forced migrants are women. Moreover, the active employment rate of women in Ukraine aged 25–49 was 76% (as of 2021).
- The active labour force among migrants is more than 2.1 million people. In particular, 1.4 million in Europe and approximately 0.7 million in Russia.
- 66% of migrants have higher education, 22% have secondary specialised education.
- More than half (2–2.5 million) of migrants are children.

The return of migrants is crucial for ensuring rapid and sustainable economic growth. To ensure at least a minimum GDP growth rate of 7% per year, Ukraine needs to recruit an additional 3.1–4.5 million people into the labour force by 2032 (assuming that most migrants return). "Without an effective state policy on the return of migrants, Ukraine could lose up to $113 billion in GDP over 10 years (in 2021 prices), which could also mean a loss of about $45 billion in tax revenues" (Livch, 2023).

For forced migrants, security is an urgent problem. People who have already returned to their home regions report difficult living conditions. The end of the war, economic development, and the rebuilding of infrastructure and housing are the main factors that will facilitate the return of Ukrainians home.

From the beginning of the full-scale invasion to the present day, the security factor has played perhaps the most important role in facilitating return home. According to the UN survey, the security situation and the occupation of the region are the main reasons for half of the respondents who do not plan to return to Ukraine. Ukrainians who lived in the northern, eastern, southern regions, and the city of Kyiv before the war pay more attention to the issue of the absence of danger when deciding to return to Ukraine. Mine clearance of frontline and war-affected regions is another component of the security factor for the post-war period (Livch, 2023).

Rebuilding infrastructure and housing is also important. According to a UN survey, forced migrants pay great attention to access to electricity and water. Educational opportunities are the most common need among migrants with children. Availability of housing is an important factor for migrants from the war zone. They will most need state support in rebuilding or obtaining housing, and this will most facilitate their return.

An extremely important factor for the return of Ukrainians is employment opportunities. According to various surveys, the availability of well-paid jobs and a relatively higher standard of living in Ukraine will facilitate the return of Ukrainians. However, over time, more and more able-bodied Ukrainians are finding work abroad, which does not contribute to their intentions to return, especially among highly qualified professionals. People who have returned to their home regions often pointed to the lack of opportunities to earn a living, which directly affects the willingness of Ukrainians to return from abroad.

According to a survey conducted by the Razumkov Centre in March 2022, the share of forced migrants who did not plan to return to Ukraine or were hesitant to answer reached almost 21% (Livch, 2023).

To return forced migrants, the state should work in the following areas:

1 Ukraine should establish an ongoing dialogue with recipient countries. The government should convey its position on the return of Ukrainians to international partners.
2 Effective formulation of demographic policy based on an understanding of the needs and interests of migrants. This requires effective data collection and analysis (from government agencies of partner countries, regular surveys of migrants and returnees, etc.)
3 Coordinate the efforts of government agencies to facilitate the adoption of a detailed action plan for the return of forced migrants.
4 Communication support, ensuring constant communication and informing Ukrainian forced migrants about the opportunities and benefits of returning to Ukraine.

Moreover, the implementation of efforts in these areas depends on the timing of the end of the war and will require significant funds to restore the country's economy. Therefore, measures to stimulate the return of migrants should be distributed over time: at the first stage (before the end of the war), analytical and communication work should be carried out, and at the second stage, incentive measures, which require significant costs, should be implemented after the victory.

The second priority area for rebuilding and developing Ukraine's economy after the war is the environment. The amount of garbage generated by the war is measured in hundreds of thousands of tonnes. Legal and illegal landfills are filled with construction waste. This waste consists of bulky and heavy materials.

During the full-scale war, Russia has committed more than 3,100 cases of environmental crimes in Ukraine, totalling more than 2.2 trillion hryvnias (Ecozagroza, 2024). According to the SES, from February 24, 2022, to January 30, 2024, 467,974 explosive devices were defused on the territory of Ukraine. An area of 114,916.81 hectares was surveyed (DSNS, 2024).

Although Russia's war in Ukraine is likely to last for a long time, studying the impact of the war on the environment will also be a long-term project. However, it is important to collect and analyse data on the country's environmental recovery now. Data collection and any research is now too complicated by the need to demine huge areas of land and clear former war zones of war debris.

On December 22, the United Nations published the Ukraine Common Country Assessment 2023 (United Nations, 2023), where in Section 4.4, Environment and Climate Change Analysis, it is stated that

> Military operations have also led to a sharp increase in the accumulation of waste, including damaged or abandoned military and civilian vehicles, equipment, shell fragments, construction debris, and uncollected household and medical waste. An estimated 10-12 million tonnes of rubbish and construction waste has accumulated across the country due to the conflict. Many of the materials are toxic, including shell fragments, medical waste and construction debris containing asbestos, polychlorinated biphenyls and heavy metals, which require special handling, transportation and disposal
>
> (United Nations, 2023)

There are already companies in Ukraine that process various types of construction waste. For example, metals are recycled by:

> Metinvest, ArcelorMittal Kryvyi Rih, Zaporizhzhia and Dnipro Metallurgical Plants.
>
> Glass is recycled by Region-2001, Vetropack and UtilVtorProm, concrete by Tsaris, TekhBudMekhanika, Agropromyslova Gruppa, Tereshchenko Group, Organa, plastic by Ekola, TIS, Region-2001, The Good Plastic Company and brick by Actis Group, Forest Ukraine and UtilVtorProm.
>
> Wood is usually processed in state forestry enterprises located in each region of Ukraine. Mercury-containing waste is disposed of by Bodnarivka (Lviv). Recycling equipment is manufactured by Hummel Ukraine LLC and JV Olnova.
>
> (BRP, 2024)

Environmentalists assure us that the decision to build new houses from recycled materials is not new to Ukraine. The problem is not in the innovation of the solution, but in the volume of construction waste that has to be recycled. In the Donetsk and Luhansk regions alone, the number of destroyed or damaged houses is around 100 000 (Zhuk & Pavliy, 2023). And the destruction continues. It continues to destroy Ukraine's housing infrastructure.

It is worth noting that today, in the face of the war's most difficult conditions, much effort is being made to save the environment.

The Ministry of Economy of Ukraine has developed a pilot project to certify mine action operators and processes to ensure mine clearance in Ukraine (Ministry of Economy of Ukraine, 2023). The aim of the project is to simplify and unify the certification process, make it more understandable and accessible to mine action actors.

It is worth noting that over 986,000 explosive devices have already been destroyed during the war; 23,000 km of railways, 435.9 km of power lines, 21.7 hectares of water areas, 800.5 km of roads, 130.1 hectares of forests, and 36.8 km of gas pipelines have been cleared (BRP, 2024).

In 2023, 18,000 square kilometres of the de-occupied territories of Ukraine were declared not to pose a threat in terms of mine safety (Ministry of Defence of Ukraine, 2023). In 2023, 115 ATCs with a total area of 50,000 square kilometres were surveyed.

For 2024, the Ministry of Defence of Ukraine (Ministry of Defence of Ukraine, 2023) plans to conduct a non-technical survey of 40,000 square kilometres on the territory of 50 ATCs in the de-occupied regions; humanitarian demining activities on 239 sites with a total area of 937 hectares.

Between the beginning of 2023 and December 15, 2,686,000 hectares of agricultural land were surveyed out of the planned 470,000 hectares. Of these, more than 200,000 hectares have been returned to operation (Svyrydenko, 2023).

In 2024, the Swiss company GCS will provide 60 remotely operated mechanical demining platforms (BRP, 2024).

On January 11, 2024, Turkey, Bulgaria, and Romania signed an agreement on joint demining of the Black Sea (AP News, 2024).

In October 2024, an international conference on humanitarian demining in Ukraine will be held in Geneva (Yevropeiska pravda, 2024).

Thus, the main priority areas of environmental protection in Ukraine are:

1 Ensure environmental safety of construction waste: sort out hazardous materials, such as asbestos (contained in slate roofs, thermal asbestos insulation of heating systems, etc.).
2 Investigate construction waste and recycle it: there are laboratories in the country that analyse the content of harmful substances in construction waste and finished materials (e.g., the State Research Institute of Building Structures). Recycle metals, glass, concrete, plastic, bricks, and wood. Dispose of mercury-containing waste.
3 Collect waste recycling statistics: calculate the recovery rate of construction and demolition waste.
4 Pay attention to specific waste resulting from shelling: the problem of waste resulting from shelling of former metallurgical enterprises is particularly relevant for Donetsk and Luhansk oblasts.

Recycling of waste, the possibility of using it to rebuild cities, towns, and roads; development of effective waste management plans at the regional and local levels;

introduction of an extended producer responsibility system; experience of effective waste management practices – such measures should bring together government officials, local government representatives, entrepreneurs, and the public.

Conclusion

The study on Ukraine's economic recovery during and after the war with Russia analyses the state of economic recovery and identifies the priority areas of economic development. The results of the study led to the following conclusions:

Without international cooperation and funding, Ukraine would not have survived. The Ukraine Recovery Conference 2023, supported by international organisations and financial institutions such as the World Bank, EBRD, EIB and others, demonstrates coordinated efforts to secure Ukraine's economic future. The allocation of significant amounts of funding, both from international partners and budgetary funds, requires transparency and proper investment management.

The right approach to cost estimation and planning is essential for economic recovery during the war. The Third Rapid Damage and Needs Assessment of Ukraine (RDNA3) has made it possible to assess the consequences of the Russian invasion until December 2023. This comprehensive assessment contributes to the planning of economic recovery projects in 2024, focusing on rebuilding infrastructure and creating additional jobs.

During the military year of 2023, a proper basis was created for a clear allocation and financing of projects for the recovery and development of Ukraine's economy. The e-platform "Monitoring of Recovery and Reconstruction of Ukraine №4" displays 1908 approved economic recovery and development projects, most of which have already been confirmed and are being implemented. While the city of Sumy leads the way in terms of confirmed funding, the capital Kyiv dominates in terms of the number of projects. The financial coverage of the total project budget varies across different sectors of the economy, but the transport services sector has reached 100%.

State and international funding is a priority. The majority of economic recovery and development projects (844) are financed by public funds, while 225 receive international support. The distribution of funding across economic sectors is uneven, which underlines the importance of international partnerships in different economic segments.

The assessment of the status of project implementation shows that 46.1% of the recovery projects have been launched, 45.8% are underway, and 7.3% have been cancelled. The key sectors for ongoing projects are industry, trade, services, education, and healthcare.

It is necessary to respond in a timely manner to the challenges of economic recovery. Despite significant progress, challenges remain. Some regions of Ukraine are recovering more slowly, and the agricultural sector lacks funding. Only the transport sector is reaching full financial coverage of the general budget.

While the war is ongoing, economic development priorities should be worked out and their order should be adapted to the current realities of martial law. In the long term, the priorities for Ukraine's post-war economic development include overcoming the impact of migration on people, the environment, and demographic shifts caused by migration. The return of forced migrants is crucial for Ukraine's sustainable economic growth.

Environmental challenges and opportunities to prevent them are also crucial. The war has caused significant environmental damage, generating millions of tonnes of waste. Waste recycling initiatives, mine clearance, and international cooperation are aimed at addressing the most pressing environmental issues.

Restoration of the workforce and human resources has a major impact on Ukraine's economic growth. The return of migrants, the creation of favourable conditions for their employment and residence, and the resolution of their security issues are critical factors in Ukraine's reconstruction. Strategic state policy and international cooperation should develop effective measures to bring Ukrainians back home.

Waste management and recycling is an important area for rebuilding the economy and life in Ukraine. Considerable efforts are being made to manage construction waste responsibly, but not enough. The introduction of hazardous materials recycling and disposal practices is essential for preserving the environment not only in Ukraine but also abroad.

To sum up, it is appropriate to state the complexity of Ukraine's economic recovery during and after the war, given the need for continuous international cooperation, strategic planning, and targeted efforts to address economic, environmental, and social issues. Migrant return and sustainable construction waste management are becoming key priorities for the country's future development.

However, the global and most important priority today is to work for Ukraine's victory!

References

AP News (11 January 2024). Turkey, Bulgaria and Romania Sign Deal to Tackle Black Sea Mines. https://apnews.com/article/turkey-bulgaria-romania-mines-black-sea-guler-149e33a227512ad043de191781c0ecff

BRP (2024, 5 January). Monitoring of Reconstruction and Recovery №5. Special Topic: Recycling of Construction Waste for Recovery – Centre for Economic Strategy. Centre for Economic Strategy is a non-Governmental Research Centre for Economic Policy. https://ces.org.ua/recovery_monitoring_5_brp/

DSNS. (2024). On the Demining of the Territory of Ukraine by the SES Units. https://dsns.gov.ua/en/map-demining

Ecozagroza. (2024, 29 January). Official Resource of the Ministry of Environmental Protection and Natural Resources of Ukraine. https://ecozagroza.gov.ua/en/feed/2575

EU Solidarity with Ukraine. (2023, 23 September). Press Corner. European Commission. https://ec.europa.eu/commission/presscorner/detail/en/ip_23_4496

Eurostat. (2023, 8 October). Nearly 4.2 Million People under Temporary Protection. Language Selection | European Commission. https://ec.europa.eu/eurostat/en/web/products-eurostat-news/w/ddn-20231006-2

Evropeiska pravda (2024, 15 January). Switzerland Will Hold an International Conference on Demining Ukraine. https://www.eurointegration.com.ua/news/2024/01/15/7177497/

Kubrakov, O. (2023, 6 November). Ukraine Launches Work with Partners on RDNA3. Government Portal, Official Website. https://www.kmu.gov.ua/en/news/oleksandr-kubrakov-ukraina-razom-iz-partneramy-rozpochala-robotu-nad-rdna3

Kubrakov, O. (2024, 15 January). Oleksandr Kubrakov: The Ministry of Recovery held a Meeting with the All-Ukrainian Association of Communities. During the Meeting, They Planned Joint Work and Identified the Main Priorities for 2024. Ministry of Infrastructure of Ukraine. https://mtu.gov.ua/news/35140.html (accessed: 28.01.2024).

Law of Ukraine. (2023, 31 March). On Waste Management. Official Web Portal of the Parliament of Ukraine. https://zakon.rada.gov.ua/laws/show/2320-20#Text

Livch, D. (2023, 1 May). Human Capital Development Project in Ukraine: Facilitating the Return of Forced Migrants. Google Docs. https://drive.google.com/file/d/1RlXw50nG2qsDskRsqYzbdHhVSstouIoL/view?fbclid=IwA R2c5ctYMJeZ8H_y8jia3EmpjlkgKswObGiZ0j8IVzBmmiUoG3ihzFXkvc8.

Ministry of Defence of Ukraine (2023, 29 December). 18 Thousand Kilometres of the de-occupied Territories Are Recognised as Not Posing a Threat in Terms of Mine Safety. Official Website of the Ministry of Defence of Ukraine. https://www.mil.gov.ua/news/2023/12/29/18- tisyach-kilometriv-deokupovanih-teritorij/

Ministry of Economy of Ukraine (2023, 27 December). Implementation of a Pilot Project on Certification of First Aid Operators Is Intended to Simplify this Process and, as a Result, Accelerate the Demining of the Territory of Ukraine, – Ihor Bezkaravaynyi | Ministry of Economy of Ukraine. Just a moment… https://www.me.gov.ua/News/Detail?lang=uk-UA&id=ebec9dc7-a0be-432e-9af3-b7642aa9892f&title=RozminuvanniaUkraini

Orekhanova, Y., Ambrosova, A., & Taran, K. (2023). The Problem of Utilisation and Recycling of Waste from Destruction. Electronic and Printed Edition. https://dtkr.com.ua/wp-content/uploads/2023/07/analiz-problemi-vidhodi-rujnuvan.pdf

Popovych, E. (2023, 10 November). Since the Beginning of the Full-Scale Invasion of Russia in Ukraine, more than 670 Thousand Tonnes of Destruction Waste Have Already Been Generated – Ministry of Environmental Protection and Natural Resources of Ukraine. Ministry of Environmental Protection and Natural Resources of Ukraine – Official website. https://mepr.gov.ua/vid-pochatku-povnomasshtabnogo-vtorgnennya-rf-v-ukrayini-vzhe-utvorylosya-ponad-670-tysyach-tonn-vidhodiv-rujnatsiyi/

Resolution of the Cabinet of Ministers of Ukraine (2023, 3 May). On Approval of the Procedure for Waste Management Generated in Connection with Damage (Destruction) of Buildings and Structures as a Result of Hostilities, Terrorist Acts, Sabotage or Works to Eliminate Their Consequences and Amendments to Certain Resolutions of the Cabinet of Ministers of Ukraine. Official web portal of the Parliament of Ukraine. https://zakon.rada.gov.ua/laws/show/1073-2022-п#Text

Resolution of the Cabinet of Ministers of Ukraine (2023, 22 December). On Amendments to Clause 1 of the Resolution of the Cabinet of Ministers of Ukraine of 3 November 2023 No. 1145. Official Website of the Parliament of Ukraine. https://zakon.rada.gov.ua/laws/show/1354-2023-п#Text

Svyrydenko, Y. (2023, 18 December). Humanitarian Demining: Since the Beginning of the year, more than 200 Thousand Hectares of the Most Valuable Agricultural Land Have Beenreturned to Economic Use | Ministry of Economy of Ukraine. Just a moment… https://www.me.gov.ua/News/Detail?lang=uk-UA&id=88980f79-9457-4a65-af17- c10cc5d7a208&title=GumRozminuvannia

The Geopolitical Landscape in Europe has Undergone Significant Shifts, Marked by the URC (2023). *Ukraine Recovery Conference on 21–22 June 2023 – London, UK.* URC-international 2017–2023. https://www.urc-international.com/

The Recovery Spending Watchdog. (2023, 22 December). Ukraine Reconstruction and Recovery Monitoring №4. Presentation of the Big Recovery Portal – Centre for Economic Strategy. Centre for Economic Strategy – Non-governmental Research Centre on Economic Policy Issues. https://ces.org.ua/en/ukraine-reconstruction-and-recovery-monitoring-№4-presentation-of-the-big-recovery-portal/

United Nations. (2023, 22 December). Ukraine Common Country Analysis 2023 – Ukraine. ReliefWeb. https://reliefweb.int/report/ukraine/ukraine-common-country-analysis- 2023

World Bank Group. (2023a, 23 March). Updated Ukraine Recovery and Reconstruction Needs Assessment. World Bank. https://www.worldbank.org/en/news/press- release/2023/03/23/updated-ukraine-recovery-and-reconstruction-needs-assessment

World Bank Group. (2023b, 16 October). MDBs to Harmonise Procurement Systems in Ukraine. World Bank. https://www.worldbank.org/en/news/press-release/2023/10/16/mdbs- to-harmonize-procurement-systems-in-ukraine

Zhuk, T., & Pavliy, I. (2023, 28 November). Ruins Will become Houses Again: How Recycling Construction Waste Can Change Reconstruction – Khmarochos. Khmarochos. https://hmarochos.kiev.ua/2023/11/28/ruyiny-znovu-stanut-budynkamy-yak-resajkling-budivelnogo-smittya-mozhe-zminyty-vidbudovu/

Postface

The research findings shed light on the multifaceted dimensions of the Russo-Ukrainian conflict and its historical context that extend beyond the immediate geopolitical landscape. The study provides insights into the historical, political, and cultural intricacies shaping the dynamics between Russia and Ukraine, revealing the origins of the conflict and its implications for global stability.

The roots of the conflict trace back to the mediaeval state of Rus, highlighting the shared historical origins of Ukrainian, Russian, Belarusian, and Lithuanian peoples. However, divergent paths over centuries have resulted in unique identities, with linguistic, cultural, and political differences shaping the geopolitical landscape of the region. The collapse of the Soviet Union in 1991 brought about the independence of Ukraine, marking the end of the Soviet occupation. However, historical interference by Moscow in Ukrainian affairs has contributed to a complex relationship, with Russia's perception of Ukraine as a key and sacred territory.

A detailed examination of military engagements involving Russia from 1991 to the full-scale attack on Ukraine in 2022 reveals a consistent pattern of military interventions and conflicts. These interventions have caused significant human casualties, geopolitical consequences, and lasting impacts on the affected regions. The study underscores that the consequences of the Russo-Ukrainian war extend beyond national borders, becoming a global concern. The war has led to the destruction of cities, infrastructure, agriculture, and the environment, with severe implications for the lives of people. The global community must recognise and address the potential for such geopolitical conflicts and their impact on world stability. Thus, the war between Russia and Ukraine is characterised as a clash between two civilisations with distinct principles. Ukrainian values of freedom, democracy, and respect for human rights stand in contrast to the authoritarianism, aggressive imperial chauvinism, and disregard for human rights evident in Russian actions.

Vladimir Putin's persistent efforts to control Ukraine, starting from the 2004 Orange Revolution to the full-scale invasion in 2022, underscore the strategic importance Moscow places on Ukraine within its geopolitical orbit. The study highlights Putin's readiness to make significant sacrifices to resolve what he perceives as the 'Ukrainian question'. Meanwhile, the aggressive military strategy employed by Russia poses a substantial risk not only to Ukraine but also to the entire world.

DOI: 10.4324/9781003435433-7

The study emphasises that the war threatens democratic systems, increases military expenses globally, reduces social expenditures, exacerbates food supply issues, and contributes to mass migration. Consequently, the Russo-Ukrainian conflict is a complex interplay of historical legacies, geopolitical dynamics, and ideological clashes with far-reaching implications. Understanding the multifaceted nature of this conflict is crucial for formulating effective strategies to address the immediate crisis and prevent similar occurrences on the global stage.

The findings also suggest several economic reasons for Russia's invasion of Ukraine, with a focus on the strategic importance of Ukraine's natural resources and its role in the global economy. Here's a summary of the key points.

- Russia has controlled numerous deposits in eastern Ukraine since 2014. The study emphasises the economic reasons for the invasion, citing the need to ensure control over valuable resources like oil, natural gas, coal, iron, nickel, titanium, chrome, uranium, gold, granite, and manganese. Control was lost over a substantial number of deposits, impacting energy independence and economic potential.
- Ukraine is considered a potential superpower in the production of important industrial metals. The country possesses commercially significant volumes of various minerals, making it a key player in the global supply chain.
- The focus on lithium is highlighted, with Ukraine possessing large deposits. The global demand for lithium, especially in the production of lithium-ion batteries for electric vehicles, has contributed to the economic significance of these reserves. International companies, including those from Australia, China, and the United States, have shown interest in Ukraine's lithium deposits. Authors suggest that Russia's invasion might be also triggered by the global attention and competition for access to these resources.
- The study also touches upon Russia's focus on food security in the Black Sea region. By seizing southern Ukrainian ports, Russia attempted to control the grain trade, influencing global food prices and causing strain in the Middle East. The war in Ukraine is suggested to have economic implications for the Middle East, particularly in terms of food prices and potential unrest.

Overall, the economic reasons for Russia's invasion of Ukraine are multifaceted, ranging from control over natural resources to influencing global markets and geopolitical dynamics.

The study also includes a detailed analysis of the economic consequences of Russia's invasion of Ukraine, including the impact on various sectors such as agriculture, energy, and metallurgy. It covers the economic situation during the war, assessing GDP growth, inflation, monetary policy, foreign exchange reserves, and financial assistance received by Ukraine.

Despite the conflict, Ukraine's GDP grew by approximately 5% in 2023, showing resilience in certain economic sectors. Various economic sectors, including public administration, defence, construction, agriculture, and manufacturing, contributed to the GDP growth. The National Bank of Ukraine implemented measures to ensure financial stability during the conflict. Exchange rate stability was maintained, with adjustments made considering the economic consequences of the war. Inflation, initially high due to war expenses, was contained with international assistance, resulting in a 5.1% rate by the end of 2023. The central bank's policy rate was reduced from 25 to 15% in 2023, contributing to exchange rate stability. Foreign aid played a crucial role in reaching historical maximums in Ukrainian foreign exchange reserves in 2023. Financial assistance from various countries covered a significant portion of Ukraine's budget needs.

Ukraine faced challenges in trade due to the Polish blockade of the land border, affecting exports and tax revenues. The metallurgical sector showed signs of recovery, operating at around 70% of capacity, with increased opportunities for black metals exports. Despite challenges, the agriculture sector benefitted from favourable weather conditions, leading to increased crop yields. Preserving logistic capabilities and negotiating to lift blockades are crucial for sustaining food exports.

Tax revenues to the general state budget remained vital for sustaining economic activities, reaching 97.7 billion UAH in December 2023. Monthly revenues from the Personal Income Tax exceeded 20 billion UAH for the first time. Business Activity Expectations Index and Consumer Sentiment Index indicated prevailing negative expectations due to the conflict, logistical issues, and workforce shortages. Job vacancies were recovering, but the labour market faced challenges, including a shortage of labour and a diminished pool of available workers in Ukraine.

Consequently, Russia's invasion resulted in severe humanitarian consequences, with mass killings, deportations, and abductions, particularly affecting children. The economic consequences of Russia's invasion of Ukraine have been severe, impacting various sectors and resources. Despite challenges, Ukraine has shown resilience in certain economic indicators, and international financial assistance has played a crucial role in stabilising the economy. Challenges in trade, logistics, and labour market dynamics remain significant, requiring ongoing efforts for recovery and adaptation to structural changes.

The European Union has responded to Russia's invasion of Ukraine by enacting 12 rounds of sanctions from 2014 to 2024, aimed at various industries and individuals. The objective of these measures was to demonstrate solidarity, weaken Russia's military strength, and affect its economy and ruling class. Despite successes, challenges in implementation and circumvention have arisen. Legislative measures were implemented for cohesive enforcement, criminalising sanctions violations. The EU's response reflects a dynamic strategy with international cooperation playing a crucial role in addressing the evolving situation.

The findings of study in Chapter 2 indicate that wars have substantial economic outcomes, both positive and negative. While boosting GDP through military production is possible, wars on a nation's territory disrupt economic activity and impose heavy fiscal cost, including the depletion of human and physical capital, disruption to production processes, and heightened uncertainty among consumers and producers. Scientists indicate that war-related disruptions can lead to stagnation and decline in education and income with long-term consequences.

The war in Ukraine presents ongoing challenges for predicting its impact on the EU economy. Asymmetric consequences exist among Member States, influenced by trade links, energy dependence on Russia, and financial market vulnerability. The war triggered a massive shock to energy and food markets, leading to supply reductions and historically unprecedented price increases. It also caused inflationary pressure in the euro area, particularly for energy and food.

Considering main aggregates of the EU economies, following a decrease in 2020, there was a rebound in consumption spending, investments, and other measures of expenditure in 2021 and 2022. Industrial production experienced a decline from August 2022 to September 2023, particularly in durable consumer goods and capital goods, impacting the overall output of the private sector. Consumer confidence across European states witnessed a significant decline, worse than during the pandemic, influenced by households' expectations about the economic situation. Business confidence also exhibited a negative trend.

European countries experienced volatile energy prices since mid-2021, exacerbated by post-COVID economic recovery, lifting travel restrictions, and unexpected increases. Unprecedented global gas price surge (170% in 2021), severe climate conditions, rising LNG demand, and economic recovery in Asia contributed to the surge in energy prices. Russia's decision to cut gas supplies in 2022 led to supply uncertainty, significant gas price hikes, and subsequently, increased electricity costs in the EU.

The EU implemented emergency regulations, including measures to reduce electricity use, cap producer revenues, and secure contributions from fossil fuel businesses, aiming to alleviate the impact on consumers and businesses. Following Russia's invasion of Ukraine, EU countries committed to reducing dependence on Russian fossil fuels. Measures include diversifying energy sources, accelerating renewables, and enhancing interconnections.

Despite a reversal in coal consumption in 2021–2022, the EU experienced a decline in solid fossil fuels overall. Oil supply security was maintained, with a 90% decline in Russian oil imports since March 2022. Electricity production saw a 28% decline compared to 2021, with renewable energy, particularly solar and wind, making substantial contributions. Sales of heat pumps soared in 2022. The EU aimed for 42.5% renewable energy in the energy mix by 2030, reinforcing its commitment to accelerate the transition to cleaner energy. In response to the energy crisis, the EU focused on renewable energy, constituted 42.5% of the EU energy mix by 2023, emphasising the commitment to further deployment.

The key conclusions of Chapter 2 highlight the multifaceted responses of the EU to the energy crisis, involving emergency measures, diversification, collaboration, and a robust focus on renewable energy to ensure energy security and transition towards sustainable sources.

Russia's invasion led to the EU granting temporary protection to refugees from Ukraine. The programme, extended until March 4, 2025, covered approximately 4.3 million non-EU citizens by November 2023. Germany, Poland, and the Czech Republic provided temporary protection to the highest number of refugees. Adult women made up a considerable proportion of recipients, specifically targeting those between the ages of 35 and 64 who had obtained a higher education. Integration efforts showed progress in employment, with Ukrainian refugees finding jobs in low-skilled sectors, facing skills discrepancies.

In order to facilitate the labour market access of Ukrainian refugees, initiatives were implemented to address challenges, such as recognising foreign qualifications. Programmes such as the EU Talent Pool and online job-search platforms were created to facilitate the integration of refugees into the workforce. The influx of Ukrainian refugees had a notable impact on the labour force and GDP growth in host countries, particularly Poland. Economic studies projected positive fiscal impacts in the long term, estimating contributions to GDP and tax payments.

The Russian military aggression against Ukraine in 2022 significantly impacted trade dynamics not only for Ukraine but also other countries and the global market. The research carried out in Chapter 3 oscillated around the analysis of the importance of Ukraine for trade with the EU and selected world countries between 2013 and 2022, particularly examining the effects of Russian aggression on Ukraine's trade dimensions. The events following the Russian invasion, including the destruction of infrastructure, significant population displacement, and the imposition of sanctions, have disrupted Ukraine's trade relations with both European countries and the rest of the world. These disruptions have led to a revaluation of Ukraine's trade policies and partnerships, with a noticeable shift away from reliance on the Russian market. Despite facing significant challenges, Ukraine has shown resilience in adapting its trade strategies to mitigate the effects of the conflict and maintain its position as a key player in the global trade landscape. As Ukraine continues to navigate the aftermath of the Russian aggression, its role in global trade is likely to evolve further, shaped by both internal dynamics and external geopolitical factors.

The main hypothesis [H] was taken to be: Ukraine is an important partner for EU countries and the world, and since the annexation of Crimea in Ukraine there followed efforts to reduce trade with Russia and target of Western countries, and Russian military aggression contributed significantly to the consolidation and deepening of Ukraine's trade with the EU. In the case of hypothesis [H1], the EU occupies an important place in Ukrainian trade and there is an increase in the share of the EU in Ukrainian exports between 2013 and 2022, it was fully confirmed. The European Union emerges as a crucial trade partner for Ukraine, with the EU's share in Ukrainian exports steadily increasing from 2013 to 2022. The Deep and Comprehensive Free Trade Area (DCFTA) played a pivotal role in enhancing bilateral trade, despite temporary setbacks such as the global COVID-19 pandemic. On the other hand, the hypothesis [H2] Ukraine is an important player in EU trade between 2013 and 2022 has not been fully confirmed. While Ukraine is an important player in EU trade, its exports are primarily concentrated in a few EU countries, indicating uneven demand within the EU market. The hypothesis [H3] the importance of Russia's trade with Ukraine between 2013 and 2022 is weakened as a result of events of a political nature (annexation of Crimea, Russia's support for separatist movements in eastern Ukraine, Russia's military aggression against Ukraine) is fully confirmed. Russia's significance in Ukraine's trade decreased significantly due to political events and military aggression. The confirmation of this assertion is evident from the data showing that Ukrainian imports from Russia experienced a significant decline from 30.19% in 2013 to 16.74% in 2014 following the events surrounding the annexation of Crimea and the conflict in the Donbass region. This downward trend persisted, reaching 6.57% in 2020 and a mere 2.52% in 2022. Similarly, Ukraine's exports to Russia decreased from 23.81% of total exports in 2013 to 7.76% in 2015, further dropping to 6.15% in 2021. Notably, following the Russian attack on Ukraine in 2022, Ukrainian exports to Russia plummeted to less than 1%, specifically 0.98%.

The hypothesis [H4] of the importance of Ukraine in the trade exchange of world states in 2013–2022 is mainly shaped by the account of agricultural production exports. This hypothesis was not confirmed. Ukraine's role in global trade extends beyond agricultural exports, encompassing various sectors, such as chemicals, machinery, and manufactured goods. Ukraine emerged as a significant exporter of raw materials, particularly in sectors like iron and steel, maize, wheat, and sunflower oil. In the case of the hypothesis [H5] following the Russian military aggression against Ukraine in 2022, there is a significant decline in trade between Ukraine and the EU, due to the operation of the Ukrainian state under martial law, the hypothesis is partially confirmed. The study indicates a decline in Ukraine-EU trade following the Russian aggression, partly attributed to the imposition of martial law in Ukraine. However, the decrease in trade is comparable to previous economic crises, highlighting the resilience of Ukraine's trade amid geopolitical challenges. However, it is important to note that while there was a significant increase of 40.08% in Ukrainian exports to the EU in 2021 compared to the previous year, this growth was followed by a decline in performance attributed to the impact of the COVID-19 pandemic at the beginning of 2022. During the first year of the war, Ukrainian exports to the EU decreased by 27.13%. However, when comparing these export results with those during the economic crisis in Ukraine from 2014 to 2015, it is evident that there were also significant declines in 2014 (−13.48%) and 2015 (−29.20%). Thus, the magnitude of the export decrease during the war is comparable to the decline experienced during the economic crisis.

The hypothesis [H6] the trade exchange between Ukraine and the countries of the world after the Russian military aggression against Ukraine is significantly limited by Russian actions blocking the flow of goods. This hypothesis is partially confirmed, as undoubtedly Russia's actions are limiting trade opportunities with world states. Although the impact is mitigated by increased trade with EU nations. Structural changes in exports and imports between Ukraine and both the EU and the rest of the world were observed post-aggression. The hypotheses [H7] the structure of exports/imports between Ukraine and the EU after the outbreak of the Russian-Ukrainian war did not change significantly and [H8] the structure of exports/imports between Ukraine and the countries of the world after the outbreak of the Russian-Ukrainian war did not change significantly, were not confirmed. Examining Ukraine's export structure to the EU, there was a notable increase in several sectors in 2022. Specifically, there was a twofold increase in the food and live animals sector. Similarly, there was an index increase for exports in the crude materials, fuels sector. Moreover, there was nearly a doubling in the mineral fuels, lubricants, and related materials sector. Regarding Ukrainian imports from the EU, growth was observed in three sectors: mineral fuels, lubricants, and related materials, animal and vegetable oils, fats, and waxes and a substantial increase in commodities and transactions not classified elsewhere in the SITC. For exports to the rest of the world, only the commodities sector of mineral fuels, lubricants, and related materials experienced an increase in 2022, while the remaining nine sectors saw a decrease in export results. As for Ukrainian imports from the rest of the world, there was an increase in the mineral fuels, lubricants, and related materials and a significant increase in commodities and transactions not classified elsewhere in the SITC with the remaining eight sectors experiencing a decrease in merchandise imports. The hypothesis [H9] EU member states with the highest share of Ukrainian exports significantly determine the overall share of Ukrainian exports in the EU economy, was confirmed. Utilising the ABC method for analysis, it was determined that one-third of EU countries contribute to as much as 80% of all Ukrainian exports to the EU. Consequently, these countries play a pivotal role in shaping the demand for Ukrainian goods within European frameworks.

The validation of a specific hypothesis [H1–9] explains that the main hypothesis is partially confirmed. The EU employs various measures to facilitate bilateral trade cooperation, particularly in light of Ukraine operating under wartime conditions. In terms of Ukraine's global trade, it exhibits a less dynamic nature. While Ukrainian goods are exported to various regions worldwide, Europe, Central Asia, East Asia Pacific, and the Middle East-North Africa emerge as indisputable leaders in this regard.

The study carried out in Chapter 4 underscores the significant influence of geopolitical events on global financial markets, with a specific focus on the Russia-Ukraine conflict. Taking into account the interplay between geopolitics, economic policy, and financial markets, the research employs an interdisciplinary perspective to gain insight into the diverse factors that influence investor behaviour and market dynamics. The study combines quantitative and qualitative methods, incorporating data analysis, synthesis, and interpretation. It references multiple scientific studies, statistical data, and international reports to provide a comprehensive analysis of the research problem. Besides, the analysis extends beyond immediate market reactions to consider the long-term consequences of geopolitical events. Questions regarding the impact on various sectors in the European stock market and the banking sector highlight the need to understand the enduring effects on economic structures and financial institutions.

Thus, findings suggest that the ongoing military clashes have led to heightened uncertainty and turmoil, impacting investor sentiment and triggering fluctuations on financial markets. The study reveals a strong relationship between Economic Policy Uncertainty and stock market performance, analysing both short and long-term perspectives. The research confirmed that global factors, such as policy uncertainty and geopolitical risk, have a significant influence on investor sentiment and financial markets. In response to these risks, investors have displayed a notable shift in their asset allocation strategies. The move towards safe assets, such as gold, government bonds, and stable currencies like the US dollar and Swiss franc indicates a flight to safety during times of heightened geopolitical tensions. Moreover, investors closely monitor actions taken by financial institutions and governments in response to geopolitical crises. The decisions and policies implemented during such times play a crucial role in shaping market responses and influencing investment choices.

The outbreak of the war caused a notable decline in various global indices. European markets, being in proximity to the conflict, experienced significant disruptions. Despite the initial market turmoil, key indices like EURO STOXX 50 reached peak levels by the end of 2023, and projections suggest a positive trajectory in the coming months. While there is a slight recovery in the overall index for the Eurozone, challenges persist, including concerns about recession. However, there is a positive trend in the medium-term outlook, driven by changing interest rate dynamics and positive inflation projections. Thus, the war in Ukraine has significantly affected investor sentiment, leading to a sharp decline in expectations, as indicated by the Sentix Economic Index. This decline is unprecedented, even when compared to events like the Covid pandemic and the banking crisis. Meanwhile, there are signs of improvement in the economic outlook. Analysts' confidence, as reflected in the ZEW Economic Sentiment Index, shows a significant surge in December 2023, surpassing market predictions and suggesting positive trends for 2024.

The European banking sector, particularly vulnerable to the effects of military conflicts, experienced a sharp decline in stock prices following the invasion of Ukraine. The banking sector faces challenges related to uncertainty, potential stagflation, and changes in investor sentiment. The ongoing war has increased market risk and impacted foreign exchange and commodity markets. There is a risk of a sudden depletion of deposits, leading to erosion of trust in financial institutions, potentially causing long-term instability in the banking sector. Moreover, the potential economic consequences, including stagflation and increased risk factors, may affect banking activity.

In conclusion, the war in Ukraine has brought about a complex and challenging economic environment, impacting investor sentiment, financial markets, and the banking sector. While signs of recovery and positive trends are emerging, the multifaceted consequences highlight the need for ongoing vigilance and adaptability in the face of uncertainty.

Thus, geopolitical tensions and the ongoing war have multifaceted consequences, impacting financial stability through direct and indirect channels. The future remains uncertain, with potential scenarios including increasing tensions with negative market implications or a stable situation without adverse effects. The interconnectedness of the global economy means that even countries not directly involved in armed conflicts, like Poland, can face significant challenges due to their geographical proximity and economic ties. Given the dynamic situation, continuous monitoring of key economic indicators, market indices, and geopolitical developments is essential to comprehend and navigate the evolving economic landscape.

The destabilisation caused by the conflicts and wars has reshaped perceptions of state security, prompting discussions on the need for robust security policies. The international community has rallied to support Ukraine, condemning Russian military actions, and providing humanitarian, financial, and military assistance. The research carried out in Chapter 5 examines the response of the EU, the UK, and the US to the war in Ukraine, particularly focusing on their aid to Ukraine and measures taken to bolster their own security. European leaders and the US have pledged substantial aid to Ukraine, emphasising the importance of upholding international norms and laws. The following statements were taken as hypotheses: [H1] involvement in aid to Ukraine has become a significant action for EU states, the UK, and the US, thus presenting support for Ukraine and condemnation of Russian actions, [H2] the hostilities in Ukraine confirmed the need to act to guarantee its own security, and to this end the EU countries, the UK, and the US have acted on increasing their defence budget spending.

The analysis revealed substantial support from EU member states, the UK, and the US for Ukraine, encompassing various forms of assistance. Notably, the US emerged as the largest contributor, followed by the EU and its member states. Germany, Poland, and the Netherlands were prominent contributors, offering extensive military aid alongside financial and humanitarian support. Examining the aid provided relative to each country's gross domestic product (GDP) highlights the significant commitment of certain nations such as Lithuania (1.31%), Estonia (1.28%), and Latvia (1.03%), which allocated a notable percentage of their GDP to aid Ukraine. Denmark (1.03%) and Poland (0.64%) were notable for their consistent contributions, both in absolute terms and relative to their GDP. Additionally, the provision of heavy weaponry and military equipment, notably tanks, by several countries including Poland, the Czech Republic, and Germany, underscores the collective effort to bolster Ukraine's defence capabilities against Russian aggression.

The European Security Strategy of 2003 highlights the shared responsibility among EU member states for security across various domains, including military, economic, environmental, and social aspects. The Versailles Declaration issued in March 2022 reaffirmed the EU's dedication to its security and collaboration with NATO, emphasising greater investments in defence and partnerships. Notably, almost all EU member states have expressed their intent to strengthen their military capacities, which implies an increase in defence spending. Specifically, European NATO members, particularly those located on the eastern flank, have demonstrated a commitment to enhancing their defence capabilities in response to perceived threats from Russia. Countries like Poland, Romania, and the Baltic States have significantly raised their defence budgets, reflecting heightened concerns about regional security. The promises made in response to Russia's aggression against Ukraine highlight the importance of strong defence strategies and global cooperation in maintaining stability worldwide and within regions. The rise in military expenditure, along with efforts to enhance alliances and collaborations, demonstrates a joint commitment to preventing aggression and fostering peace and security in the face of changing geopolitical complexities.

In Chapter 6, in order to identify priorities for the recovery and development of Ukraine's economy after the war, the study was carried out in two stages: the first stage analyses the state of economic recovery in Ukraine during the war, and the second stage identifies priority areas for economic recovery and development after the war. A detailed review of the current state of Ukraine's economic recovery during the war, highlighting aspects of international support, financial initiatives, project details, regional differences, and environmental challenges, has led to the following conclusions:

International support is crucial for Ukraine. The 2023 Ukraine Recovery Conference (URC) held in London underscores the commitment of the international community to support Ukraine's economic recovery. Ukraine's long-term economic stability is possible through the mobilisation of international support, including emergency assistance and private sector financing.

The war has caused significant economic damage. The World Bank has estimated the cost of rebuilding Ukraine at $411 billion over ten years. The direct destruction of buildings and infrastructure in the first year of the war alone is estimated at more than US$135 billion, with total damage reaching around US$290 billion.

Financial support for Ukraine and coordination of actions is declared in the Memorandum of Intent signed by the heads of the four development banks. This underlines the need for clear coordination between Ukraine's partners to ensure effective financial assistance. The cooperation is aimed at harmonising and streamlining procurement procedures for public sector investments.

The Government of Ukraine, together with international partners, such as the World Bank and the European Commission, has initiated the Third Rapid Damage and Needs Assessment of Ukraine (RDNA3). This initiative aims to provide an updated analysis of the consequences of the Russian invasion and to enhance funding for projects to restore and develop Ukraine's economy until 2024.

The study provides an overview of the number and types of projects to restore and develop various sectors of Ukraine's economy. These projects are aimed at rebuilding infrastructure, supporting education and healthcare, and promoting economic recovery.

A breakdown of approved projects and confirmed funding by region shows differences in the number of projects and the amount of funding. Sumy, Kyiv, Kharkiv, and Chernihiv regions stand out in terms of the number of projects and the amount of funding.

The financial coverage of project budgets is presented, indicating sectors with 100% financial coverage and sectors with lesser coverage. Sources of funding include public funds and funds from international partners.

The study identifies organisations and institutions that have confirmed investments of more than UAH 100 million in projects, as well as participation of more than 45% in project co-financing. These investors include both state funds and international partners.

The important issue of construction waste generated during the war is considered. The importance of their proper management, recycling, and the need for coordination at the state level to address environmental issues is emphasised.

The study identified two priority areas for the recovery and development of Ukraine's economy.

The first priority area is people: (1). Population and demography. The war has led to significant migration, with millions of Ukrainians seeking refuge abroad. Demographic changes pose challenges to socio-economic conditions and defence capabilities. It is important to create favourable conditions for the employment of internally displaced persons. (2). Labour migration. A significant number of Ukrainians, especially skilled workers, have migrated abroad. The return of migrants is crucial for economic growth, with a potential loss of GDP in the absence of effective policies. (3). Security and return of migrants. Security is a vital factor influencing migrant returns. War-affected regions need to be demined to ensure security, and rebuilding infrastructure and housing is crucial. (4). Economic growth and employment. Providing well-paid jobs and higher living standards are important to encourage the return of Ukrainians. The lack of economic opportunities in their home regions may deter returnees. (5). Policy recommendations. The state should establish a dialogue with recipient countries and formulate an effective demographic policy. Government coordination, communication support, and funding are crucial for migrant return programmes.

The second priority area is environmental challenges: (1) The impact of the war on the environment. The war has caused significant environmental damage, generating large amounts of waste, including hazardous materials. Russia's environmental crimes and explosive devices further complicate the situation. (2). Efforts to restore the environment. Certification projects for mine action operators and processes should be introduced. Significant progress has been made in mine clearance and demining activities. International cooperation for joint demining efforts is a positive development. (3). Environmental protection priorities. Focus on safe disposal of construction waste and hazardous materials. Initiatives to recycle metals, glass, concrete, plastic, bricks, and wood. Collection and analysis of waste recycling statistics. Special attention to waste generated by shelling, especially in Donetsk and Luhansk oblasts.

Thus, the consequences of the war are not limited to human suffering, but also cause economic and environmental problems. Restoring Ukraine's economy requires a comprehensive approach that involves governments, local authorities, businesses, and the public. Post-war reconstruction is a long-term project that requires careful planning and resource allocation. This study highlights the complexity of the post-war challenges facing Ukraine and the need for multifaceted strategies to address demographic change, security, and environmental issues for sustainable economic development.

Index

aggressor 10, 31
agricultural 15, 19, 24, 44, 77, 88, 101, 103, 110, 134, 136, 179, 180, 182, 189
agriculture i, viii, 1–2, 5, 16, 22, 79, 82, 88, 162, 166, 169, 184–186
annexation of Crimea v, ix, 4, 15, 36, 75–78, 80, 82, 85, 87, 89, 109–110, 155, 188, 189
asset 18, 22, 37–38, 41, 115, 117–118, 120–121, 130–134, 190

banking sector i, vi–vii, x–xi, 115–116, 130–136, 190–191
banks vii, 19–20, 36, 39, 42, 123, 128, 130–134, 163, 165, 193
Black Sea 11, 13–14, 21, 31, 102, 179, 185
budget 17, 20, 23–25, 27, 81, 117, 143, 150, 152–153, 155, 157–159, 162–163, 169–172, 180, 186, 192–193
business vii, x, xi, 17, 19, 25, 27–28, 44, 46–50, 52–55, 65–68, 120, 127, 130–131, 133, 136, 162, 186–187, 194

capacity 21–22, 27, 40, 42, 60, 117, 150, 186
capital i, 38, 42–47, 81, 115–117, 120, 125, 131, 133–134, 169–170, 180, 186, 187
challenges i, ix, xii, 2, 21, 25, 35–36, 55, 65, 67–68, 115, 124, 133, 136, 150, 158–159, 162, 164, 180–181, 186–189, 191, 193–94
confidence 28–29, 32, 48–52, 67, 122, 129, 130, 136, 187, 191
conflict viii, ix–xii, 1–5, 10, 22, 25, 44, 78–80, 82, 115, 117–125, 129–130, 133–136, 143, 149–150, 152, 164, 178, 184–186, 188–191
consequences i, v, vii–viii, x–xi, 2, 4, 6, 14, 17, 22, 35–36, 43–45, 67, 83, 115, 117, 121, 133, 149, 154, 162, 166, 173–174, 180, 184–187, 190–194
consumption viii, 45–47, 52–53, 58, 67–68, 120, 134, 187
cooperation ix, xii, 1, 3, 9, 35–37, 41, 75, 80–81, 87–88, 112, 148, 150, 152, 154, 159, 162–163, 165, 180–181, 186, 190, 192–194
cost vii–viii, xii, 9, 14, 43, 45, 48, 53–54, 67, 134, 162, 165–166, 170, 174–175, 177, 180, 186–187, 193
Crimea v, ix, 1, 3–4, 8–9, 11, 15, 29, 36, 75–78, 80, 82, 85, 87, 89, 109–110, 152, 155, 188–189
crisis ix, xii, 2, 35, 46–47, 53–54, 60, 68, 78–83, 103, 110–111, 117–118, 120, 122, 127, 136, 154, 185, 187, 189, 191
currency xii, 17–19, 21, 80–82, 116, 121, 134

DCFTA 81–82, 88, 110, 188
decline 16, 18–19, 22, 25–26, 44–48, 51–52, 55, 58–60, 66–68, 77, 81–83, 92–95, 111–112, 120, 122–124, 126–128, 130–132, 134–136, 186–187, 189, 191
decrease 13, 18–19, 21–22, 24, 26–27, 43–44, 46–48, 52, 55, 57–60, 66–67, 81, 83, 87, 92–93, 95, 103, 106, 111–112, 120, 122–123, 126–127, 130–132, 134, 136, 155, 187–190
defence i, vii, xi, 1, 3, 16, 20, 28, 37–38, 40, 42, 78–79, 142–143, 149–159, 175, 179, 185, 192, 194
demand viii, 12–13, 19, 31, 48–49, 52, 53–55, 57–58, 61, 78, 81, 108, 110, 112, 134, 185, 187–188, 190
deposits viii, 10, 11–13, 15–16, 19, 21, 117, 131–132, 135, 185, 191

destruction ix, xi, 2, 5, 9, 29, 44, 75, 101, 142, 162, 164, 166, 171, 174, 178, 184, 188, 193
development ii, vi–viii, xi–xii, 10, 12–13, 15–16, 26, 29, 37, 40, 44, 56–57, 63–64, 68, 115–117, 129, 133, 136, 143, 150–151, 157, 162–166, 168, 171–172, 175–176, 179–181, 191–194
dynamics i, ix, 2, 24, 26–27, 79, 109, 121, 123–124, 126, 163, 184–186, 188, 190–191

EBRD 43, 69, 163, 165, 180
economic crisis 79, 82–83, 111, 189
economic policy iii, vi–vii, x, 75, 81–82, 101, 115–117, 121, 190
economy i–ii, v–xii, 1–4, 10, 16–17, 27–28, 35–37, 44–46, 49, 59, 66–67, 73, 76–77, 80–82, 88, 101, 105, 108–109, 112, 115, 117–118, 121, 123, 129–131, 133–136, 144, 163–164, 166–168, 170, 174–175, 177, 179–181, 185–187, 190–194
education i, 35, 44, 61, 63–67, 164, 170–171, 173, 176, 180, 186, 188, 193
electricity 51–54, 58–60, 67–68, 177, 187
emergency ix, 22, 35, 53–54, 59, 67, 133, 164, 165, 187, 193
employment i, ix, xii, 26–27, 30, 35, 44, 47–49, 61, 63–66, 68, 120, 175–177, 181, 188, 194
energy i, v–ix, xii, 2, 11–13, 15, 22, 31, 35–39, 41–42, 44–47, 51–57, 59–60, 67–68, 70–71, 79–81, 115, 117, 122, 125, 128, 134, 136, 151, 166, 174, 185, 187
escalation 26, 36, 80, 82, 120, 122–123, 125, 136
EU economy ix–x, 35, 45–46, 59, 67, 76–77, 105, 108–109, 112, 130, 187, 190
euro area 46, 48–50, 52, 67, 122–123, 125–126, 129–131, 136, 187
European Commission 36–37, 41–42, 46–47, 50, 52, 60, 82, 162, 166, 176, 193
European Union xii, 1, 3, 13, 20, 38, 46, 53, 64, 67, 78, 81–82, 85, 89–98, 103, 112–113, 134, 150, 158, 186, 188
exports vi, x, 16, 21, 24, 26, 38–40, 42, 47, 60, 75–78, 80, 82–98, 100–112, 186, 188–190

financial i, vi–viii, x–xii, 2, 4, 16–18, 20, 25–26, 36, 38–40, 42, 45, 49, 53, 67, 79–80, 115–118, 120–122, 124–126, 129–136, 140, 142–147, 151–153, 157–158, 162–164, 166, 169–172, 180, 185–187, 190–193
financial aid 20, 143–144, 146
financial market i, vi–vii, x, 38, 42, 45, 67, 115–118, 120–121, 124–126, 129–130, 134, 136, 187, 190–191
fluctuations 19, 52, 59, 115, 117, 118, 120, 122, 190
Food and live animals 89, 91, 95, 98, 99, 110–111, 189
full-scale attack viii, 1, 2, 3, 184
full-scale war 1–2, 5, 19, 21, 27, 67, 80, 175, 178

gas 5, 11, 15, 31, 37–38, 40, 42, 46–47, 51–60, 67, 80, 122, 179, 185, 187
GDP ix, 2, 16–17, 25, 35, 43–46, 66–68, 79, 82, 121, 146–149, 151–159, 161, 176, 185–186, 188, 192, 194
geopolitical i, x, 1–6, 10–11, 14, 31, 35, 68, 79, 80, 115, 117–118, 121–122, 130, 133, 135–136, 159, 184–185, 188–192
global implications 2, 31, 52, 185
global market ix, 57, 75, 96, 109, 128, 188
global risks 1, 5
government 3–4, 7–9, 14, 16–17, 20, 28, 38, 44, 46, 63, 78, 79, 117, 120, 122, 133, 146, 151–154, 157, 162, 164, 166, 174, 177, 180, 190–191, 193–194
growth ix, xi, 2, 12, 16, 17, 35, 43–46, 48–49, 58, 60, 66, 68, 82, 92, 112, 115–116, 120, 129, 131–134, 154, 164, 176, 181, 185, 188–190, 194

healthcare xii, 61, 65–66, 164, 170–171, 180, 193
humanitarian aid 143–144, 146–147

imports 16, 21, 24, 31, 37, 39, 40–42, 47, 53, 55–60, 71, 75–78, 80–103, 105–112, 136, 187, 189–190
independence viii, 2, 8–9, 15, 29, 47, 54, 68, 78, 143, 152, 182, 185
index 21–22, 26, 33, 47, 50–51, 55, 57, 71, 111, 114, 120, 122–126, 129, 131, 136, 139, 140, 189, 191
indices 33, 47, 118, 120, 122, 124–125, 127–128, 136, 191
industries 32, 44, 47–49, 51, 53, 67, 79, 82, 88, 115, 117–118, 125, 127, 130–131, 135, 148, 150, 164, 169, 174, 180, 186
inflation xii, 2, 17–19, 35, 46–48, 51–52, 68, 83, 121, 123–124, 129, 134, 185, 187, 191

influence 14, 42, 49, 53, 66, 68, 80, 83, 116, 123, 126, 133–135, 190
influx 60, 61, 66, 68, 188
information 3, 39, 40, 47–49, 63, 72, 79, 106, 144, 150, 157, 162, 165, 169
infrastructure 1, 5, 22, 55, 75, 78–79, 81, 101, 109, 117, 142–143, 153, 163–164, 166, 176–178, 184, 188, 193, 194
initiatives 58, 160, 163, 181, 188, 193
instability 29, 53, 75, 120, 121–122, 125, 136, 191
international 1–5, 12, 18–19, 25, 33, 35–36, 79, 81, 102, 116, 121, 142, 144, 150–152, 155, 158–159, 163–165, 168–170, 172, 177, 179–181, 183, 186, 190, 192–193
International Monetary Fund 20, 162, 165
invasion vii–viii, xi–xii, 1–3, 9, 11–13, 15, 18, 27–29, 31–32, 35, 38–39, 55, 60–61, 67–68, 75, 79, 101, 115, 117–118, 121, 131, 133, 151–152, 160, 162–163, 166–167, 173, 175–176, 180, 184–188, 191, 193
investment 44, 46, 80–81, 115, 117, 120, 130, 135, 150–151, 162–163, 165, 172–173, 180, 191
investors 12, 115–118, 120–126, 130, 164, 170, 190–191, 193

labour force 30, 35, 61, 66–68, 176, 188
law 7, 77, 79, 81, 111, 142, 151–152, 155, 162, 165, 180, 189
legislation 37, 61, 81

machinery and transport equipment 90, 98, 110, 112
manufacturing 16, 35, 44, 47–48, 51, 66, 70, 82, 131, 185
market viii, ix–xi, 16, 18, 27, 40, 42, 47, 52–56, 57–59, 61, 63–68, 70, 72, 75–78, 81–82, 87–88, 89, 91, 100–102, 115–118, 120–127, 129–130, 134, 136, 140, 164, 186, 188, 190–191
measures 2, 16, 35–42, 46–47, 53–54, 57–59, 67, 69–70, 76, 80–82, 87, 89, 102, 109–110, 113, 115, 142, 149, 152–153, 159, 163–164, 177, 180–181, 185–187, 190
Member States 35–38, 45, 55, 58–59, 61, 67–69, 105–106, 112, 144, 146, 148, 150, 152, 159, 187
migrants 66–67, 164, 175–177, 181, 194
migration 2, 10, 29, 63, 66, 75, 101, 175, 181, 185, 194
military aid 143–144, 146, 158, 192
minerals 11–13, 15, 31, 185
monetary policy 16, 18, 20, 52, 116, 123, 134, 185

NATO 1, 3, 9, 11, 150–161, 192
natural resources 2, 10, 31, 185

occupied territories 15–16, 76, 102, 164, 179
OECD 49–51, 61, 64–68
oil 11–12, 14–15, 31–32, 38–42, 47, 54–55, 58–59, 80, 88, 111, 118, 122, 129, 185, 187, 189
OSCE 150

PMI 47–49, 70, 73
policy 9, 18, 24, 33, 52, 75, 79, 80, 82–83, 89, 91, 108, 110, 120–122, 142–143, 146, 149, 150–152, 154–155, 157–158, 160, 164, 176–177, 181, 186, 190, 194
political 2, 4–8, 28, 77–81, 110, 115, 117–118, 120, 124, 131, 184–185, 188
population 4–5, 14, 26, 43–45, 61, 66, 68, 78, 101, 143, 188
post-war 163–165, 175, 177, 194
prices 12–14, 17, 31, 45–48, 51–55, 67, 70, 83, 121–123, 125, 127, 129, 134, 176, 185, 187, 191
production 12–13, 15, 21–22, 25, 37–38, 43–44, 47–49, 51, 56, 58–60, 67, 71, 79, 81, 88, 101–102, 110, 120, 174, 185–187
public funds 163, 168–169, 171, 180, 193

rebuilding 162–163, 165, 176–177, 180–181, 193–194
recession 46, 52, 79, 122, 191
reconstruction xi, 81, 143, 162–165, 171, 175, 181, 183, 194
recovery vii, xi–xii, 16, 19, 21–22, 33, 45–47, 52, 55, 58, 67, 70–71, 136, 162–175, 178–181, 183, 186–187, 191–193
refugees ix–xi, 4–5, 35, 43, 61, 64–66, 68, 71–73, 142, 144, 146, 187–188
regulations 35, 38, 57, 61, 67, 116, 133, 187
Revolution of Dignity 78, 80–81
risk vi–vii, x, 10, 29, 57–58, 116, 118, 120–122, 130–131, 133–136, 175, 184, 190, 191
Russian aggression viii–ix, xi, 10, 79, 82, 87–88, 101, 143, 150–152, 154–155, 157–159, 188–189, 192
Russian Federation 14, 38, 73, 75, 78, 80–81, 85, 151, 155

Russian market 75, 81, 89
Russian military aggression 75–78, 88, 95–96, 102, 109, 111, 153, 188–189
Russian-Ukrainian war 76, 82, 111, 189

safety 60, 175, 179, 191
sanctions 36–42, 54, 59, 67, 69, 70, 73, 75, 80, 109, 118, 134, 136, 186
security vii–viii, xi–xii, 13, 31, 35, 38, 53–54, 59, 68, 70, 79, 81, 115, 117, 135, 142–143, 149, 150–152, 154, 155, 157, 158–161, 166, 176–177, 181, 185, 187, 191–192, 194
security policy 79, 151
separatist movements 5, 75, 77, 79–80, 110, 152, 188
services 19–20, 24, 35, 38–40, 42, 44, 46, 48–49, 61, 63–66, 68, 70, 75, 77, 79, 80–82, 117, 162, 164, 169–170, 180
shortages 25, 35, 47, 56, 57, 186
social 2, 4, 10, 64, 143, 150, 154, 164–165, 171, 181, 185, 192
solidarity 36, 53–54, 57, 67, 70, 109, 150, 186
Soviet Union 1–3, 8–9, 184
stability 2, 16–20, 24, 52, 82, 129, 130, 133, 135, 143, 149, 150–152, 154, 159, 164, 184, 186, 191–193
stock market viii, 115, 118, 120, 122, 126, 134, 190
strategic importance viii, 2, 31, 154, 184–185
supply 2, 10, 22, 35–36, 42, 45–47, 53, 54–60, 67–68, 70, 103, 117, 122, 125, 134–136, 170, 185, 187
support viii, xi–xii, 18, 36, 57, 61, 63–66, 75, 77, 80, 103, 110, 123, 142–149, 151–152, 157–161, 163–166, 177, 180, 188, 192–194

temporary protection ix, 35, 60–64, 67–68, 176, 187
trade viii, ix, 16, 19–20, 31, 36, 38, 39–41, 45–47, 67, 75–83, 87–98, 101–105, 108–113, 118, 124, 134, 136, 164, 169–170, 180, 185–190
transport 24, 26, 36, 38, 39–42, 66, 79, 88, 90, 94, 96, 98–99, 101–102, 109–110, 112, 162, 166, 169–170, 180

Ukrainian grain 102–105, 109
uncertainty vii–viii, x, 25, 42–43, 53, 67, 115, 118–122, 130–131, 134, 186–187, 190–191
United Nations 13, 162, 178, 183

vulnerability 45, 67, 117, 187

war 1–6, 9, 10, 13–19, 21, 24–25, 27–29, 31–36, 42–46, 49, 51, 54, 61, 66–67, 69, 71, 75–80, 82–83, 85, 90–92, 94, 98, 101–103, 109–112, 115–118, 122, 124–127, 130–131, 133–136, 142–143, 152–154, 158, 161–167, 174–181, 184–194
waste 60, 162, 164, 170, 173–175, 177–181, 193–194
World Bank 3, 20, 82, 83, 87–89, 162–163, 165–166, 180, 193

Made in the USA
Las Vegas, NV
19 September 2026

f1b4a56b-f4c6-43a8-a6c9-639fd8374e5dR01